MATTHEW ERMAN   STEFANO SIMEONE

GOOD LUCK ™

Published by

BOOM! STUDIOS

SERIES DESIGNER
MICHELLE ANKLEY

COLLECTION DESIGNER
MARIE KRUPINA

ASSISTANT EDITOR
GAVIN GRONENTHAL

EDITOR
JONATHAN MANNING

SENIOR EDITOR
ERIC HARBURN

GOOD LUCK, MARCH 2022. Published by BOOM! Studios, a division of Boom Entertainment, Inc. Good Luck is ™ & © Matthew Erman. Originally published in single magazine form as GOOD LUCK No. 1-5. ™ & © 2021 Matthew Erman. All rights reserved. BOOM! Studios™ and the BOOM! Studios logo are trademarks of Boom Entertainment, Inc., registered in various countries and categories. All characters, events, and institutions depicted herein are fictional. Any similarity between any of the names, characters, persons, events, and/or institutions in this publication to actual names, characters, and persons, whether living or dead, events, and/or institutions is unintended and purely coincidental. BOOM! Studios does not read or accept unsolicited submissions of ideas, stories, or artwork.

BOOM! Studios, 5670 Wilshire Boulevard, Suite 400, Los Angeles, CA 90036-5679.
Printed in China. First Printing.

ISBN: 978-1-68415-813-3, eISBN: 978-1-64668-446-5

Withdrawn

CHAPTER

1

SAFE & SOUND

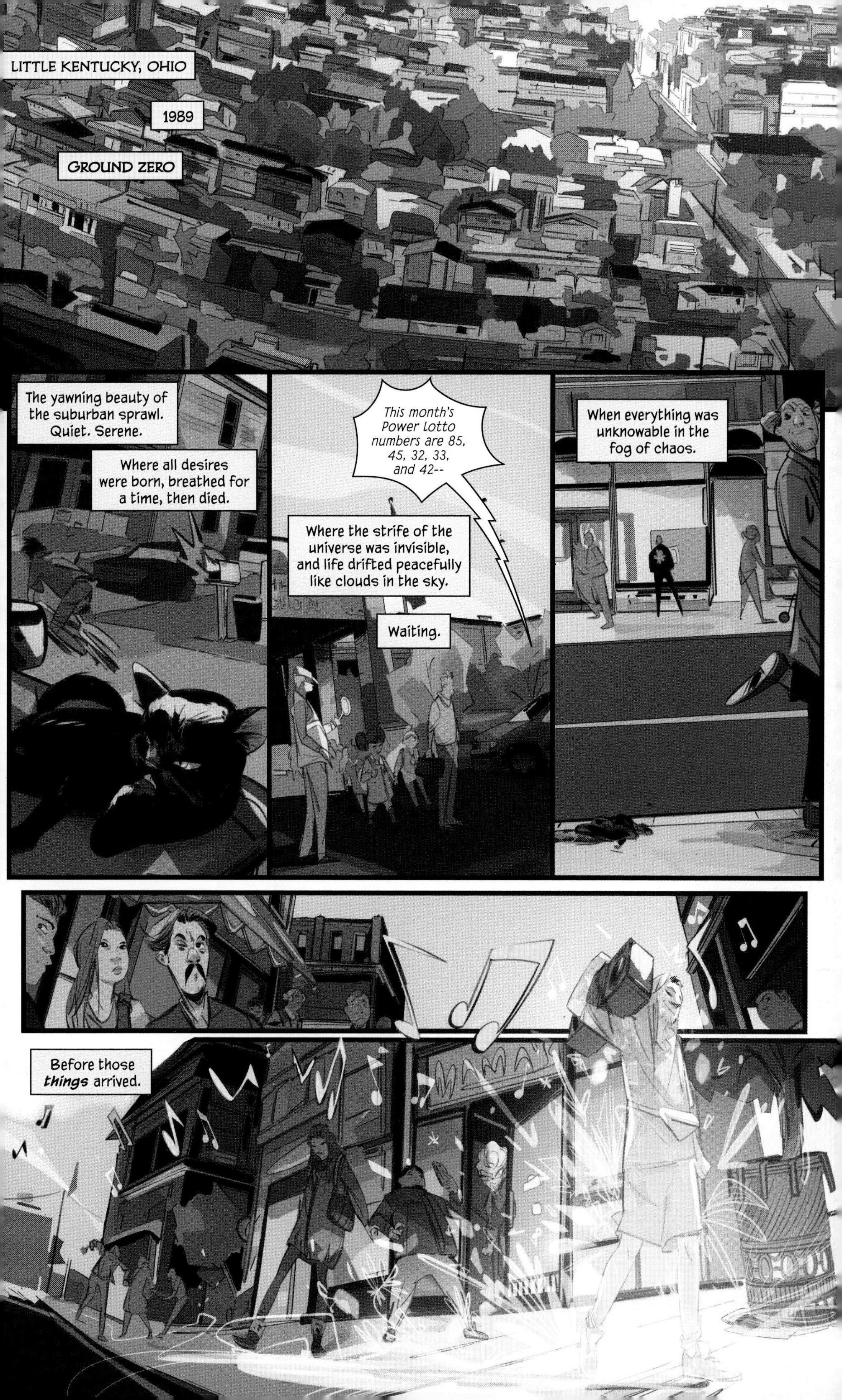
LITTLE KENTUCKY, OHIO
1989
GROUND ZERO
The yawning beauty of the suburban sprawl. Quiet. Serene.
Where all desires were born, breathed for a time, then died.
This month's Power Lotto numbers are 85, 45, 32, 33, and 42--
Where the strife of the universe was invisible, and life drifted peacefully like clouds in the sky.
Waiting.
When everything was unknowable in the fog of chaos.
Before those *things* arrived.

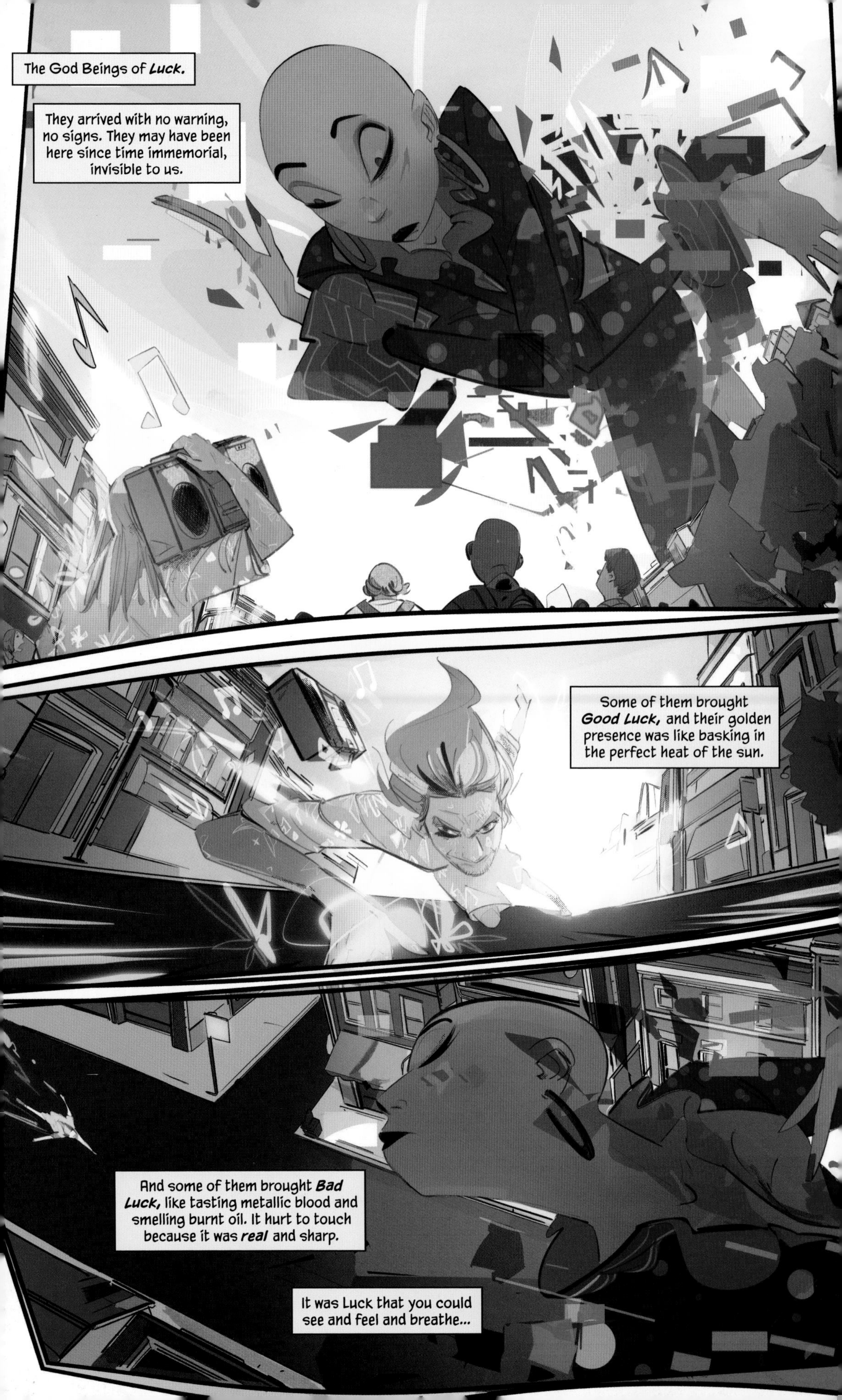
The God Beings of *Luck.*
They arrived with no warning, no signs. They may have been here since time immemorial, invisible to us.
Some of them brought *Good Luck,* and their golden presence was like basking in the perfect heat of the sun.
And some of them brought *Bad Luck,* like tasting metallic blood and smelling burnt oil. It hurt to touch because it was *real* and sharp.
It was Luck that you could see and feel and breathe...

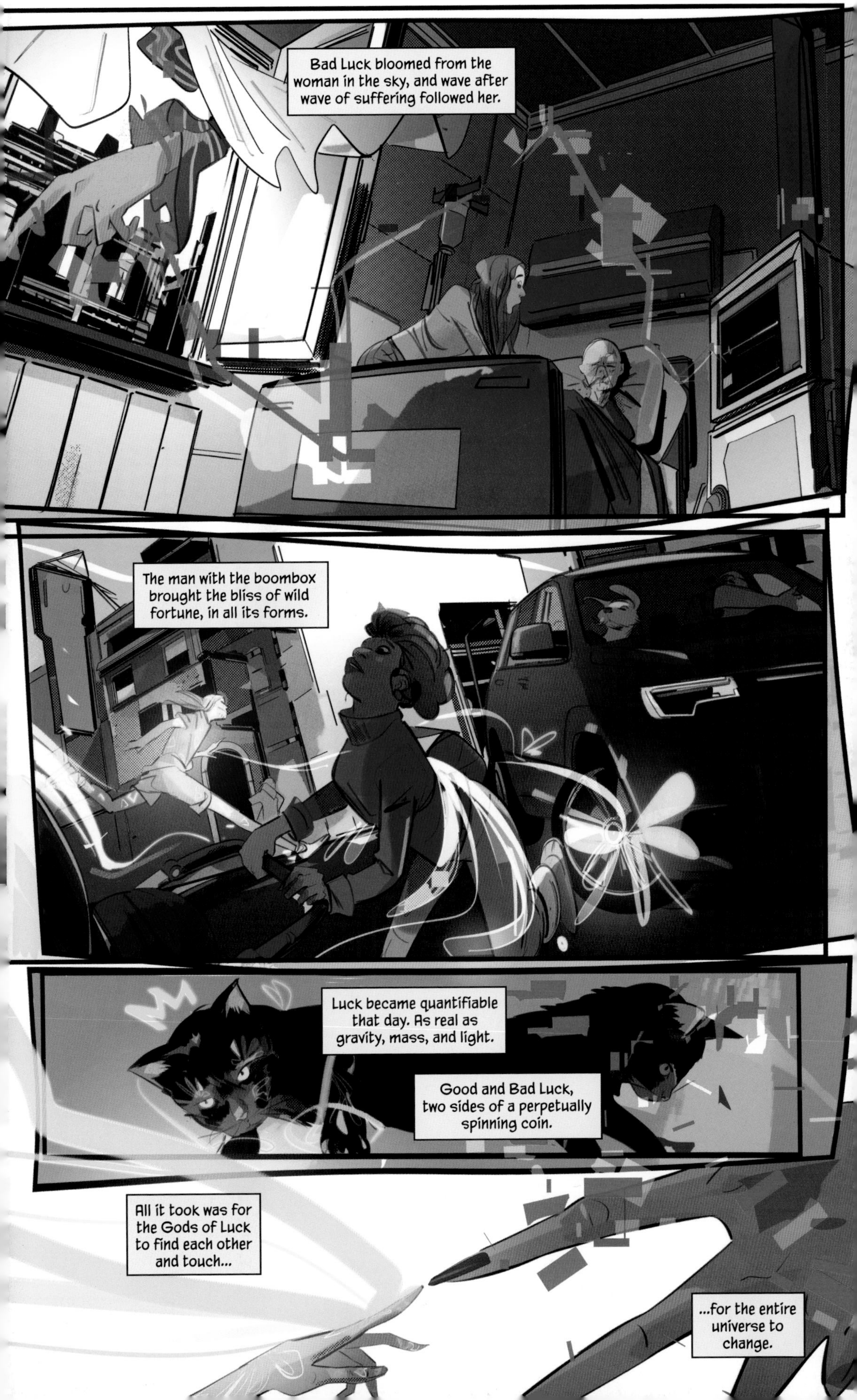
Bad Luck bloomed from the woman in the sky, and wave after wave of suffering followed her.
The man with the boombox brought the bliss of wild fortune, in all its forms.
Luck became quantifiable that day. As real as gravity, mass, and light.
Good and Bad Luck, two sides of a perpetually spinning coin.
All it took was for the Gods of Luck to find each other and touch...
...for the entire universe to change.

GOOD

LUCK™

WRITTEN BY
MATTHEW ERMAN

ILLUSTRATED BY
STEFANO SIMEONE

LETTERED BY
MIKE FIORENTINO

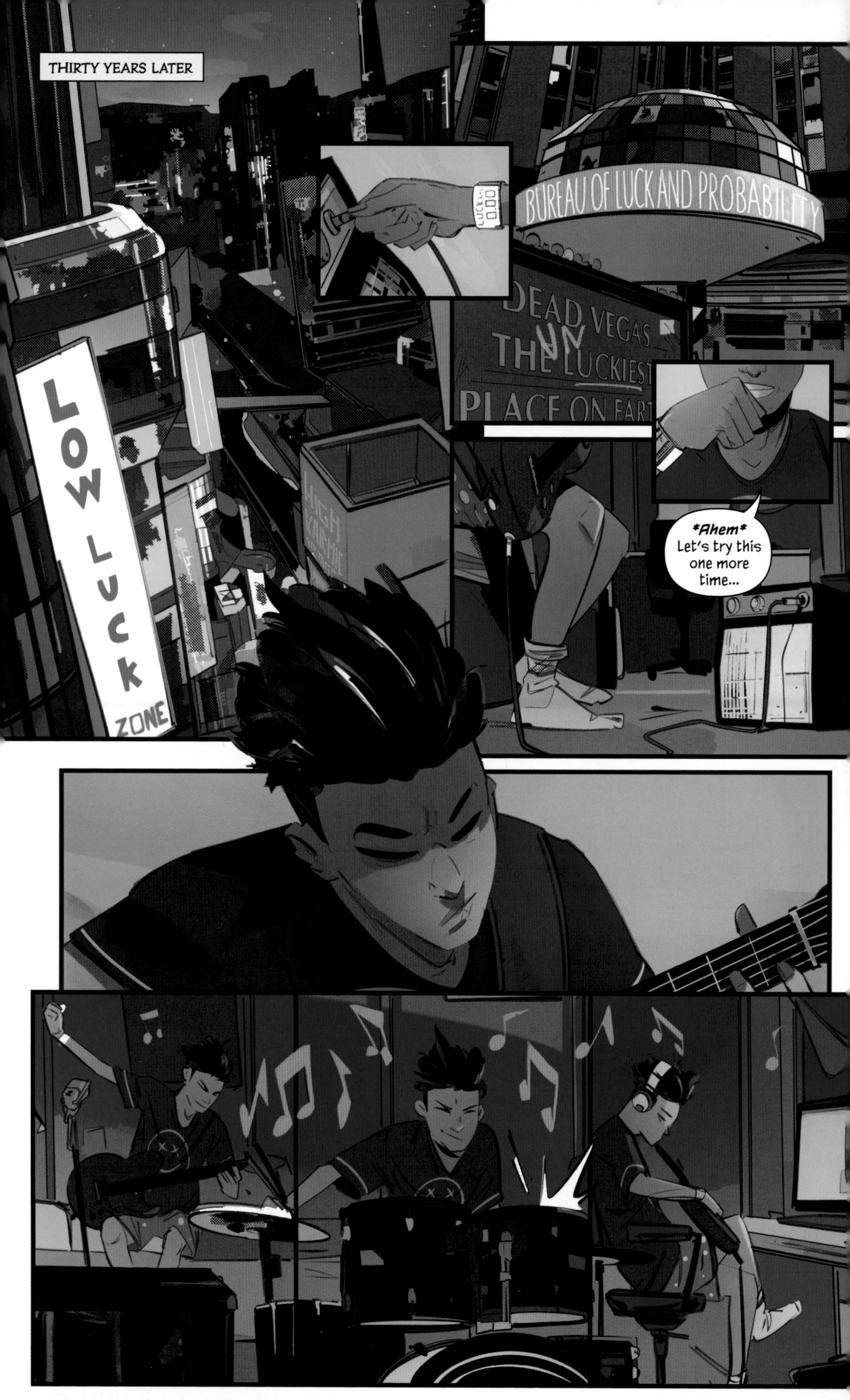
THIRTY YEARS LATER
LOW LUCK ZONE
LUCK 0.00
BUREAU OF LUCK AND PROBABILITY
DEAD VEGAS
UN
THE LUCKIEST
PLACE ON EART
Ahem Let's try this one more time...

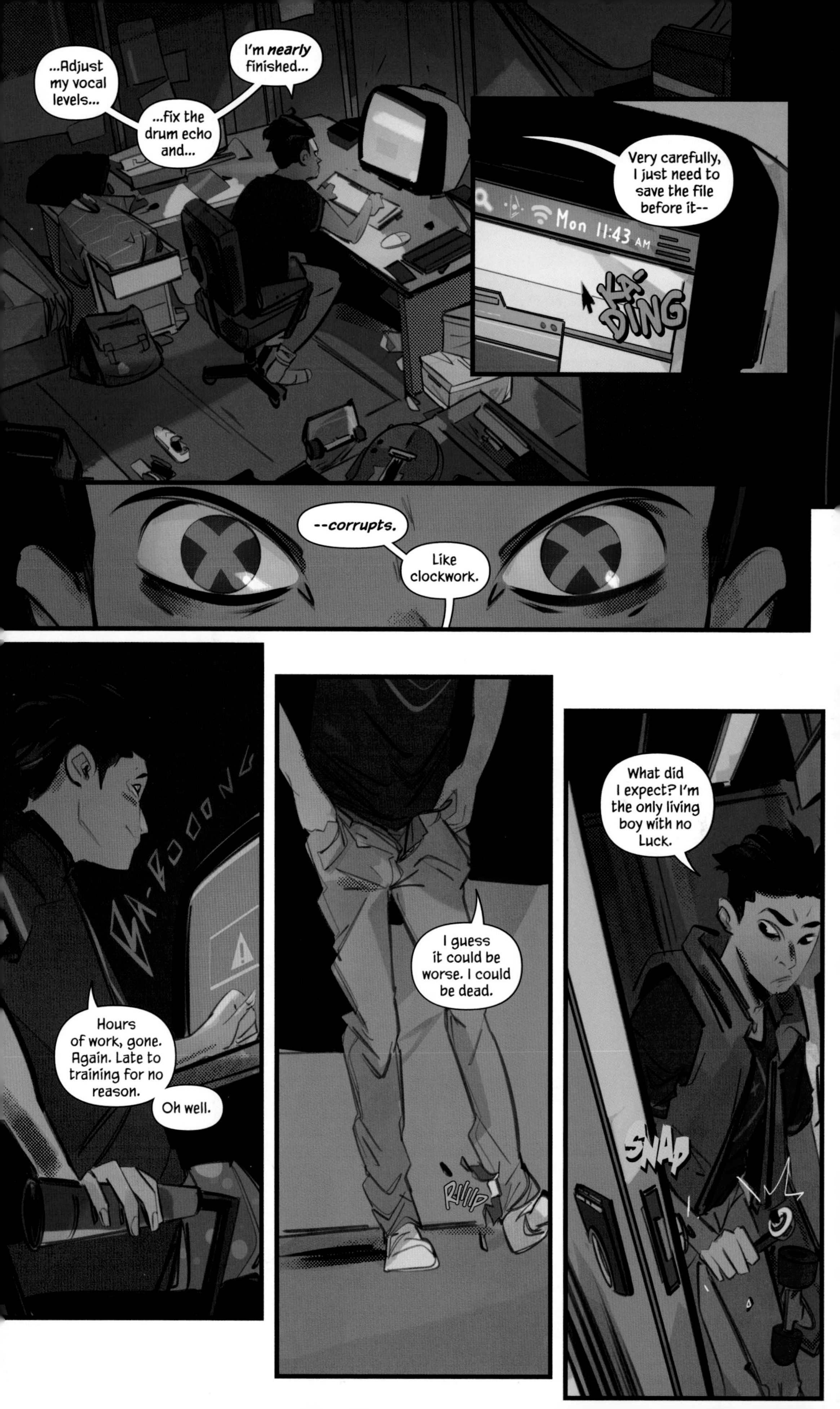
...Adjust my vocal levels...
...fix the drum echo and...
I'm *nearly* finished...
Very carefully, I just need to save the file before it--
Mon 11:43 AM
KA-DING
--*corrupts.*
Like clockwork.
KA-BOOONG
Hours of work, gone. Again. Late to training for no reason.
Oh well.
I guess it could be worse. I could be dead.
RIIIP
What did I expect? I'm the only living boy with no Luck.
SNAP

Artemis?! What are you doing in *this* sector? You're going to *kill us!*

He can't be here! Sound the alarms!

Good god! He's coming! Out of the way!

He's going to karmically obliterate us! Put on your safety gear! Hurry!

--It's happening! Oh no! This is it! Get to safety!

How many times do we have to tell you to take the sealed tunnel to the training simulation!

Hnng--ouch. My bones...

Artie. You and your friends are responsible for the fate of all existence.

Be more careful.

Please.

Don't worry, the fate of the world is in pretty good hands!

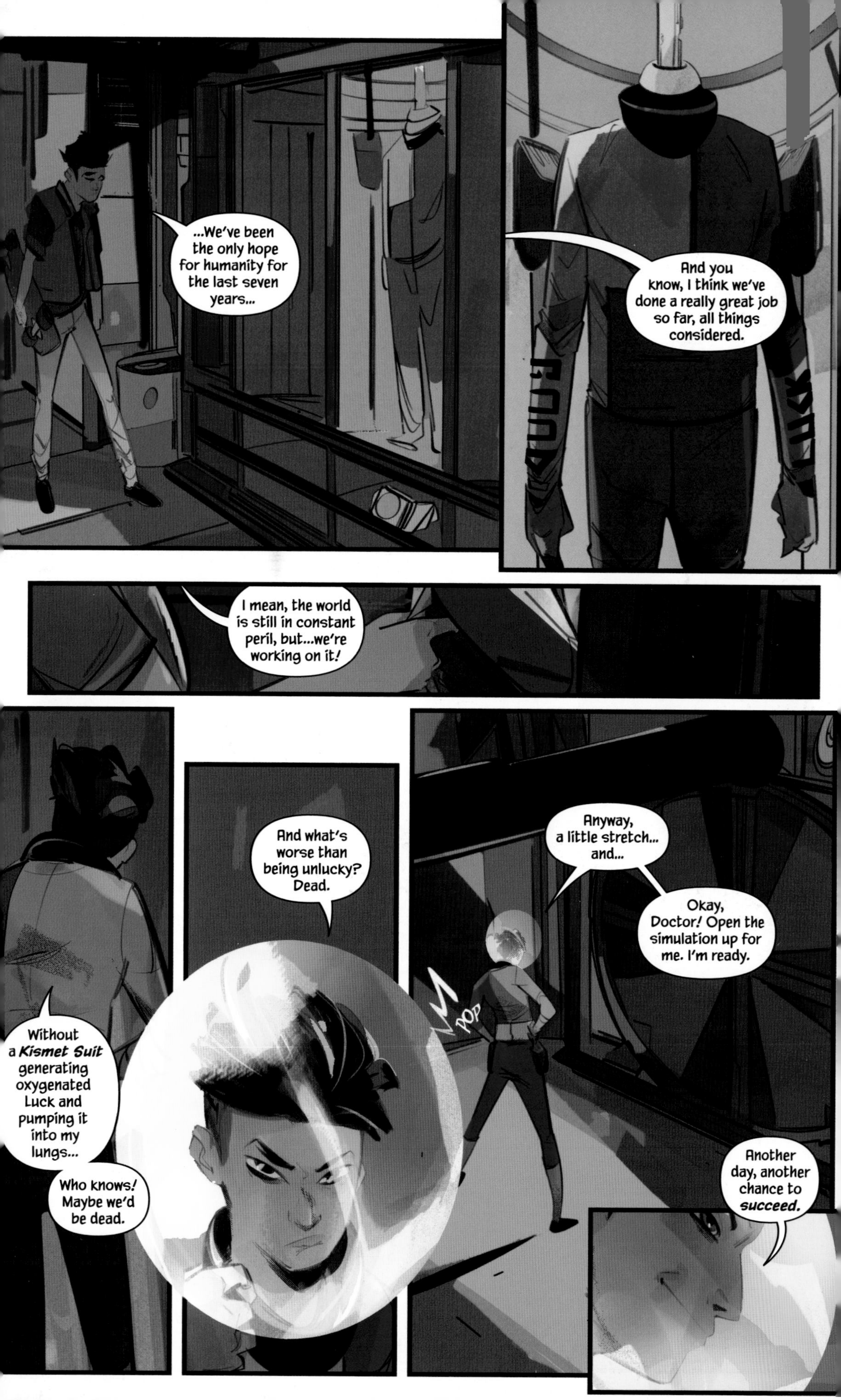
...We've been the only hope for humanity for the last seven years...
And you know, I think we've done a really great job so far, all things considered.
GOOD
LUCK
I mean, the world is still in constant peril, but...we're working on it!
Without a *Kismet Suit* generating oxygenated Luck and pumping it into my lungs...
Who knows! Maybe we'd be dead.
And what's worse than being unlucky? Dead.
Anyway, a little stretch... and...
Okay, Doctor! Open the simulation up for me. I'm ready.
POP
Another day, another chance to ***succeed.***

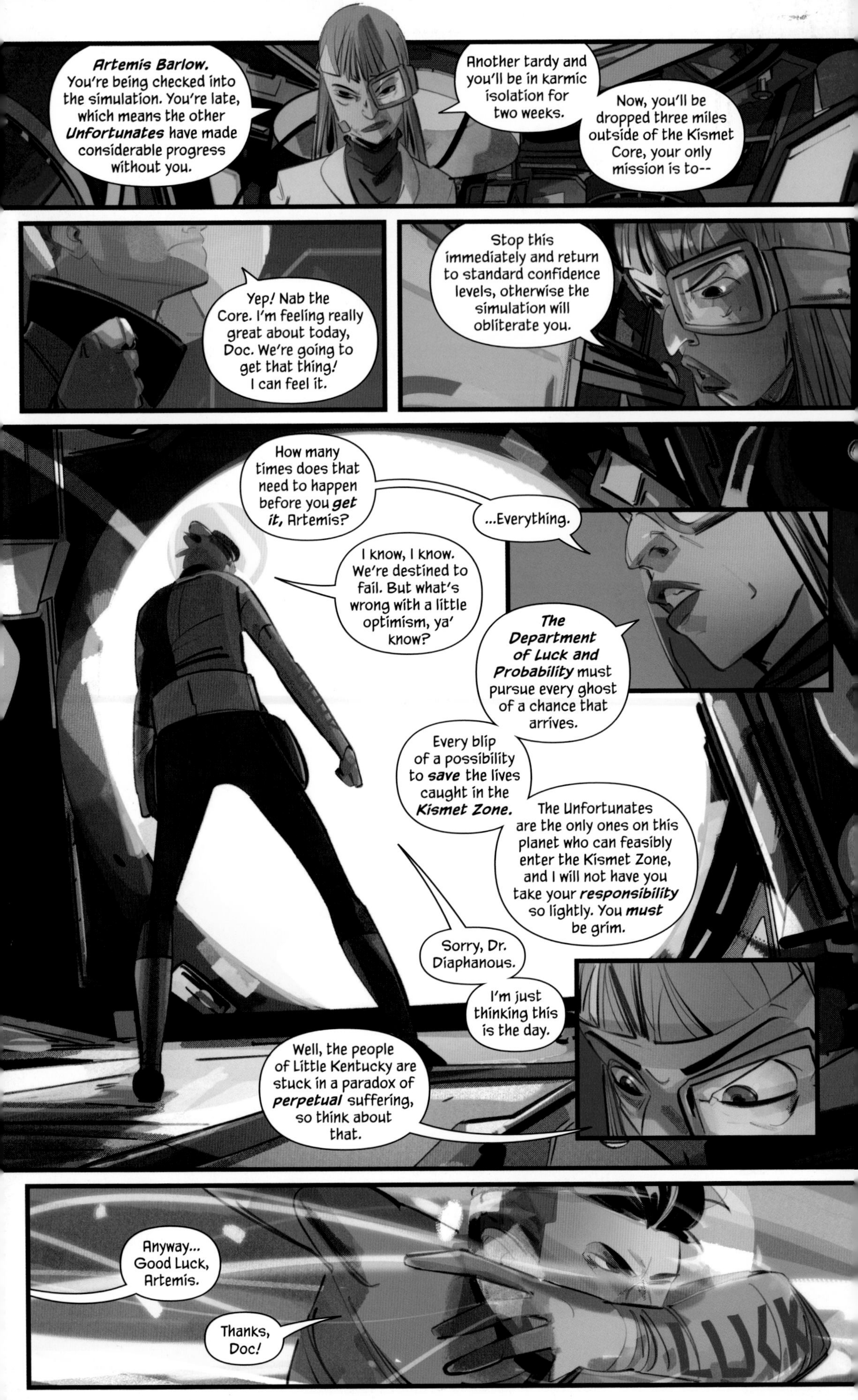

Artemis Barlow. You're being checked into the simulation. You're late, which means the other ***Unfortunates*** have made considerable progress without you.
Another tardy and you'll be in karmic isolation for two weeks.
Now, you'll be dropped three miles outside of the Kismet Core, your only mission is to--
Yep! Nab the Core. I'm feeling really great about today, Doc. We're going to get that thing! I can feel it.
Stop this immediately and return to standard confidence levels, otherwise the simulation will obliterate you.
How many times does that need to happen before you ***get it,*** Artemis?
...Everything.
I know, I know. We're destined to fail. But what's wrong with a little optimism, ya' know?
The Department of Luck and Probability must pursue every ghost of a chance that arrives.
Every blip of a possibility to ***save*** the lives caught in the ***Kismet Zone.***
The Unfortunates are the only ones on this planet who can feasibly enter the Kismet Zone, and I will not have you take your ***responsibility*** so lightly. You ***must*** be grim.
Sorry, Dr. Diaphanous.
I'm just thinking this is the day.
Well, the people of Little Kentucky are stuck in a paradox of ***perpetual*** suffering, so think about that.
Anyway... Good Luck, Artemis.
Thanks, Doc!
LUCK

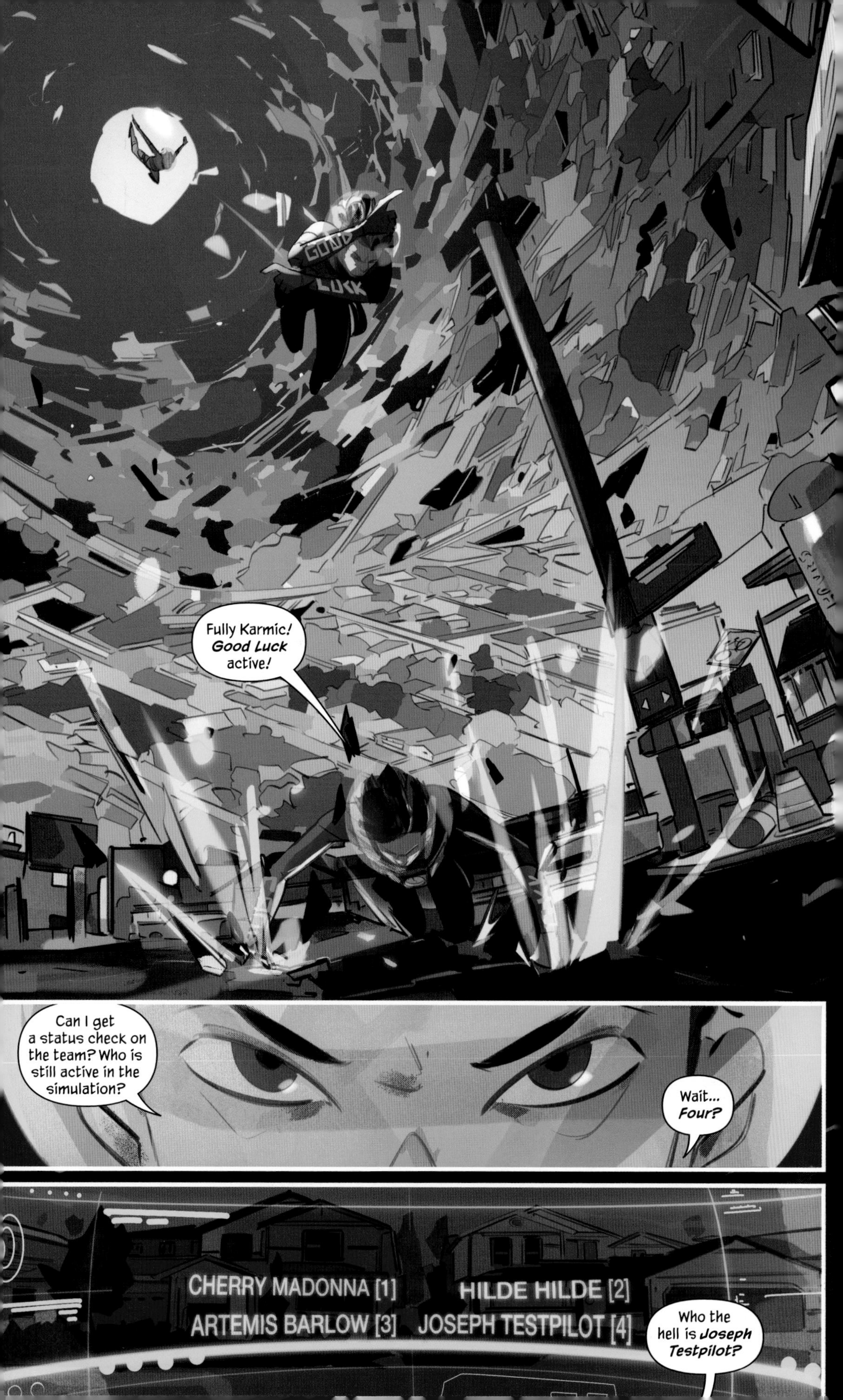
Fully Karmic! ***Good Luck*** active!
Can I get a status check on the team? Who is still active in the simulation?
Wait... ***Four?***
CHERRY MADONNA [1]
HILDE HILDE [2]
ARTEMIS BARLOW [3]
JOSEPH TESTPILOT [4]
Who the hell is ***Joseph Testpilot?***

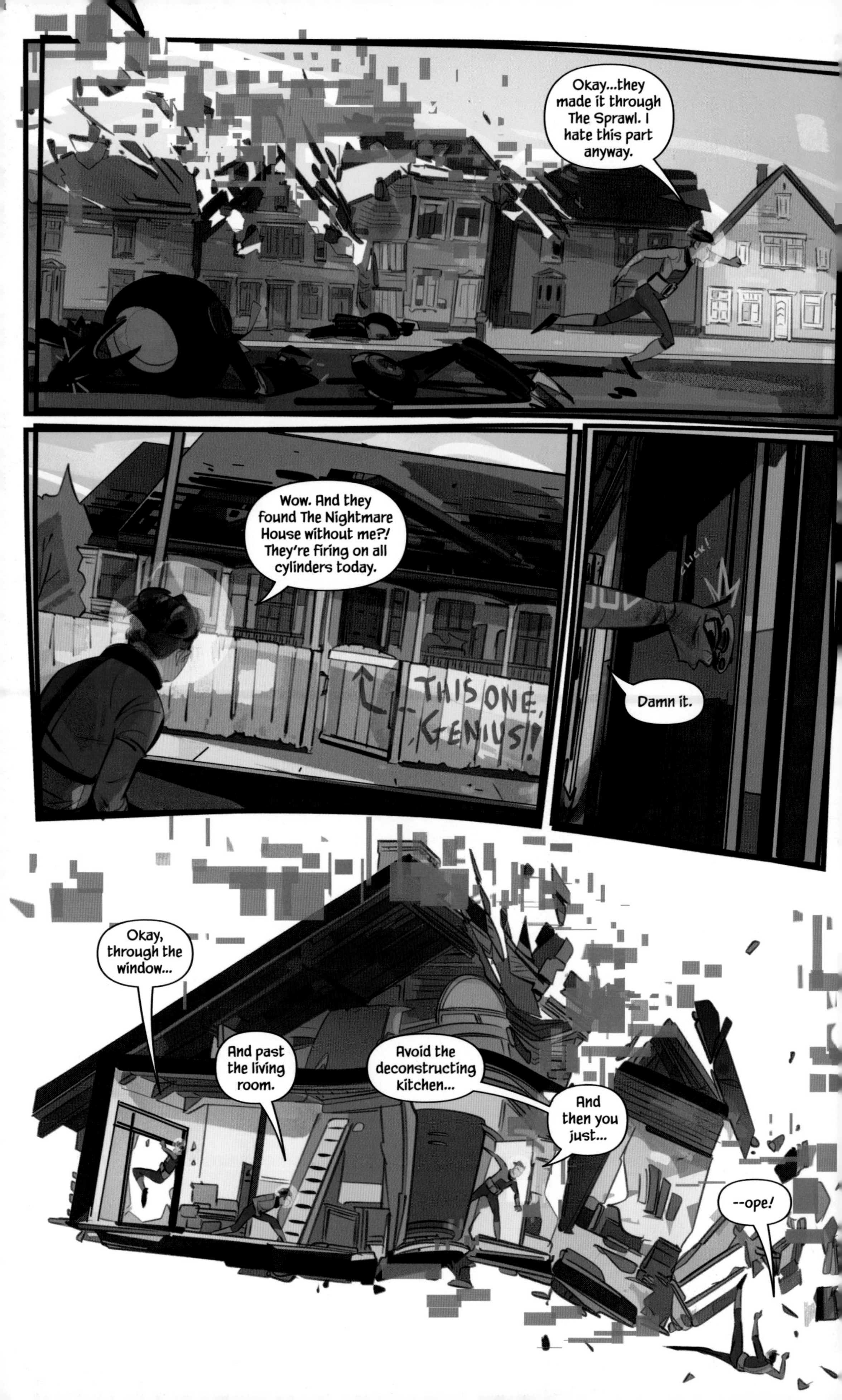

Okay...they made it through The Sprawl. I hate this part anyway.
Wow. And they found The Nightmare House without me?! They're firing on all cylinders today.
THIS ONE, GENIUS!
CLICK!
Damn it.
Okay, through the window...
And past the living room.
Avoid the deconstructing kitchen...
And then you just...
--ope!

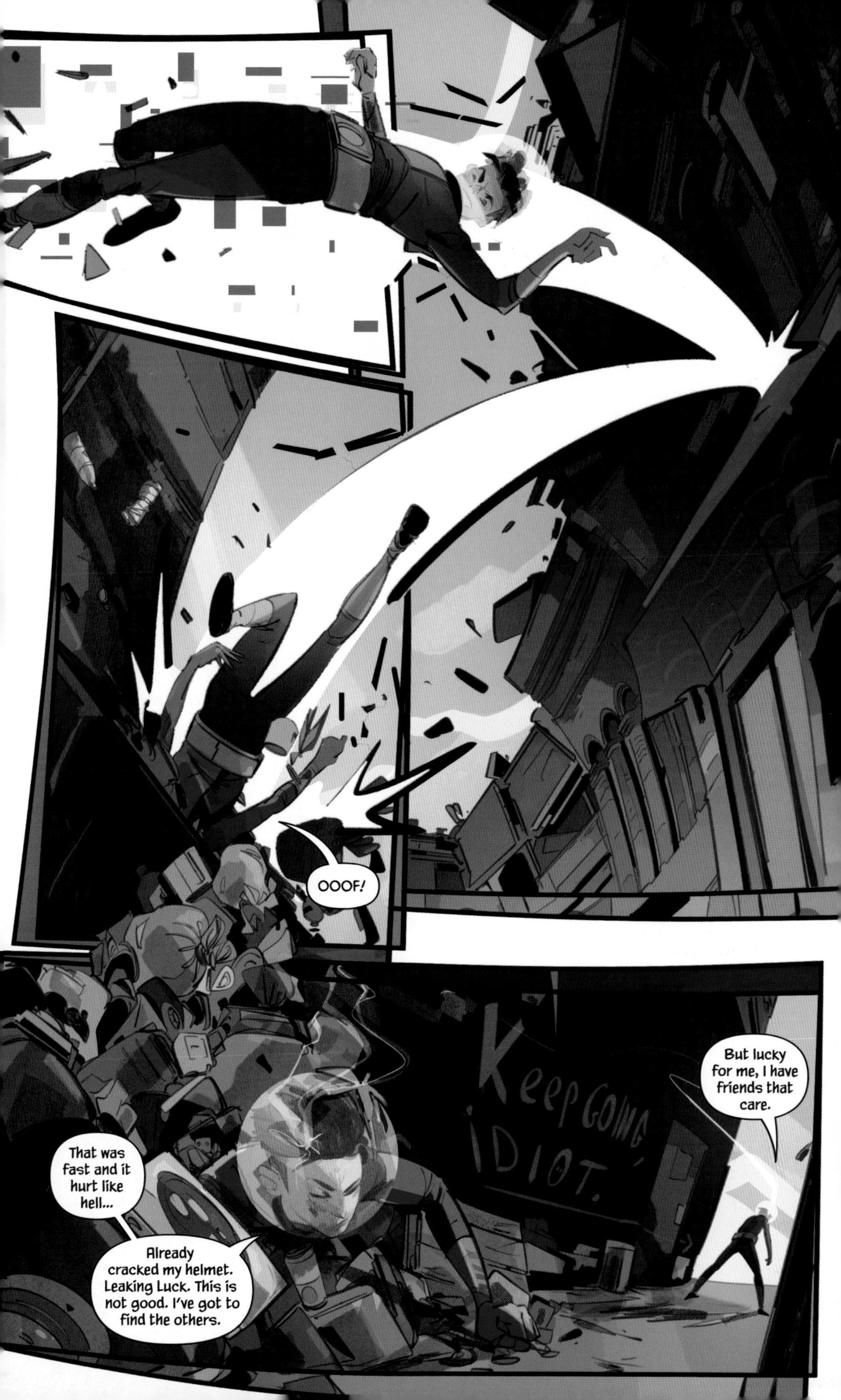
OOOF!
That was fast and it hurt like hell...
Already cracked my helmet. Leaking Luck. This is not good. I've got to find the others.
KEEP GOING IDIOT.
But lucky for me, I have friends that care.

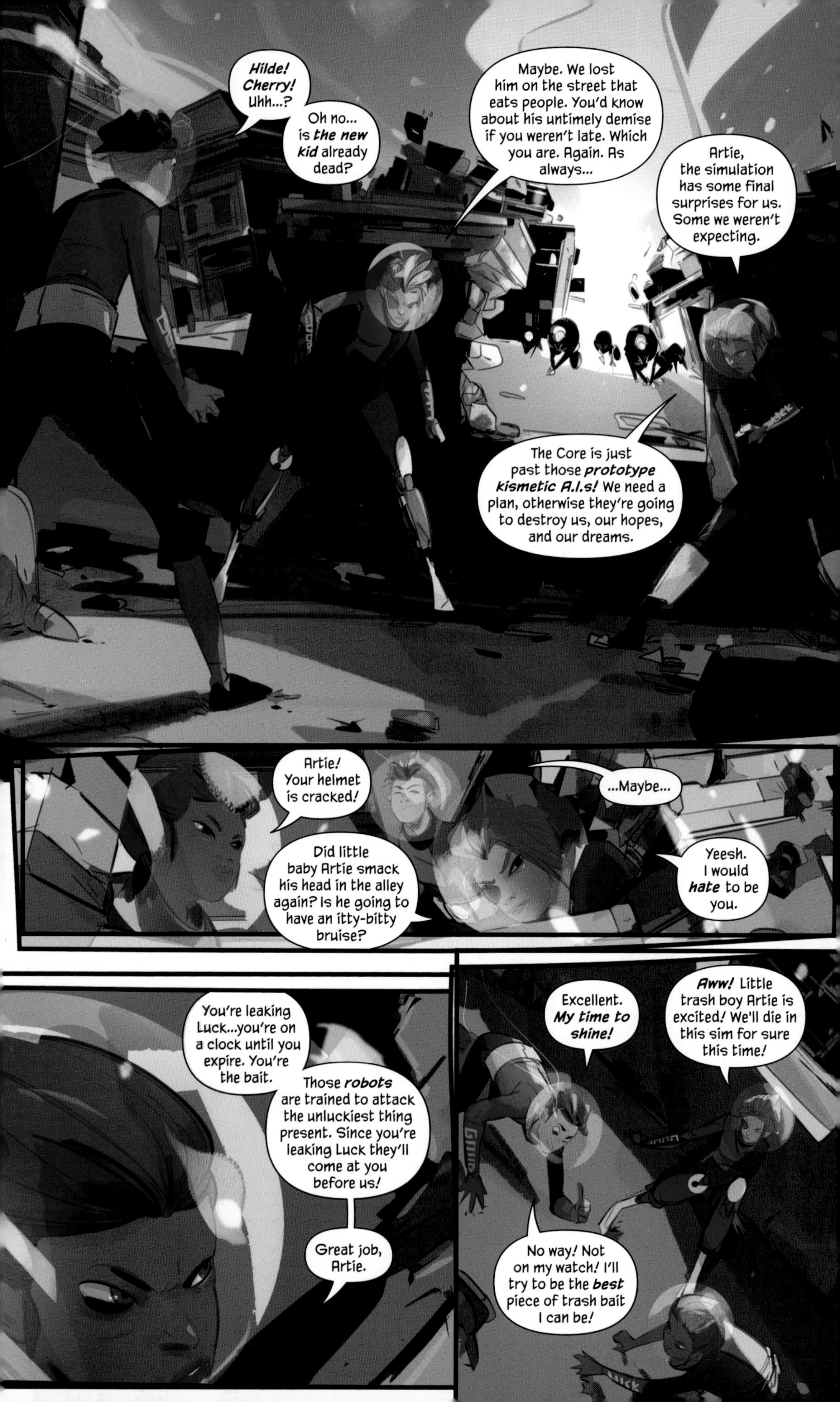
Hilde! Cherry! Uhh...?
Oh no... is the new kid already dead?
Maybe. We lost him on the street that eats people. You'd know about his untimely demise if you weren't late. Which you are. Again. As always...
Artie, the simulation has some final surprises for us. Some we weren't expecting.
The Core is just past those prototype kismetic A.I.s! We need a plan, otherwise they're going to destroy us, our hopes, and our dreams.
Artie! Your helmet is cracked!
Did little baby Artie smack his head in the alley again? Is he going to have an itty-bitty bruise?
...Maybe...
Yeesh. I would hate to be you.
You're leaking Luck...you're on a clock until you expire. You're the bait.
Those robots are trained to attack the unluckiest thing present. Since you're leaking Luck they'll come at you before us!
Great job, Artie.
Excellent. My time to shine!
Aww! Little trash boy Artie is excited! We'll die in this sim for sure this time!
No way! Not on my watch! I'll try to be the best piece of trash bait I can be!

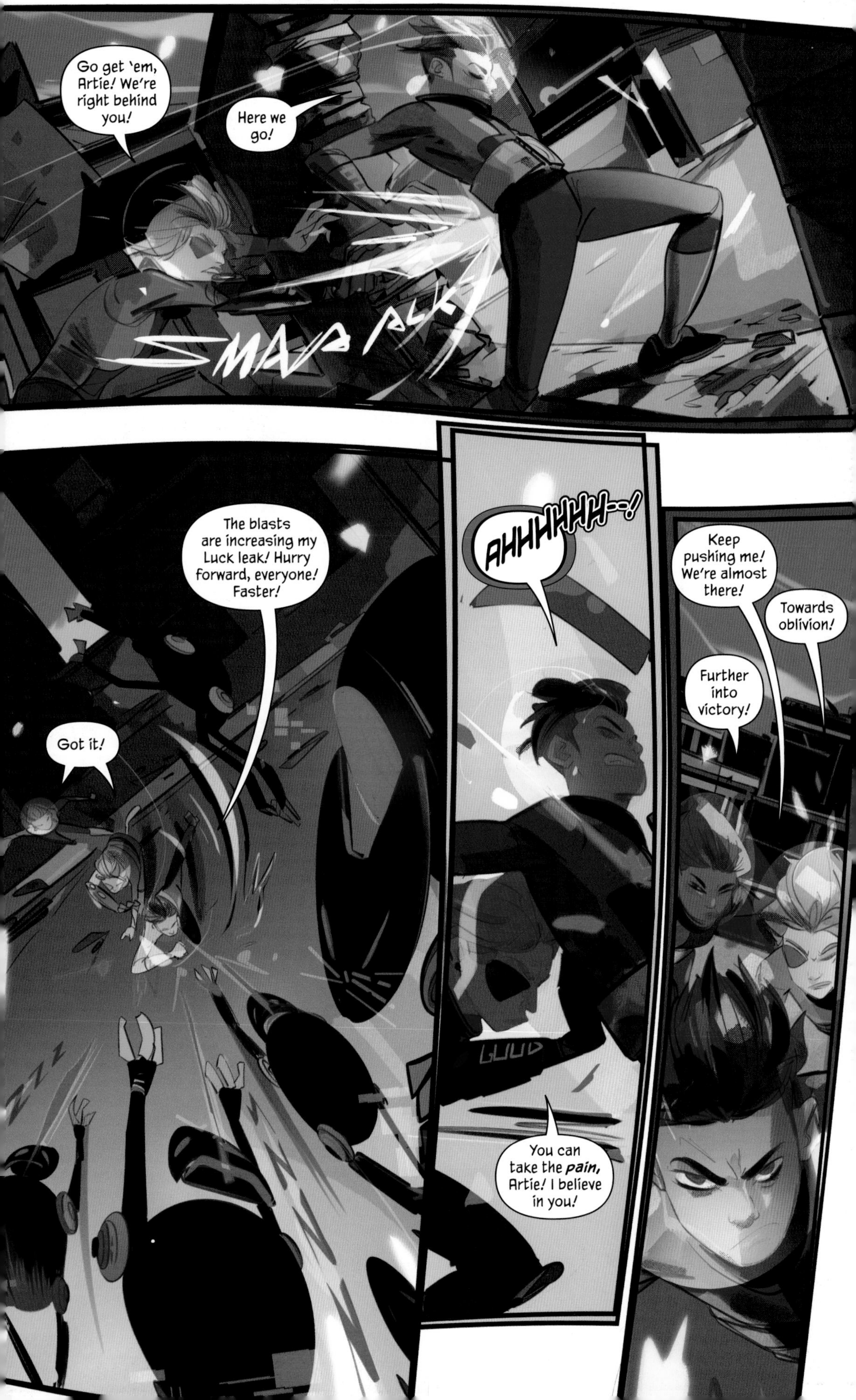
Go get 'em, Artie! We're right behind you!
Here we go!
The blasts are increasing my Luck leak! Hurry forward, everyone! Faster!
Got it!
AHHHHHH--!
You can take the *pain,* Artie! I believe in you!
Keep pushing me! We're almost there!
Towards oblivion!
Further into victory!

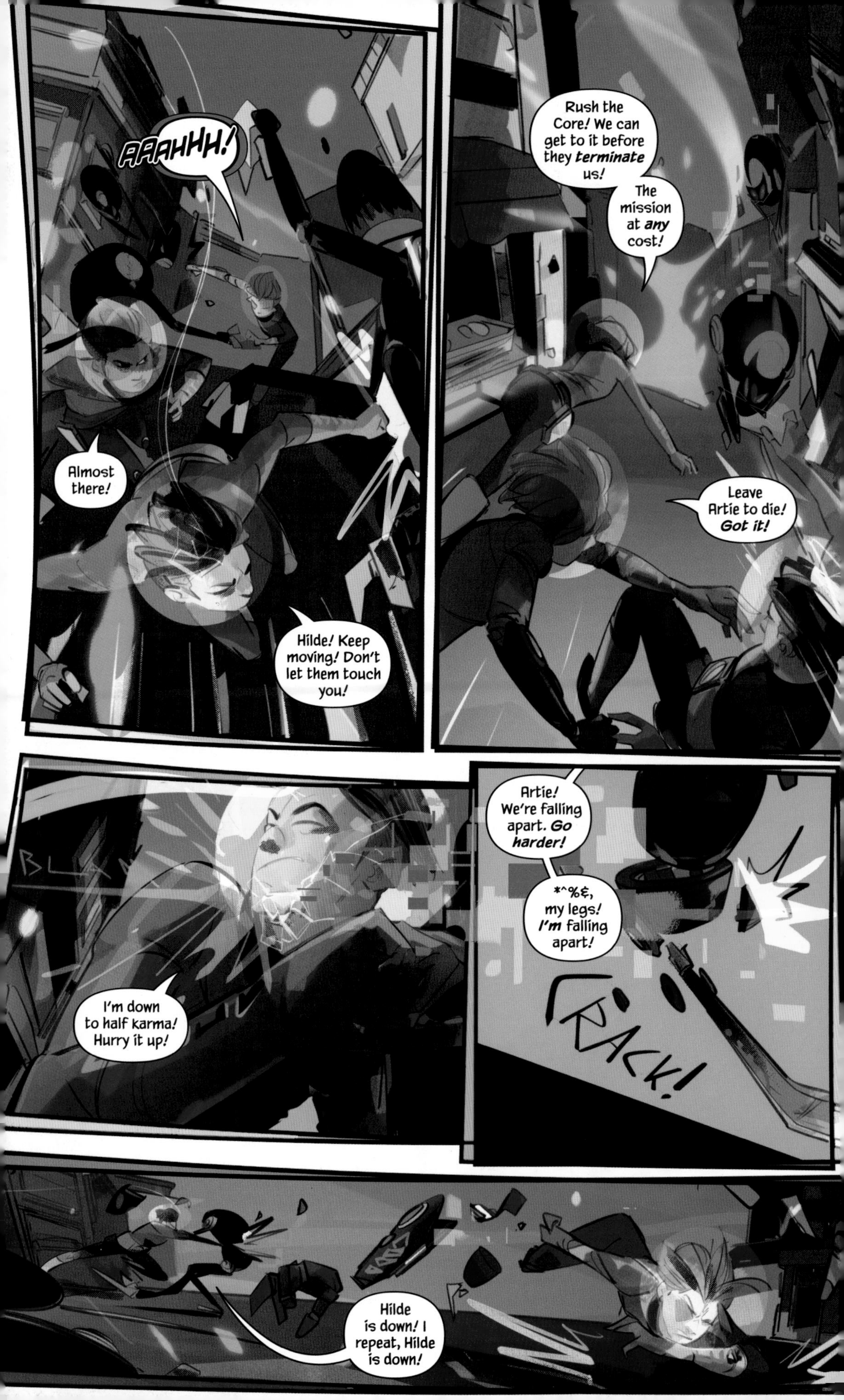
AAAHHH!
Almost there!
Hilde! Keep moving! Don't let them touch you!
Rush the Core! We can get to it before they *terminate* us!
The mission at *any* cost!
Leave Artie to die! ***Got it!***
I'm down to half karma! Hurry it up!
Artie! We're falling apart. ***Go harder!***
*^%&, my legs! ***I'm*** falling apart!
CRACK!
Hilde is down! I repeat, Hilde is down!

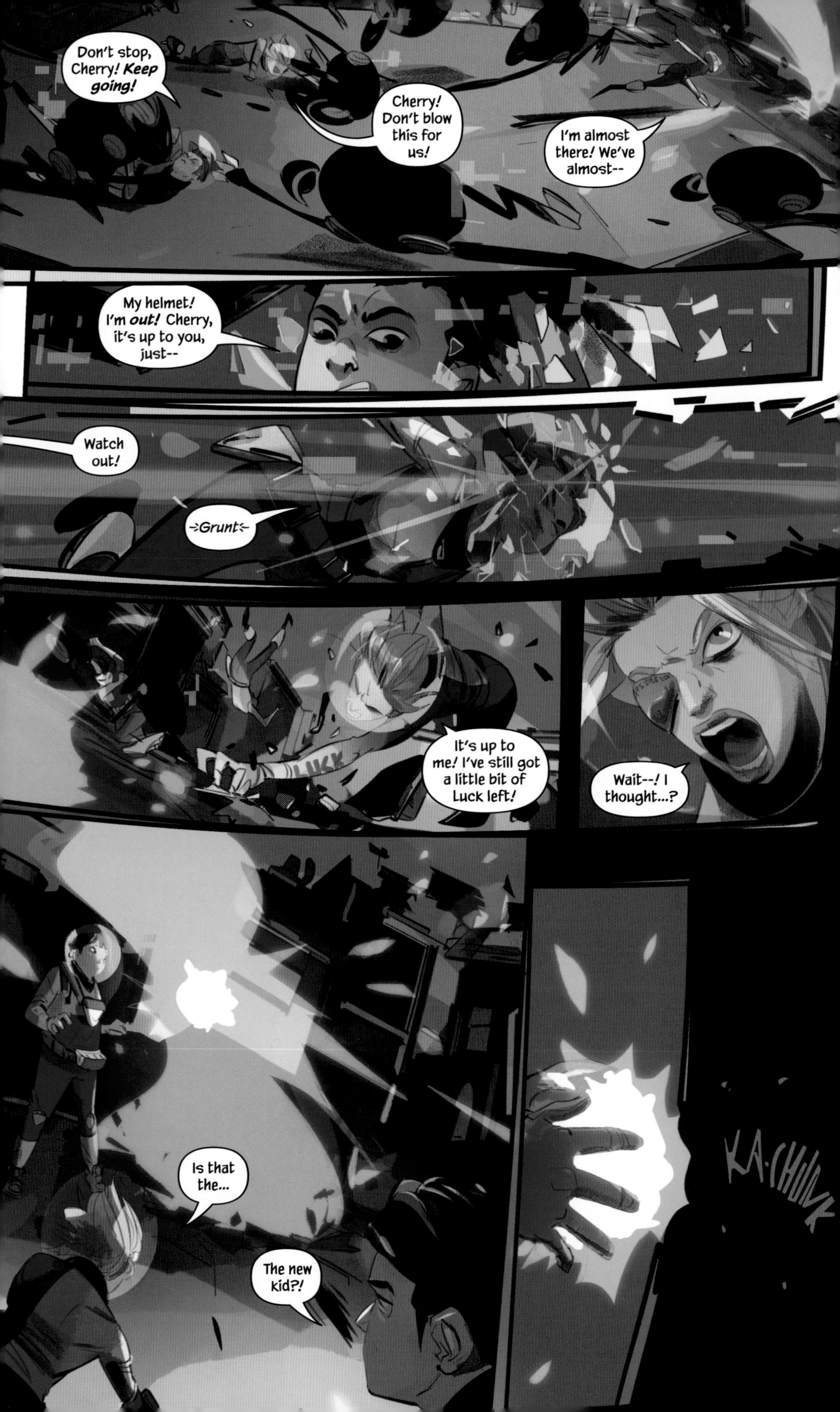
Don't stop, Cherry! ***Keep going!***
Cherry! Don't blow this for us!
I'm almost there! We've almost--
My helmet! I'm ***out!*** Cherry, it's up to you, just--
Watch out!
Grunt
It's up to me! I've still got a little bit of Luck left!
Wait--! I thought...?
Is that the...
The new kid?!
KA-CHUNK

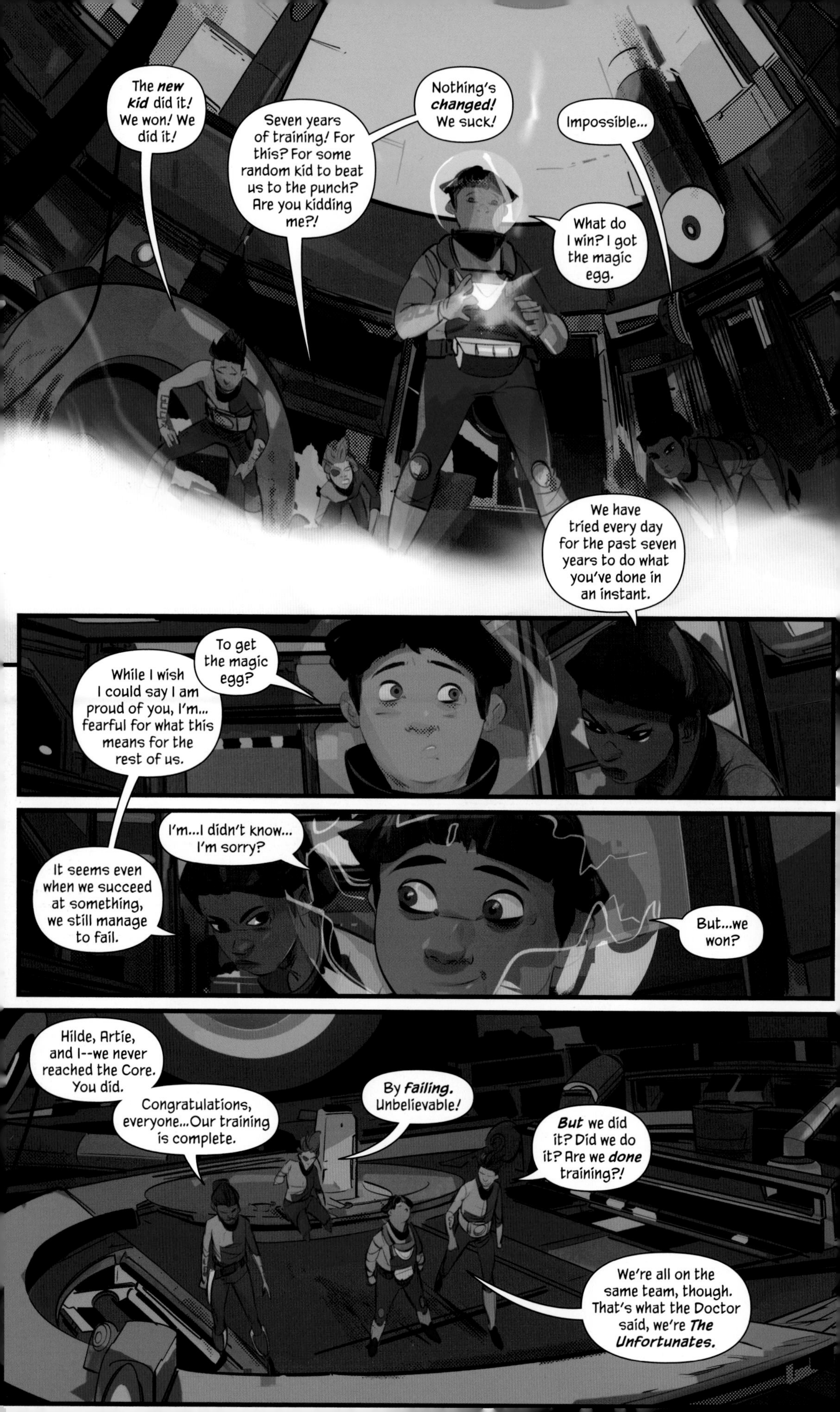
The *new kid* did it! We won! We did it!
Seven years of training! For this? For some random kid to beat us to the punch? Are you kidding me?!
Nothing's *changed!* We suck!
Impossible...
What do I win? I got the magic egg.
We have tried every day for the past seven years to do what you've done in an instant.
To get the magic egg?
While I wish I could say I am proud of you, I'm... fearful for what this means for the rest of us.
I'm...I didn't know... I'm sorry?
It seems even when we succeed at something, we still manage to fail.
But...we won?
Hilde, Artie, and I--we never reached the Core. You did.
Congratulations, everyone...Our training is complete.
By *failing.* Unbelievable!
But we did it? Did we do it? Are we *done* training?!
We're all on the same team, though. That's what the Doctor said, we're *The Unfortunates.*

Yes. We are the only people on this planet with approximately zero Luck. Nothing good will ever happen to us.

It is science.

Wait. *Hold up.*

If this little twerp has zero Luck, *like the rest of us*, how was he able to get to the Core? That doesn't make any sense? He should have failed like the rest of us.

I just pretended it was like a video game and before I knew it, I was at the end of the level. I thought there was going to be a boss.

Am I going crazy? Does this make sense to anyone else?

Hilde. We don't ask questions, we just put our head down and do the job.

Anyway, Joseph, this is Artie--he is usually late to the training simulation.

I used to think I was the only boy with this kind of Luck. It's *nice* to know I'm not alone anymore.

Great to meet you, Joey.

So this kid exists to torture us. Okay, I get it. Anytime the three of us would succeed, we fail and *he* succeeds. The Gods of Luck are really rubbing our faces in it, huh?

Hey, it's not *his* fault. He's unlucky like the rest of us! Cut him some slack.

I'm sorry, I can leave. I don't want to be a problem...

Yes! Leave!

No, stay!

...

Hilde. Artie. *Enough.*

We're sorry, little dude. Emotions run high around here.

Don't apologize for me, because I'm not sorry. He's a walking, talking paradox and we've got enough weird %¢^$ to worry about!

We're *worms*, Artie, and anything that comes into our lives is just a *bird waiting to eat us.*

Shut the hell up, Artie!

Both of you, stop. Now.

You're a bird, Joey! An evil bird, and I will not be your dinner!

...What? I'm not a bird...

Geez! You are so negative. Maybe Joey here is just what we needed! What if *he's* the missing member of the band! Sometimes you need a rhythm *and* a lead, Hilde!

Maybe he's our lead now!

Congratulations.

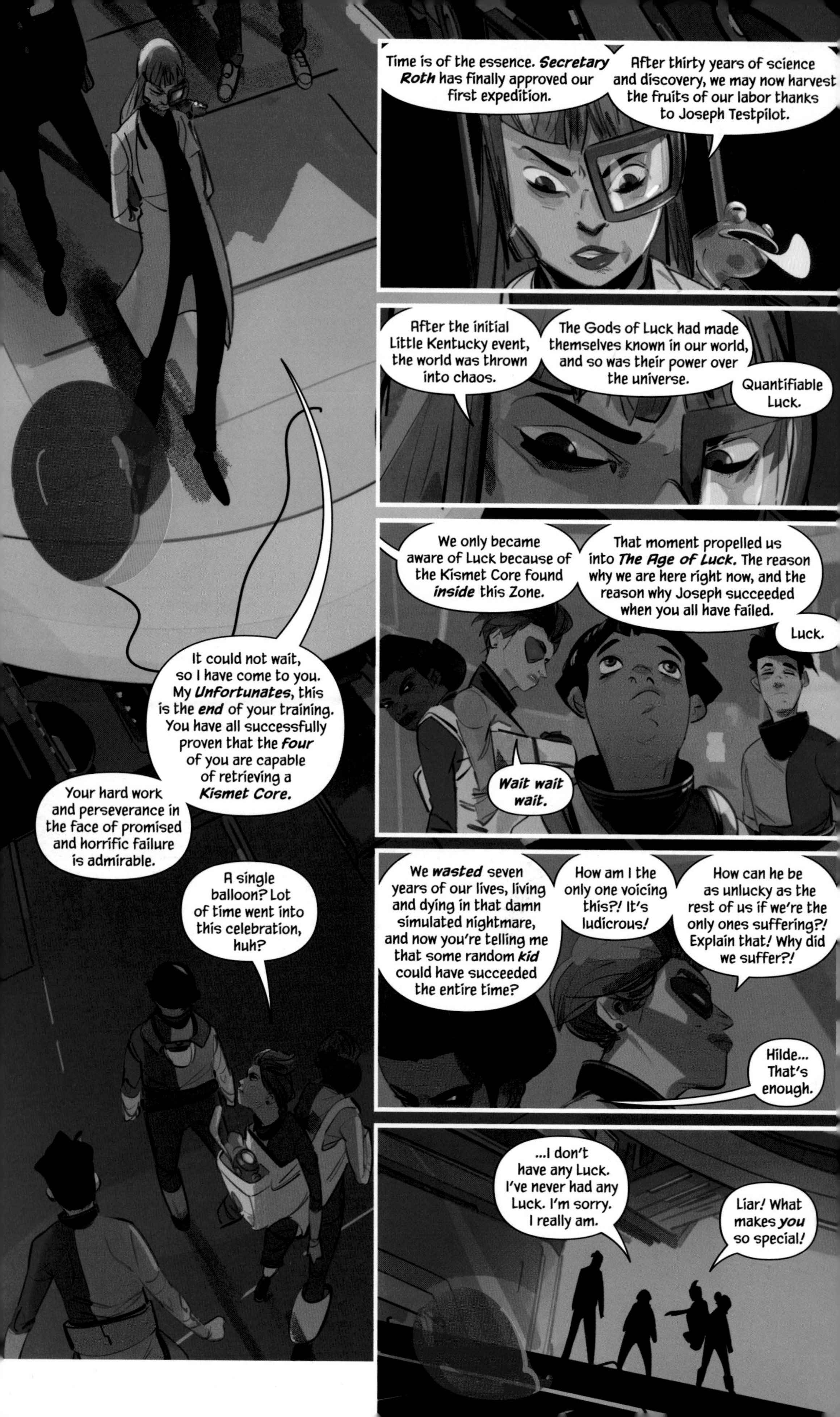
It could not wait, so I have come to you. My *Unfortunates*, this is the *end* of your training. You have all successfully proven that the *four* of you are capable of retrieving a *Kismet Core.*
Your hard work and perseverance in the face of promised and horrific failure is admirable.
A single balloon? Lot of time went into this celebration, huh?
Time is of the essence. ***Secretary Roth*** has finally approved our first expedition.
After thirty years of science and discovery, we may now harvest the fruits of our labor thanks to Joseph Testpilot.
After the initial Little Kentucky event, the world was thrown into chaos.
The Gods of Luck had made themselves known in our world, and so was their power over the universe.
Quantifiable Luck.
We only became aware of Luck because of the Kismet Core found *inside* this Zone.
That moment propelled us into *The Age of Luck.* The reason why we are here right now, and the reason why Joseph succeeded when you all have failed.
Luck.
Wait wait wait.
We *wasted* seven years of our lives, living and dying in that damn simulated nightmare, and now you're telling me that some random *kid* could have succeeded the entire time?
How am I the only one voicing this?! It's ludicrous!
How can he be as unlucky as the rest of us if we're the only ones suffering?! Explain that! Why did we suffer?!
Hilde... That's enough.
...I don't have any Luck. I've never had any Luck. I'm sorry. I really am.
Liar! What makes *you* so special!

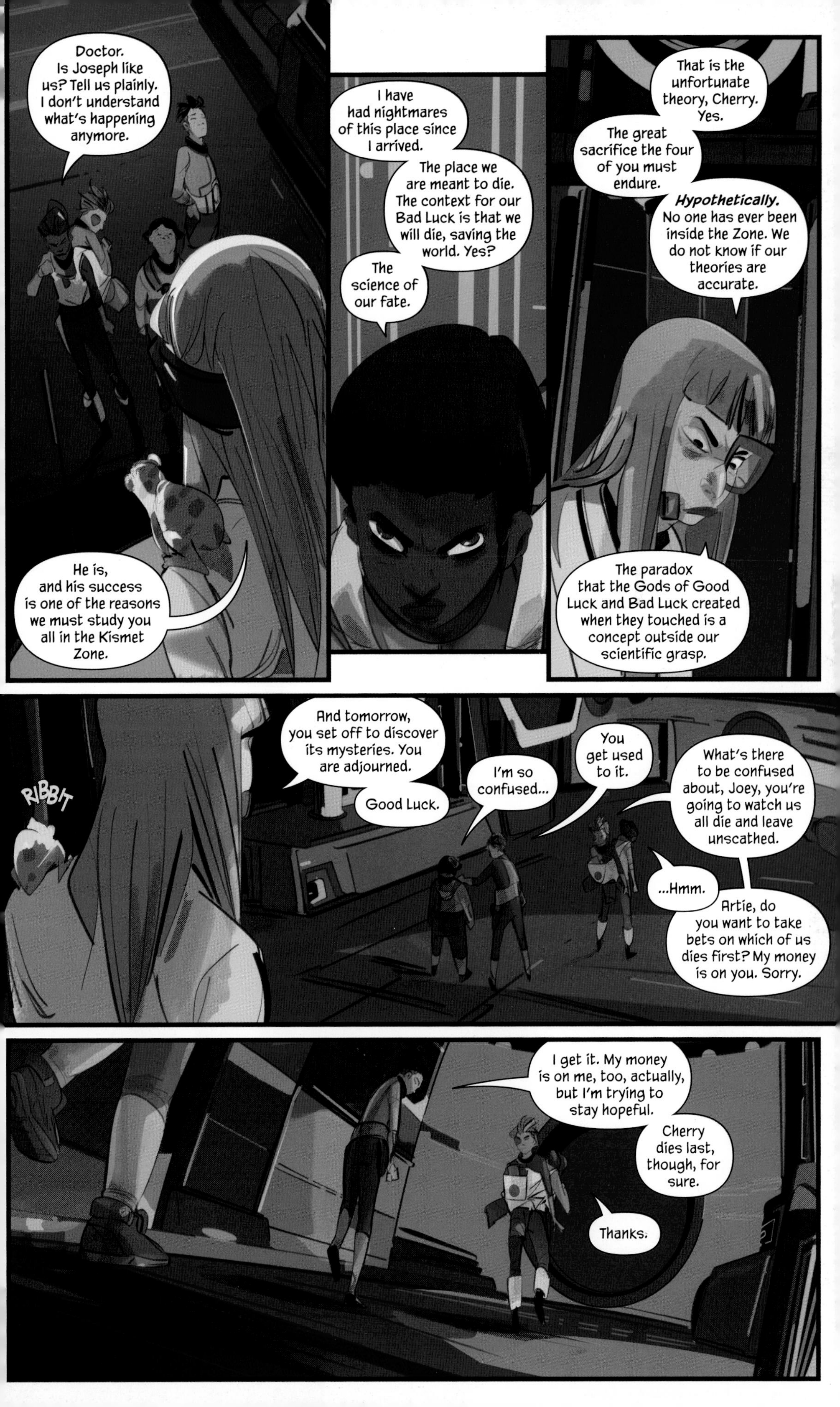
Doctor. Is Joseph like us? Tell us plainly. I don't understand what's happening anymore.
He is, and his success is one of the reasons we must study you all in the Kismet Zone.
I have had nightmares of this place since I arrived.
The place we are meant to die. The context for our Bad Luck is that we will die, saving the world. Yes?
The science of our fate.
That is the unfortunate theory, Cherry. Yes.
The great sacrifice the four of you must endure.
Hypothetically. No one has ever been inside the Zone. We do not know if our theories are accurate.
The paradox that the Gods of Good Luck and Bad Luck created when they touched is a concept outside our scientific grasp.
RIBBIT
And tomorrow, you set off to discover its mysteries. You are adjourned.
Good Luck.
I'm so confused...
You get used to it.
What's there to be confused about, Joey, you're going to watch us all die and leave unscathed.
...Hmm.
Artie, do you want to take bets on which of us dies first? My money is on you. Sorry.
I get it. My money is on me, too, actually, but I'm trying to stay hopeful.
Cherry dies last, though, for sure.
Thanks.

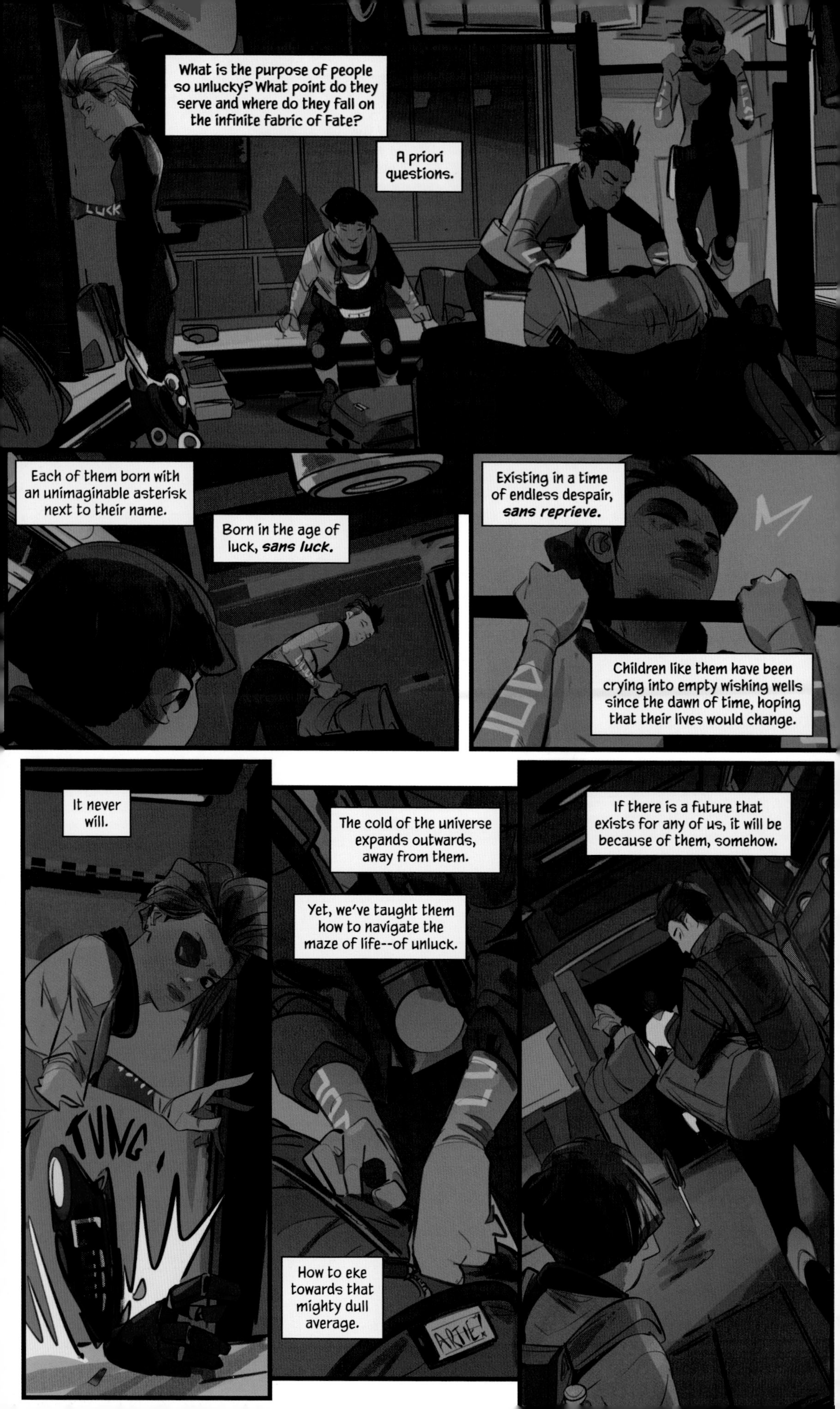
What is the purpose of people so unlucky? What point do they serve and where do they fall on the infinite fabric of Fate?
A priori questions.
LUCK
Each of them born with an unimaginable asterisk next to their name.
Born in the age of luck, *sans luck.*
Existing in a time of endless despair, *sans reprieve.*
Children like them have been crying into empty wishing wells since the dawn of time, hoping that their lives would change.
It never will.
TUNG
The cold of the universe expands outwards, away from them.
Yet, we've taught them how to navigate the maze of life--of unluck.
How to eke towards that mighty dull average.
ARTIE!
If there is a future that exists for any of us, it will be because of them, somehow.

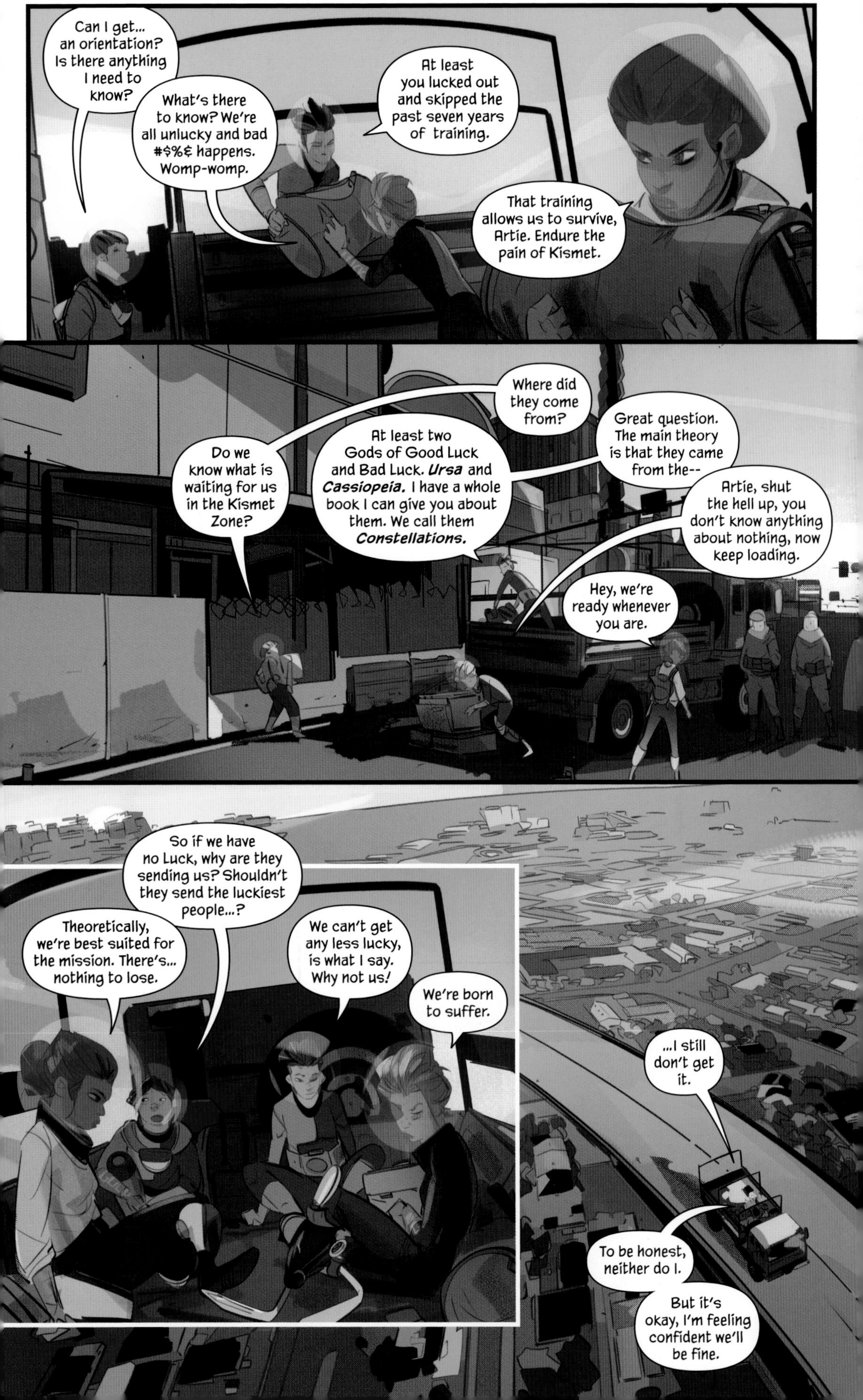
Can I get... an orientation? Is there anything I need to know?
What's there to know? We're all unlucky and bad #$%& happens. Womp-womp.
At least you lucked out and skipped the past seven years of training.
That training allows us to survive, Artie. Endure the pain of Kismet.
Do we know what is waiting for us in the Kismet Zone?
Where did they come from?
At least two Gods of Good Luck and Bad Luck. *Ursa* and *Cassiopeia.* I have a whole book I can give you about them. We call them ***Constellations.***
Great question. The main theory is that they came from the--
Artie, shut the hell up, you don't know anything about nothing, now keep loading.
Hey, we're ready whenever you are.
So if we have no Luck, why are they sending us? Shouldn't they send the luckiest people...?
Theoretically, we're best suited for the mission. There's... nothing to lose.
We can't get any less lucky, is what I say. Why not us!
We're born to suffer.
...I still don't get it.
To be honest, neither do I.
But it's okay, I'm feeling confident we'll be fine.

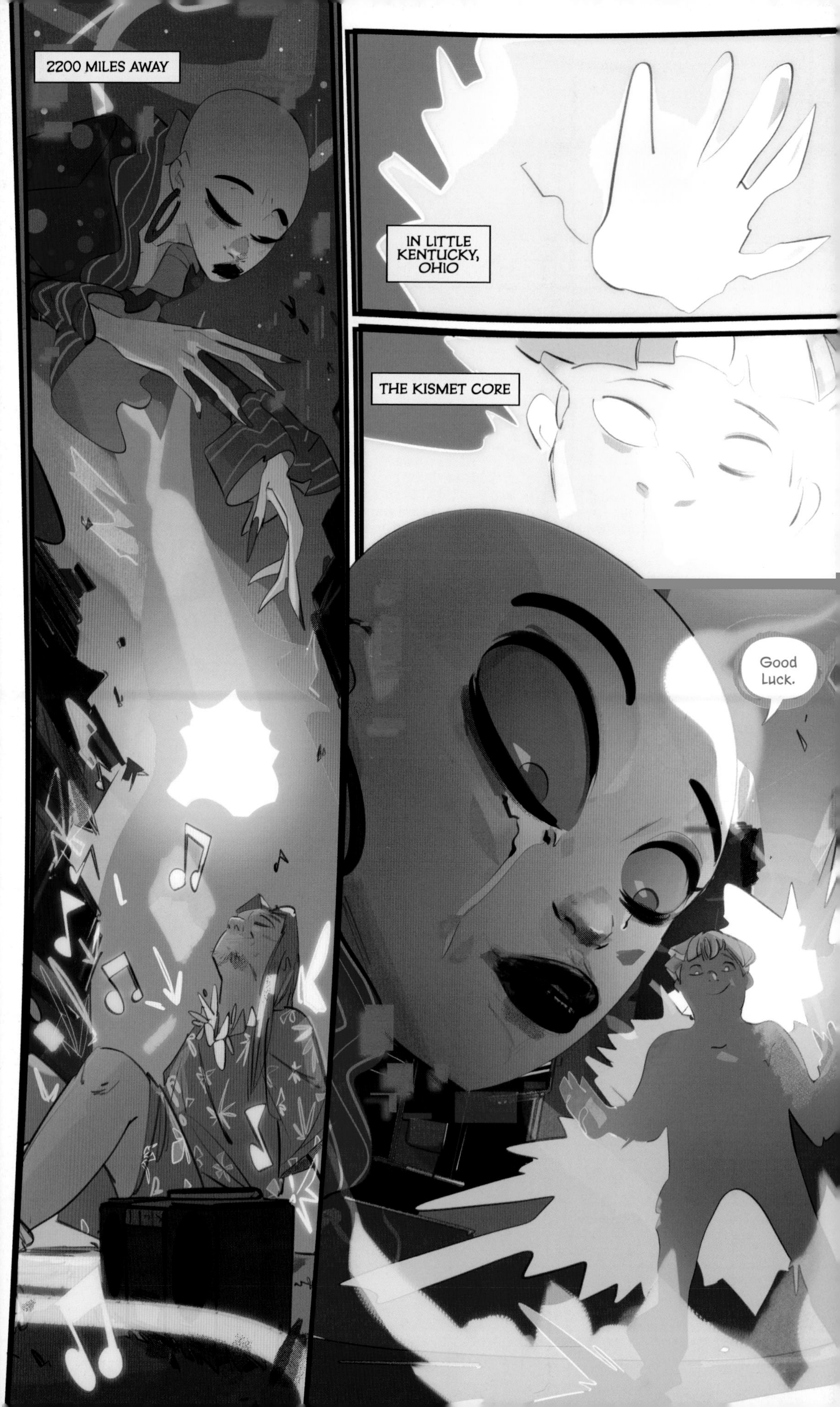
2200 MILES AWAY
IN LITTLE KENTUCKY, OHIO
THE KISMET CORE
Good Luck.

CHAPTER

2

WINDY SUMMER, 1989

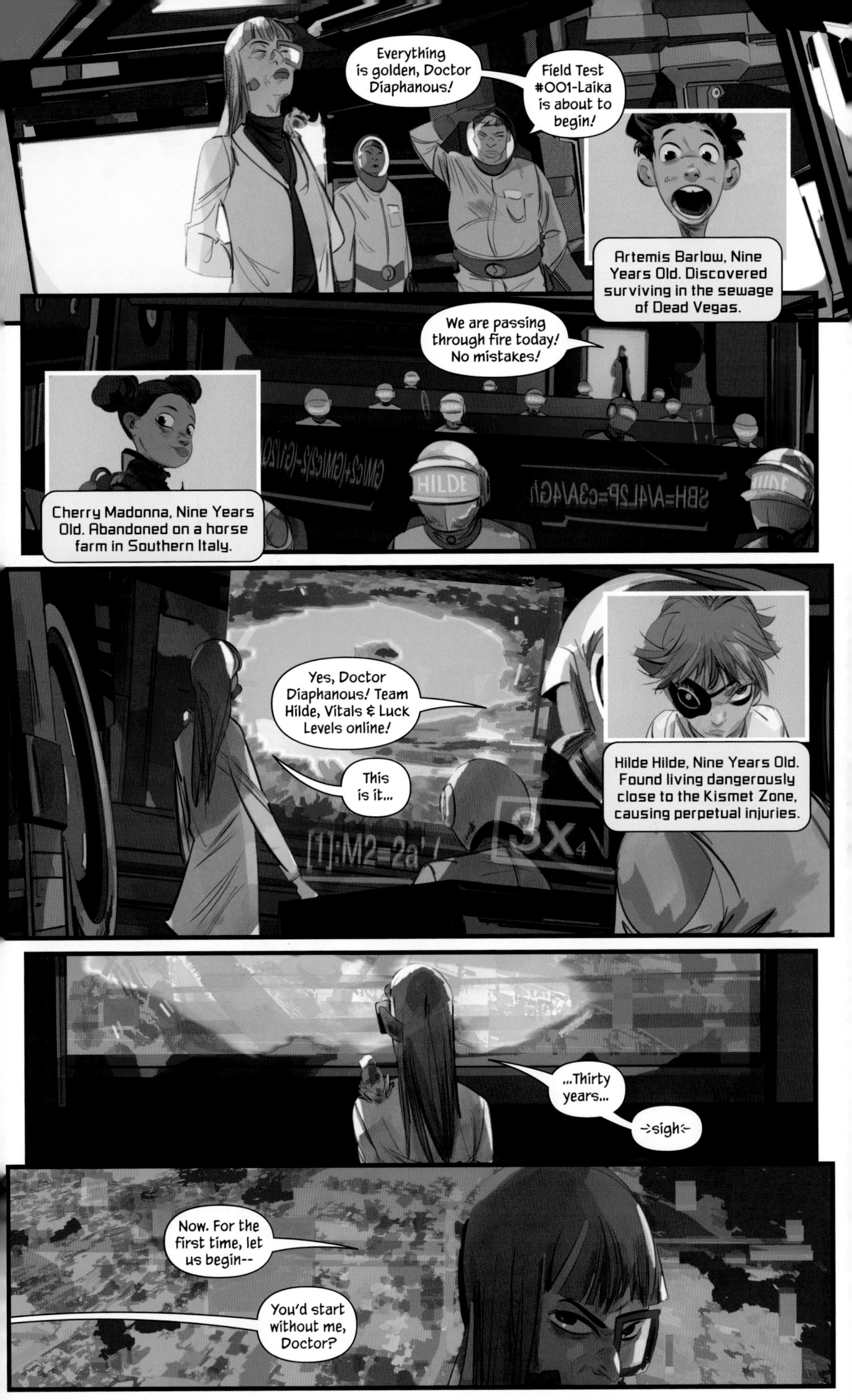
Everything is golden, Doctor Diaphanous!
Field Test #001-Laika is about to begin!
Artemis Barlow, Nine Years Old. Discovered surviving in the sewage of Dead Vegas.
Cherry Madonna, Nine Years Old. Abandoned on a horse farm in Southern Italy.
We are passing through fire today! No mistakes!
HILDE
Yes, Doctor Diaphanous! Team Hilde, Vitals & Luck Levels online!
This is it...
Hilde Hilde, Nine Years Old. Found living dangerously close to the Kismet Zone, causing perpetual injuries.
...Thirty years...
sigh
Now. For the first time, let us begin--
You'd start without me, Doctor?

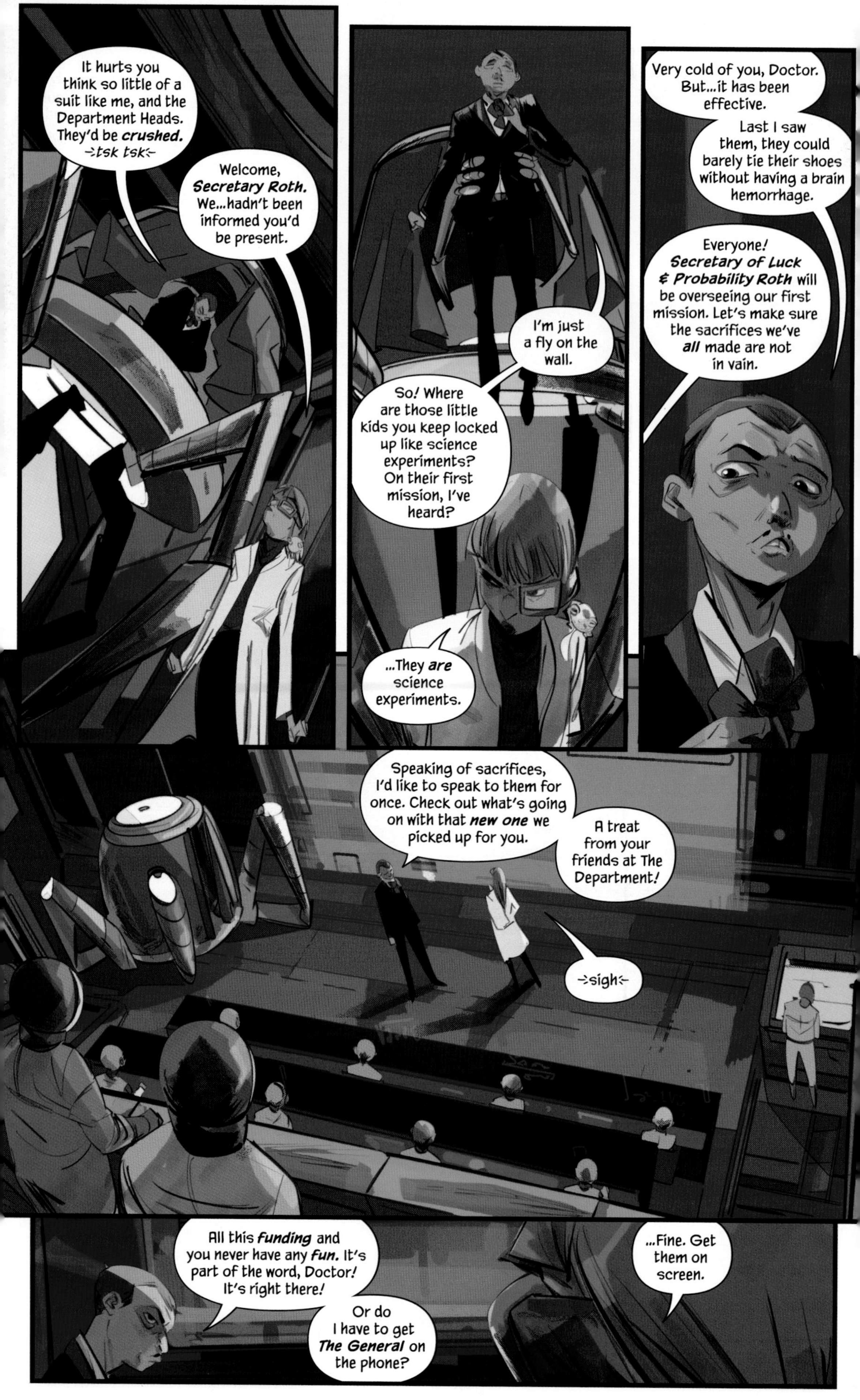
It hurts you think so little of a suit like me, and the Department Heads. They'd be *crushed.* ->tsk tsk<-
Welcome, *Secretary Roth.* We...hadn't been informed you'd be present.
I'm just a fly on the wall.
So! Where are those little kids you keep locked up like science experiments? On their first mission, I've heard?
...They *are* science experiments.
Very cold of you, Doctor. But...it has been effective.
Last I saw them, they could barely tie their shoes without having a brain hemorrhage.
Everyone! *Secretary of Luck & Probability Roth* will be overseeing our first mission. Let's make sure the sacrifices we've *all* made are not in vain.
Speaking of sacrifices, I'd like to speak to them for once. Check out what's going on with that *new one* we picked up for you.
A treat from your friends at The Department!
->sigh<-
All this *funding* and you never have any *fun.* It's part of the word, Doctor! It's right there!
Or do I have to get *The General* on the phone?
...Fine. Get them on screen.

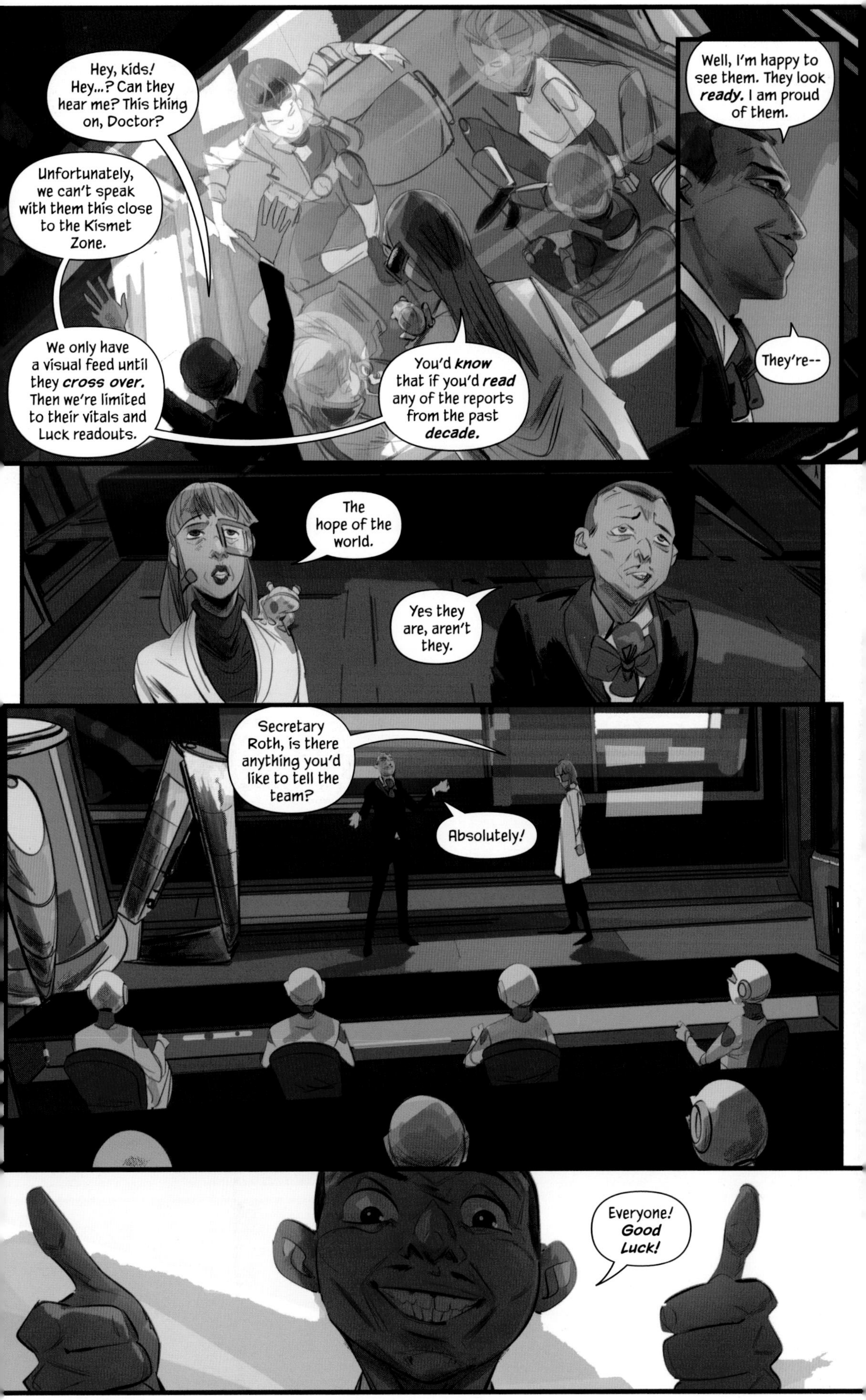

Hey, kids! Hey...? Can they hear me? This thing on, Doctor?
Unfortunately, we can't speak with them this close to the Kismet Zone.
We only have a visual feed until they *cross over.* Then we're limited to their vitals and Luck readouts.
You'd *know* that if you'd *read* any of the reports from the past *decade.*
Well, I'm happy to see them. They look *ready.* I am proud of them.
They're--
The hope of the world.
Yes they are, aren't they.
Secretary Roth, is there anything you'd like to tell the team?
Absolutely!
Everyone! *Good Luck!*

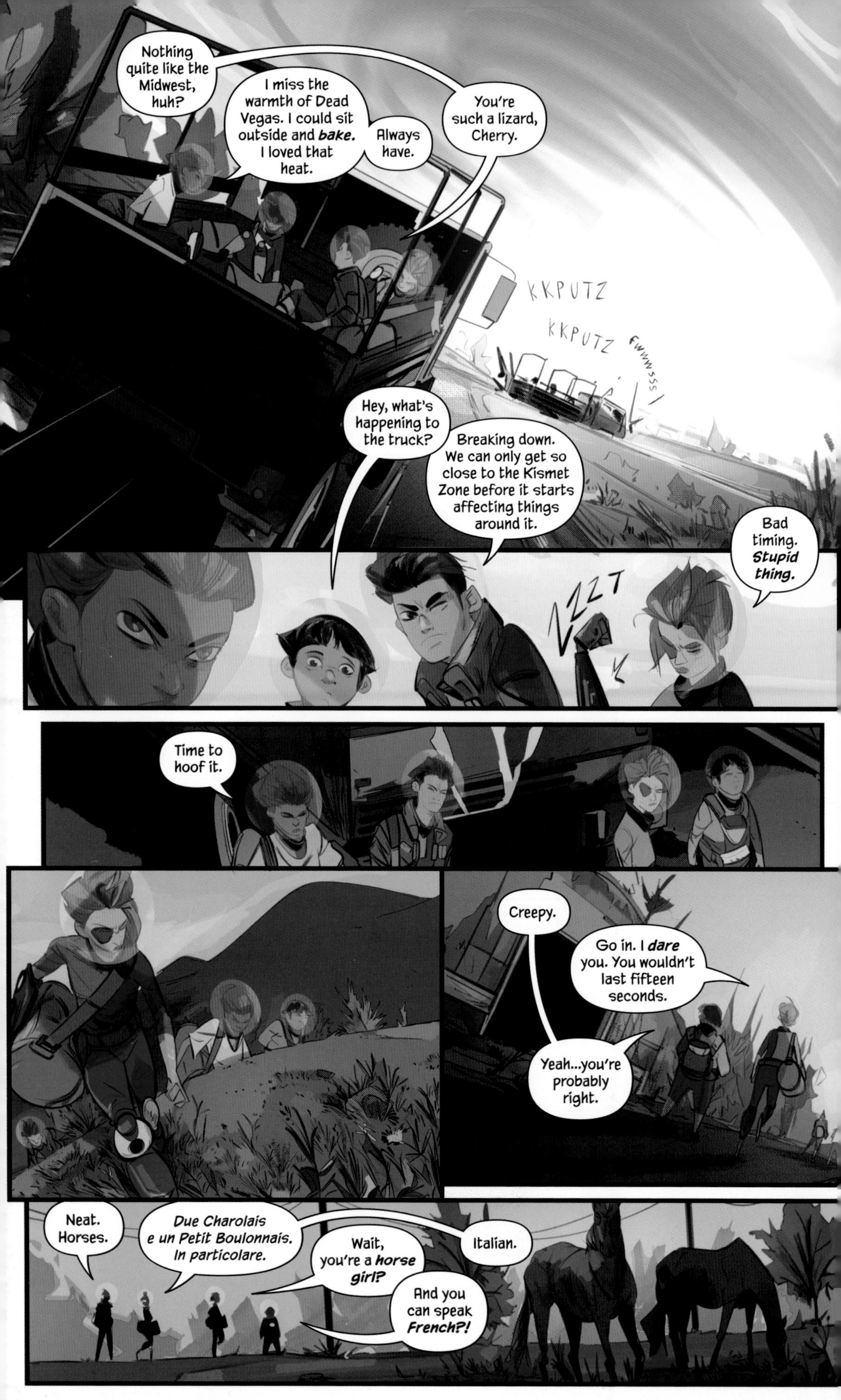
Nothing quite like the Midwest, huh?
I miss the warmth of Dead Vegas. I could sit outside and *bake.* I loved that heat.
Always have.
You're such a lizard, Cherry.
KKPUTZ
KKPUTZ
FWWWSSS!
Hey, what's happening to the truck?
Breaking down. We can only get so close to the Kismet Zone before it starts affecting things around it.
Bad timing. *Stupid thing.*
ZZZT
Time to hoof it.
Creepy.
Go in. I *dare* you. You wouldn't last fifteen seconds.
Yeah...you're probably right.
Neat. Horses.
Due Charolais e un Petit Boulonnais. In particolare.
Italian.
Wait, you're a *horse girl?*
And you can speak *French?!*

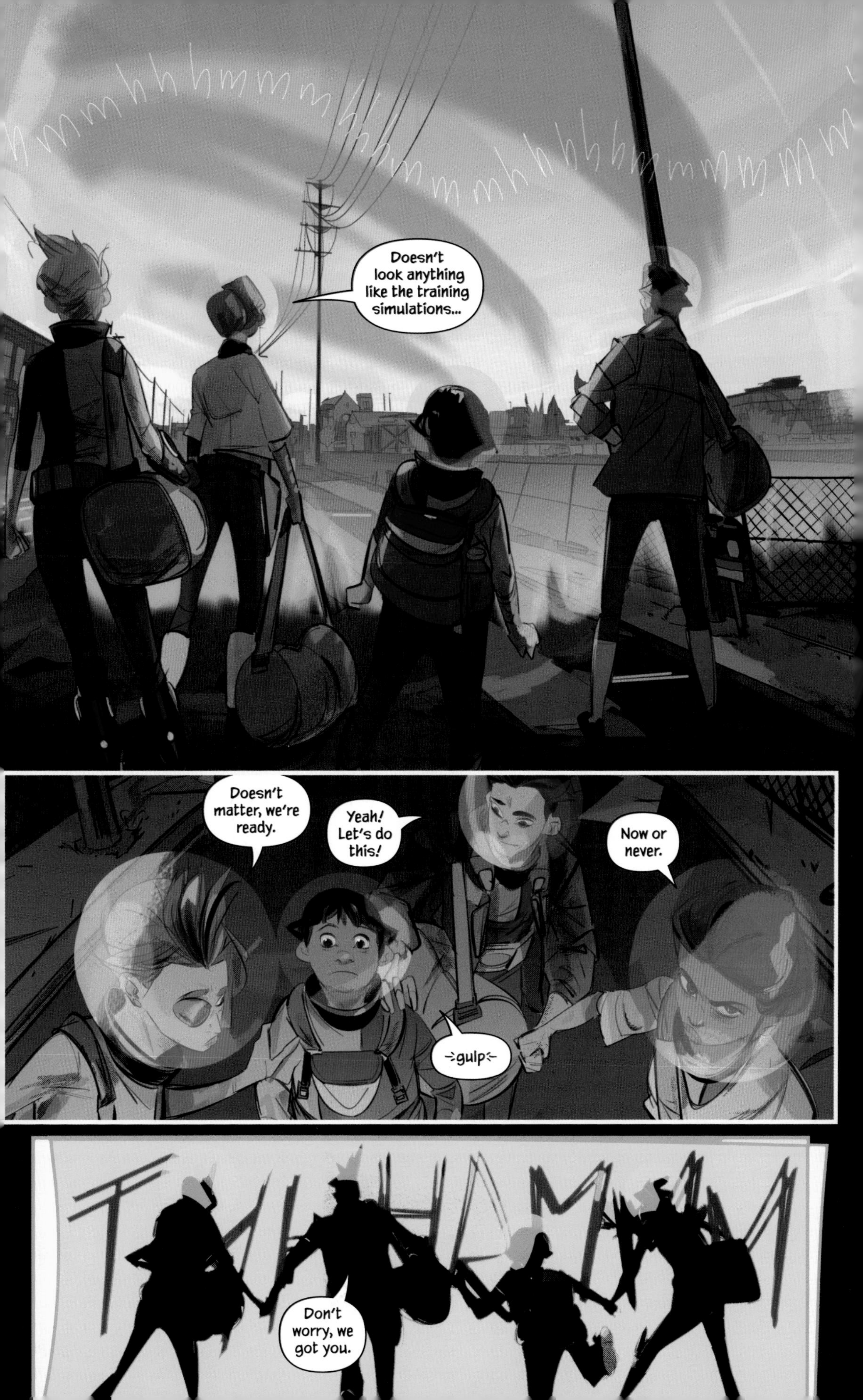
hmmhhhmmmhh hhmmmhhhhhhmmmmm
Doesn't look anything like the training simulations...
Doesn't matter, we're ready.
Yeah! Let's do this!
Now or never.
gulp
THHMM
Don't worry, we got you.

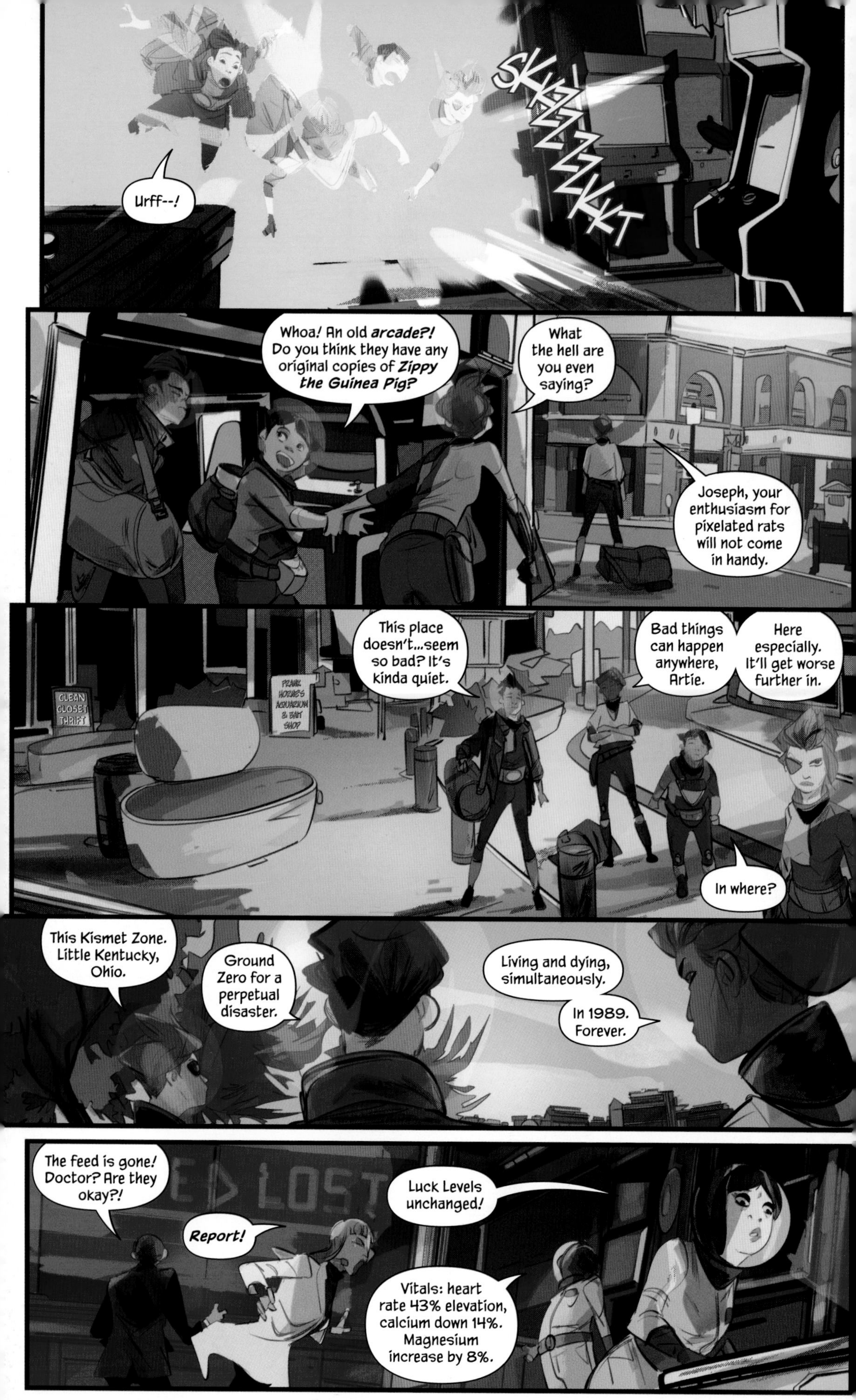
Urff--!
SKKZZZZKKT
Whoa! An old *arcade?!* Do you think they have any original copies of ***Zippy the Guinea Pig?***
What the hell are you even saying?
Joseph, your enthusiasm for pixelated rats will not come in handy.
CLEAN CLOSET THRIFT
FRANK HORNE'S AQUARIUM & BAIT SHOP
This place doesn't...seem so bad? It's kinda quiet.
Bad things can happen anywhere, Artie.
Here especially. It'll get worse further in.
In where?
This Kismet Zone. Little Kentucky, Ohio.
Ground Zero for a perpetual disaster.
Living and dying, simultaneously.
In 1989. Forever.
The feed is gone! Doctor? Are they okay?!
ED LOST
Report!
Luck Levels unchanged!
Vitals: heart rate 43% elevation, calcium down 14%. Magnesium increase by 8%.

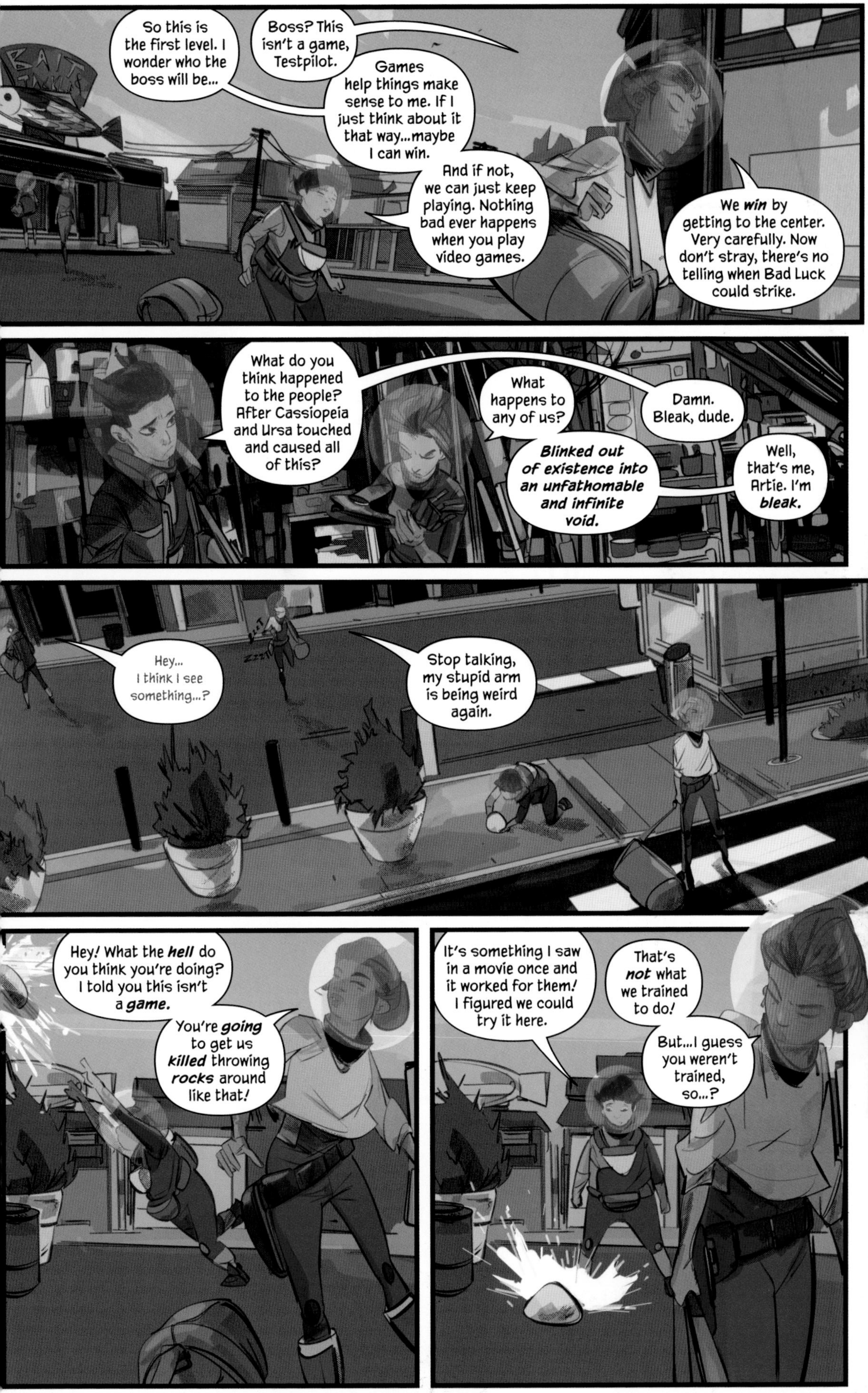

BAIT
So this is the first level. I wonder who the boss will be...
Boss? This isn't a game, Testpilot.
Games help things make sense to me. If I just think about it that way...maybe I can win.
And if not, we can just keep playing. Nothing bad ever happens when you play video games.
We *win* by getting to the center. Very carefully. Now don't stray, there's no telling when Bad Luck could strike.
What do you think happened to the people? After Cassiopeia and Ursa touched and caused all of this?
What happens to any of us?
Blinked out of existence into an unfathomable and infinite void.
Damn. Bleak, dude.
Well, that's me, Artie. I'm ***bleak.***
Hey... I think I see something...?
Stop talking, my stupid arm is being weird again.
Hey! What the ***hell*** do you think you're doing? I told you this isn't a ***game.***
You're ***going*** to get us ***killed*** throwing ***rocks*** around like that!
It's something I saw in a movie once and it worked for them! I figured we could try it here.
That's ***not*** what we trained to do!
But...I guess you weren't trained, so...?

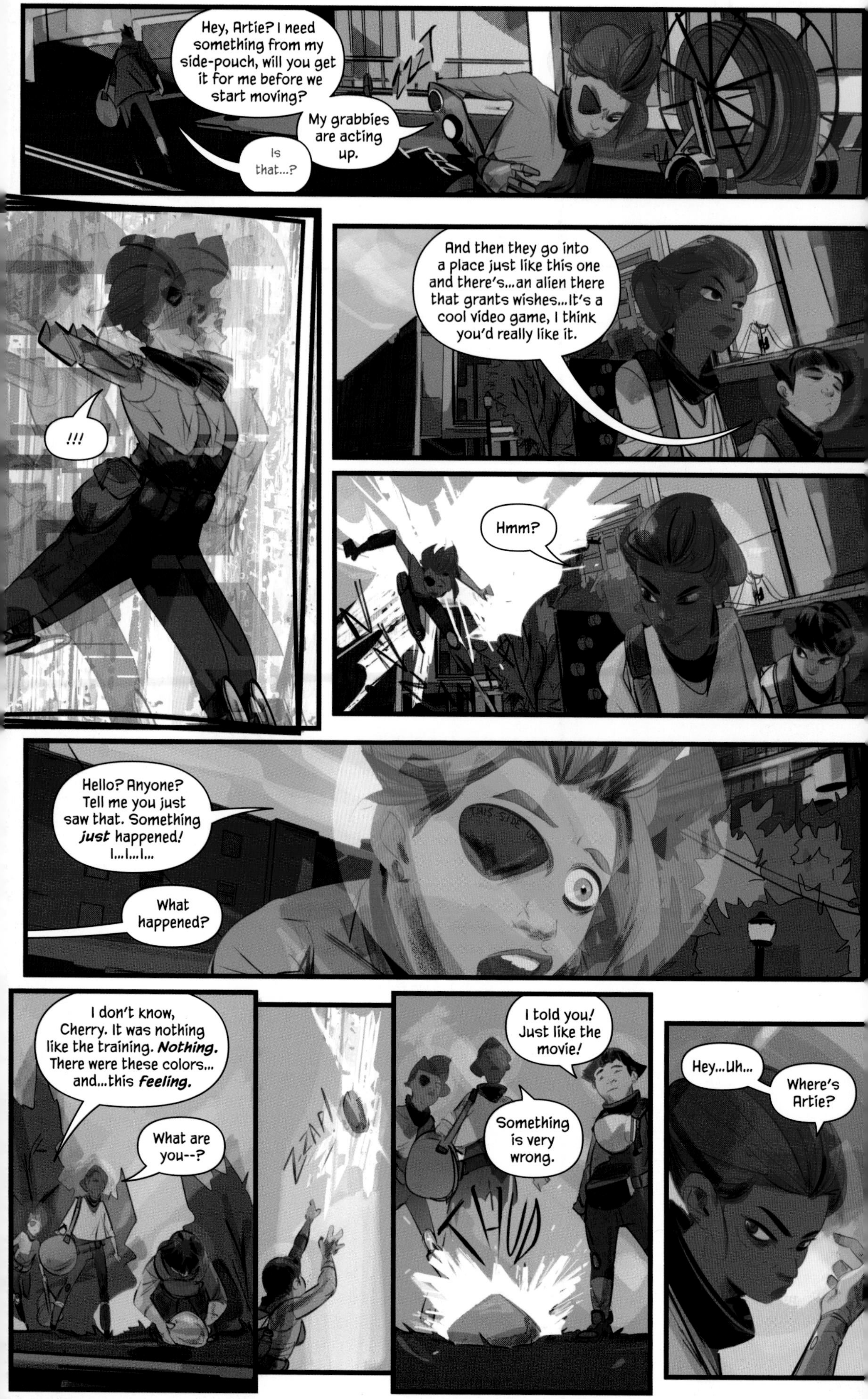
Hey, Artie? I need something from my side-pouch, will you get it for me before we start moving?
ZZZT
My grabbies are acting up.
Is that...?
!!!
And then they go into a place just like this one and there's...an alien there that grants wishes...It's a cool video game, I think you'd really like it.
Hmm?
Hello? Anyone? Tell me you just saw that. Something *just* happened! I...I...I...
THIS SIDE UP
What happened?
I don't know, Cherry. It was nothing like the training. **Nothing.** There were these colors... and...this ***feeling.***
What are you--?
Z-ZAP!
I told you! Just like the movie!
Something is very wrong.
THUD
Hey...uh...
Where's Artie?

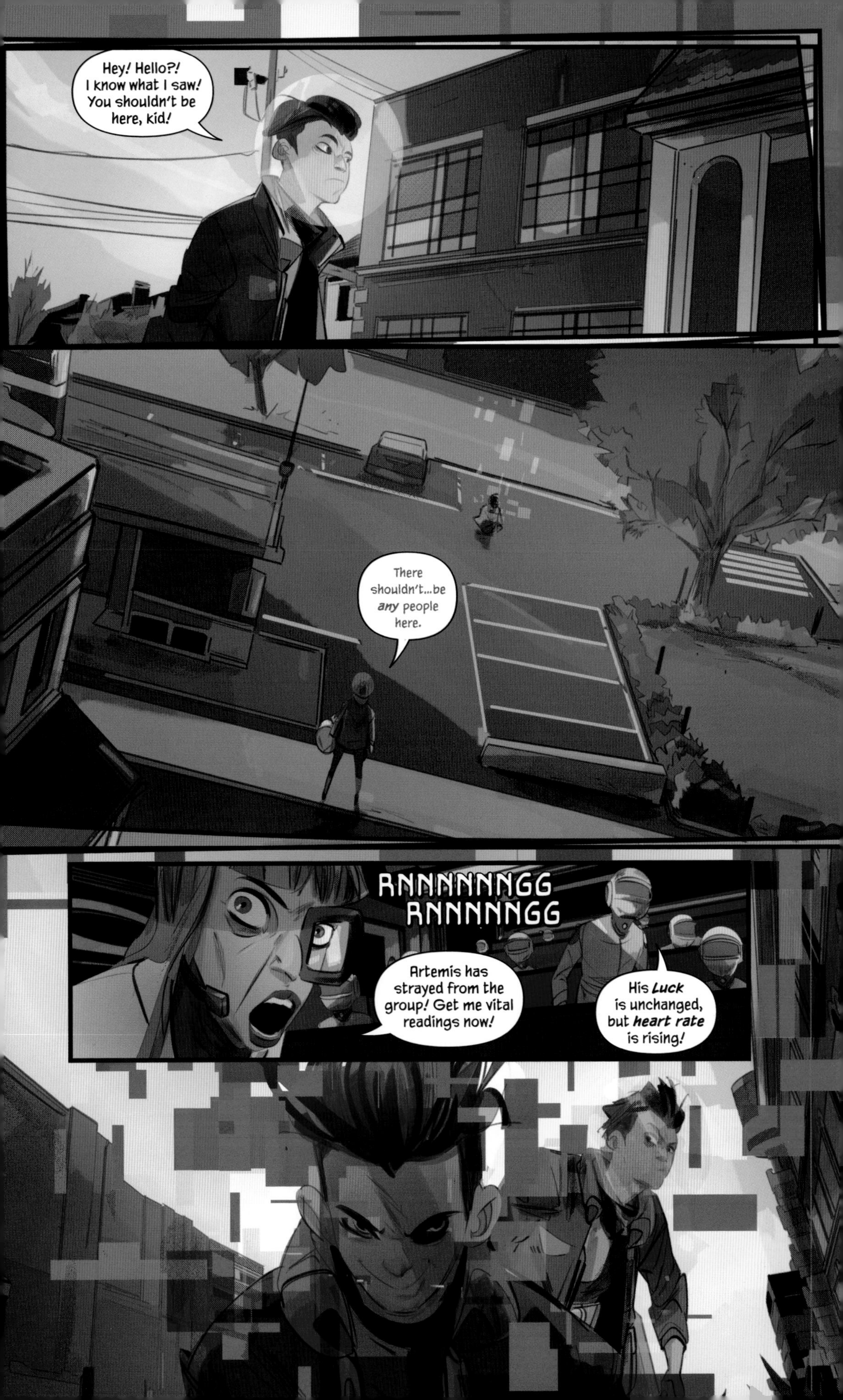

Hey! Hello?! I know what I saw! You shouldn't be here, kid!
There shouldn't...be *any* people here.
RNNNNNNGG RNNNNNGG
Artemis has strayed from the group! Get me vital readings now!
His *Luck* is unchanged, but *heart rate* is rising!

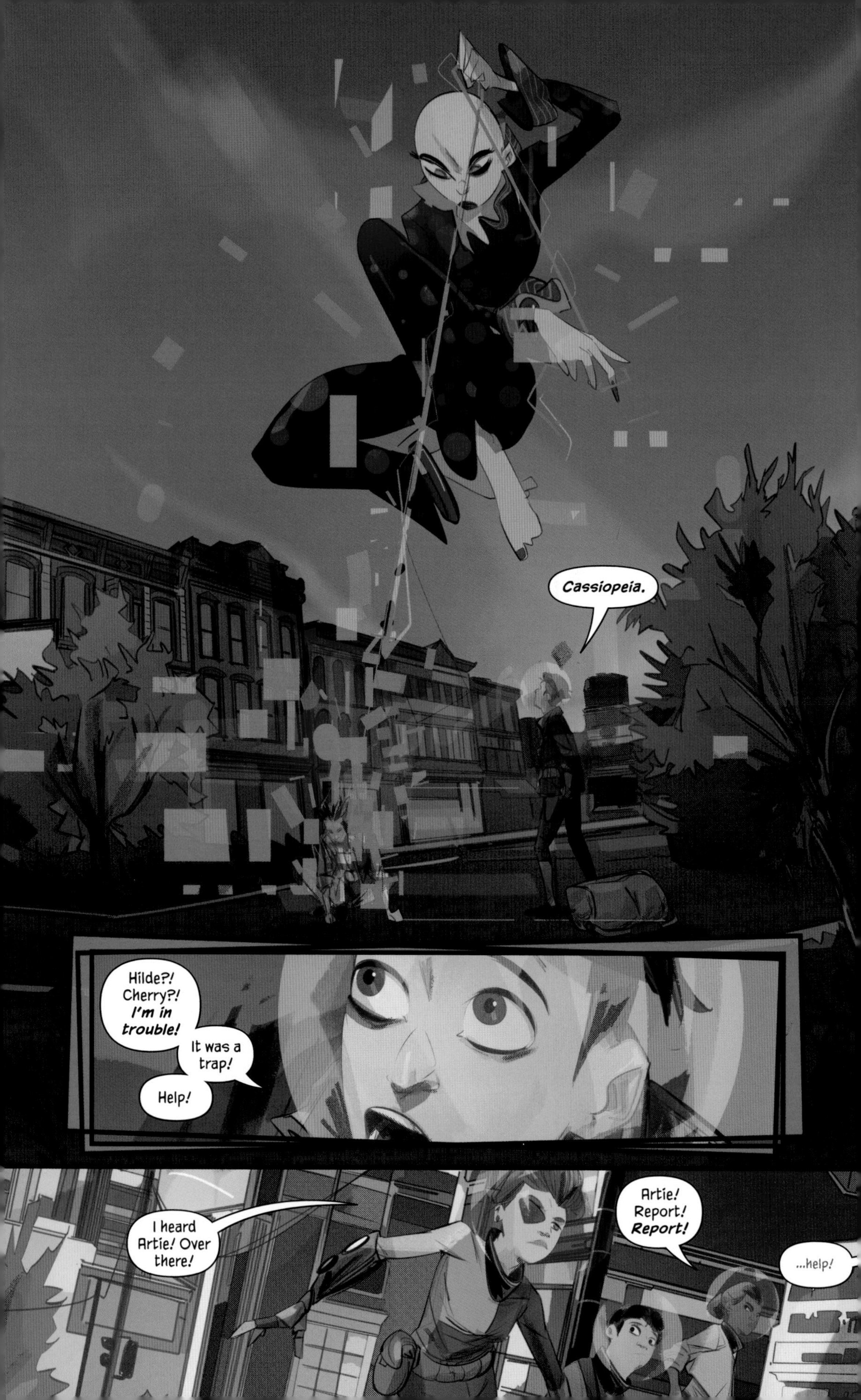

Cassiopeia.
Hilde?! Cherry?! ***I'm in trouble!***
It was a trap!
Help!
I heard Artie! Over there!
Artie! Report! ***Report!***
...help!

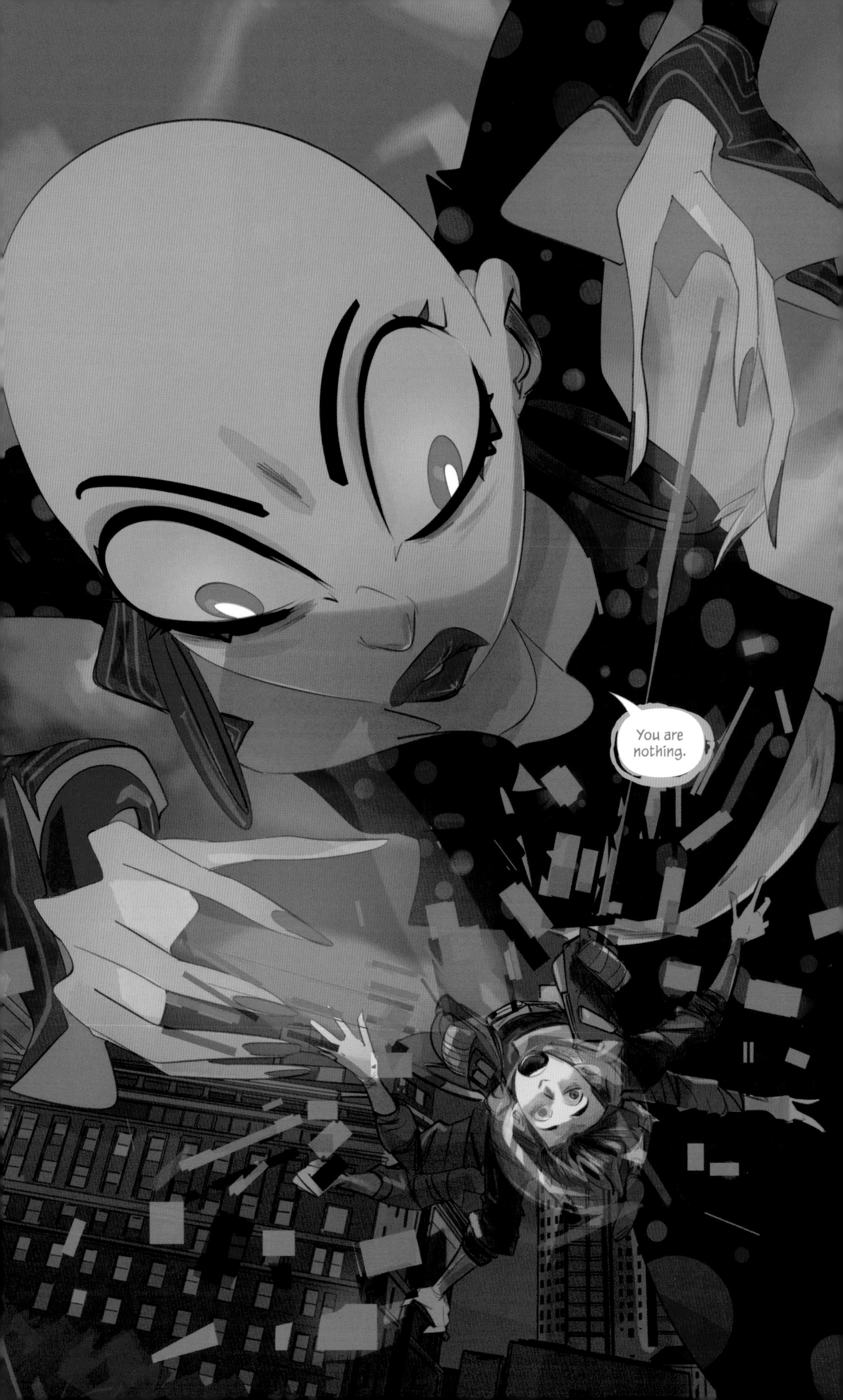
You are nothing.

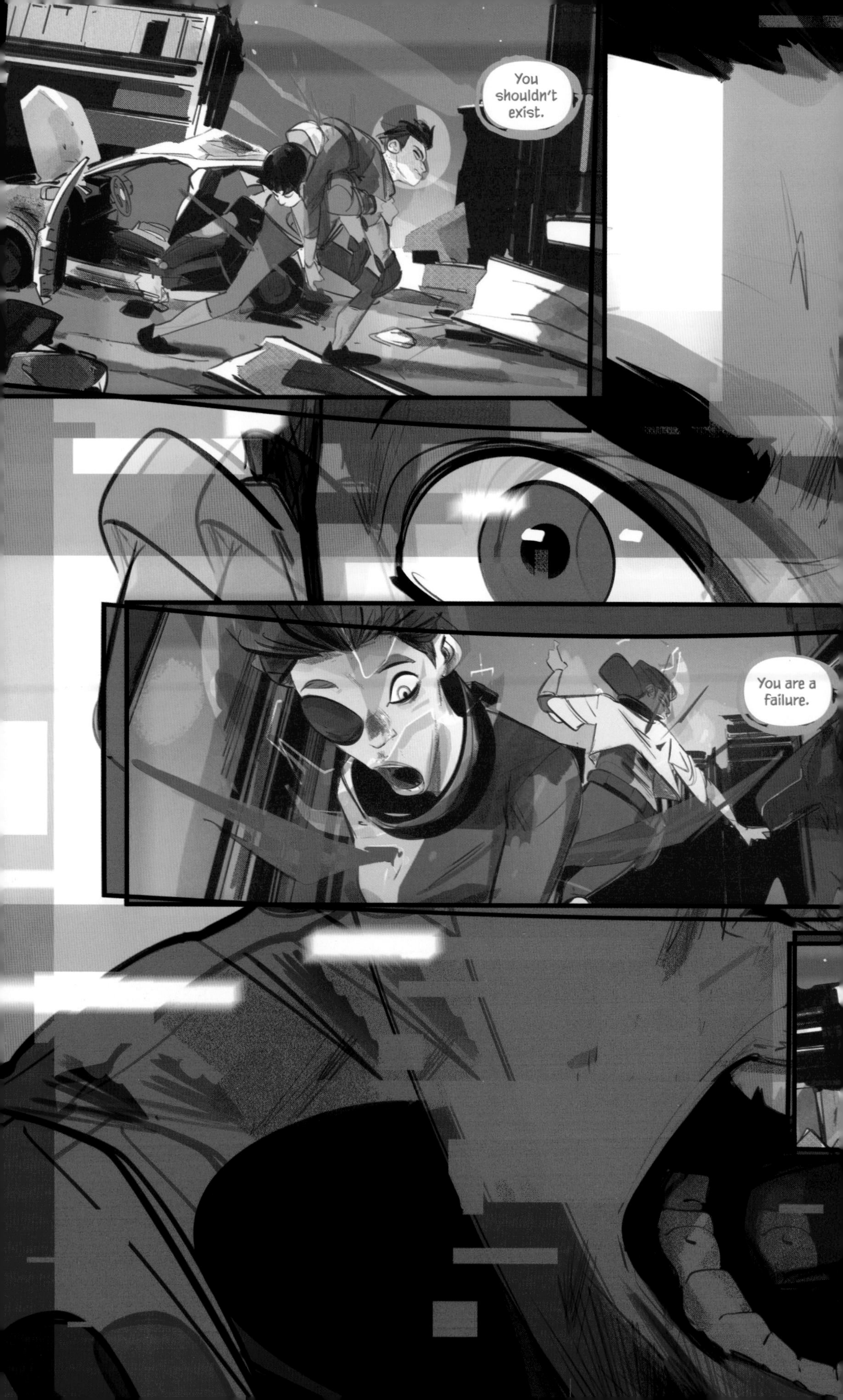
You shouldn't exist.
You are a failure.

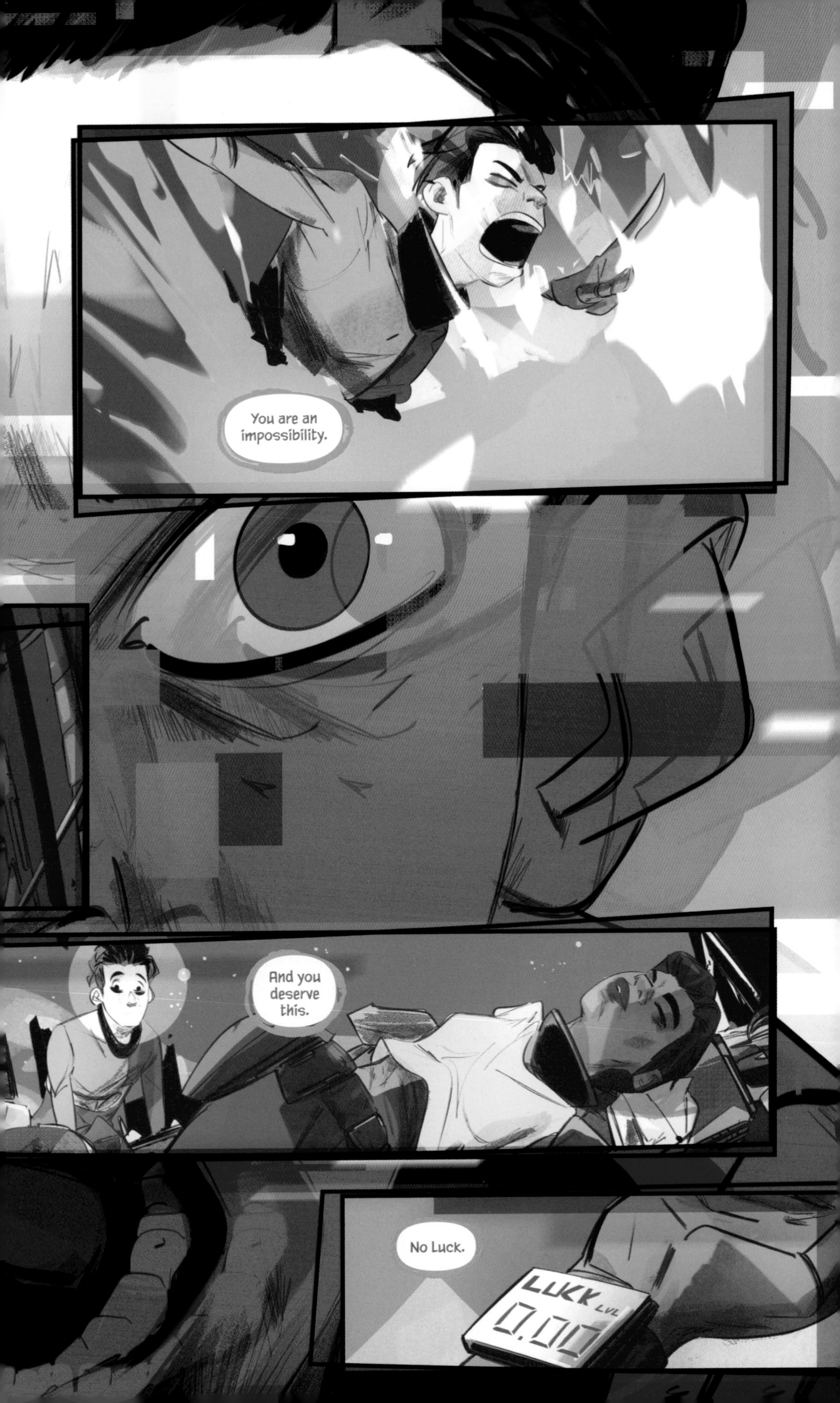
You are an impossibility.
And you deserve this.
No Luck.
LUCK LVL
0.00

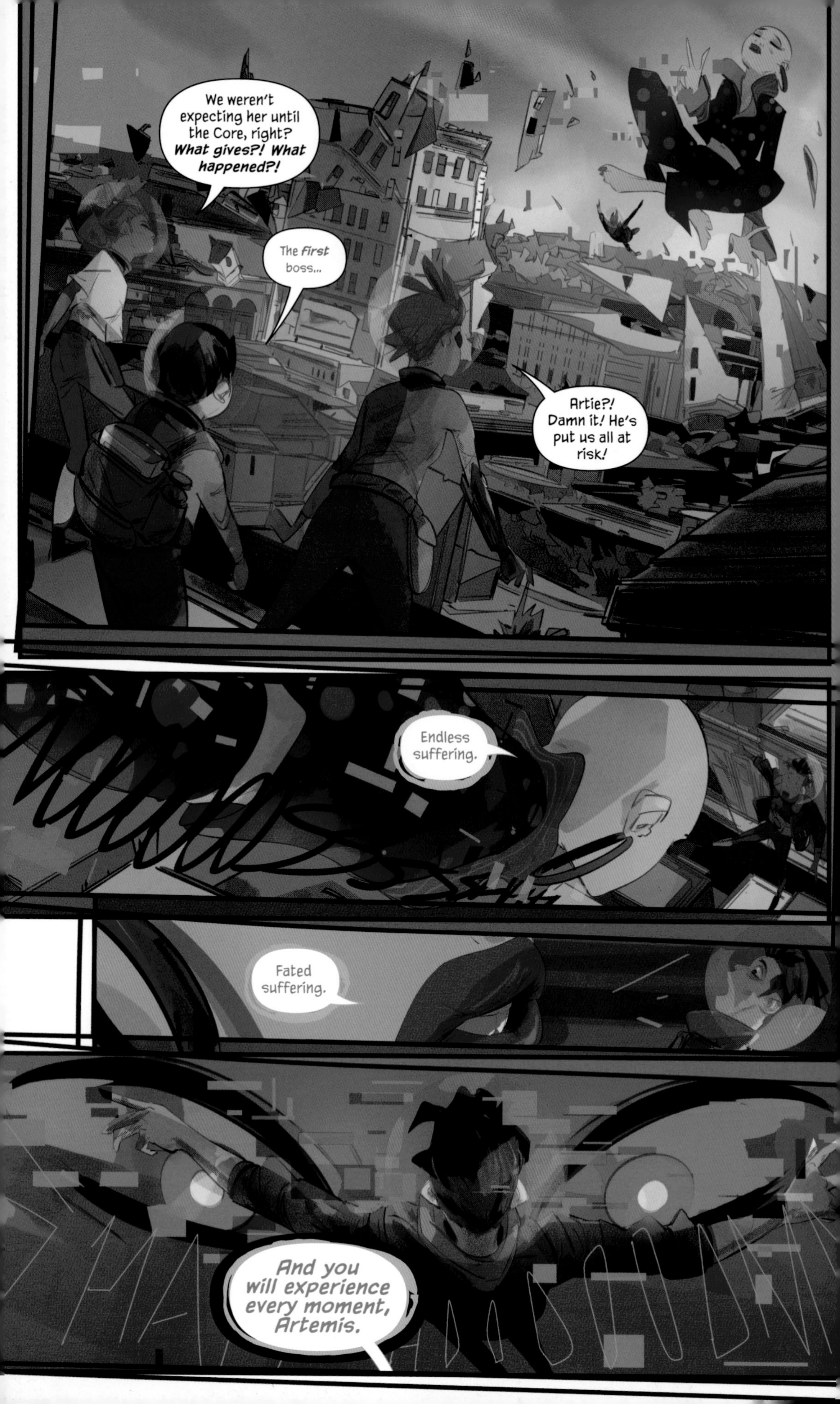
We weren't expecting her until the Core, right? **What gives?! What happened?!**
The *first* boss...
Artie?! Damn it! He's put us all at risk!
Endless suffering.
Fated suffering.
And you will experience every moment, Artemis.

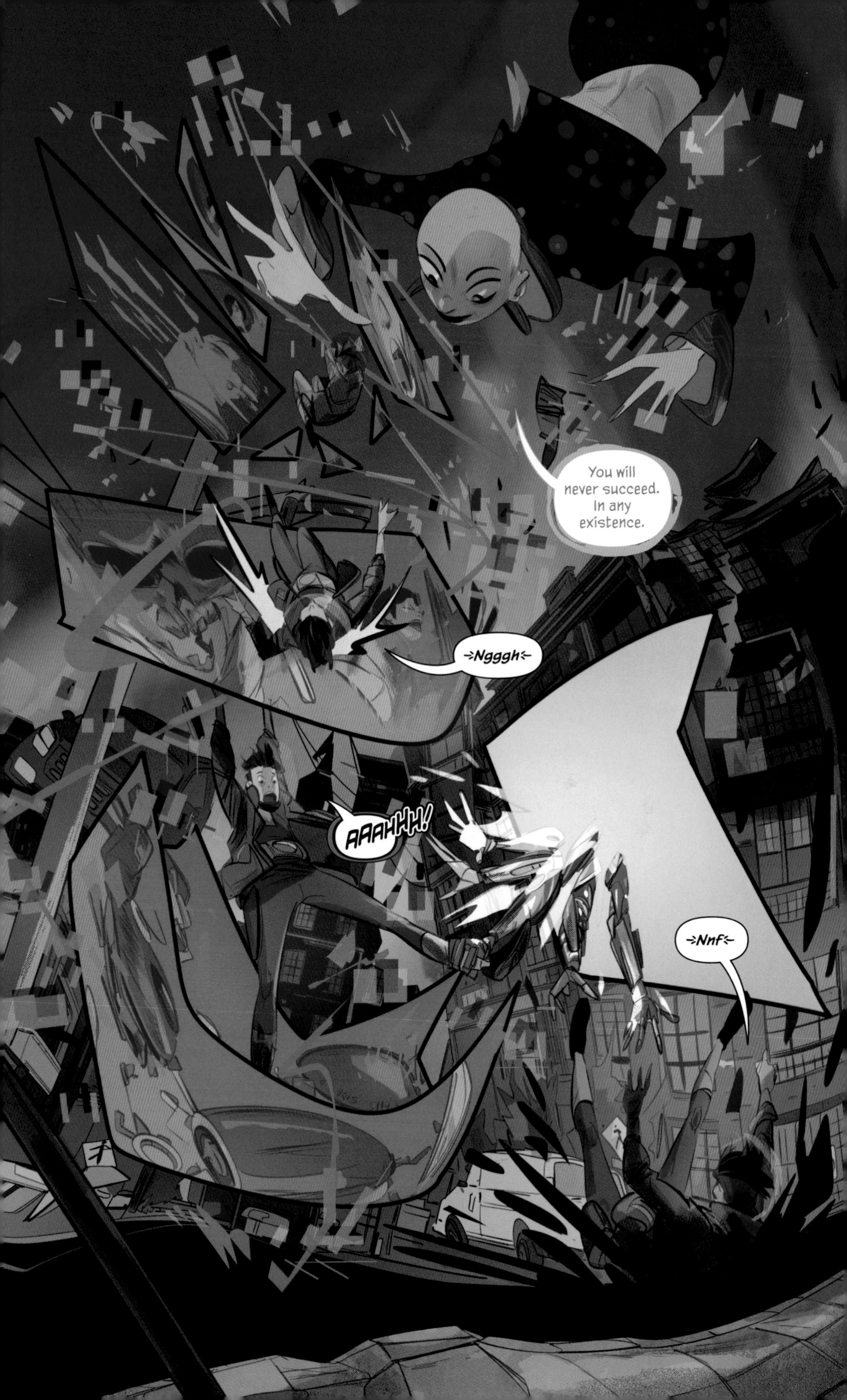

You will never succeed. In any existence.
Ngggh
AAAHHH!
Nnf

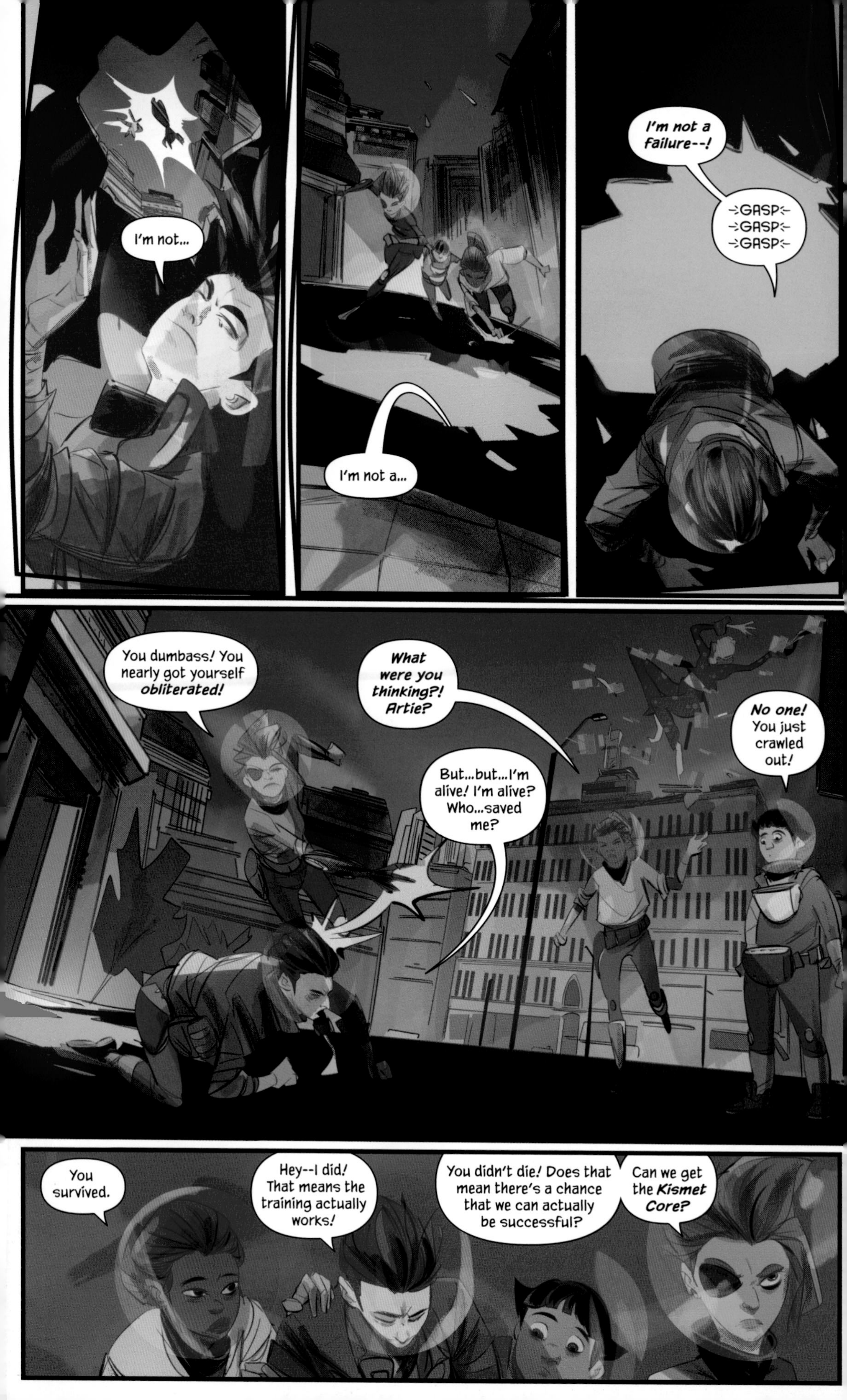
I'm not...
I'm not a...
I'm not a failure--!
GASP GASP GASP
You dumbass! You nearly got yourself obliterated!
What were you thinking?! Artie?
But...but...I'm alive! I'm alive? Who...saved me?
No one! You just crawled out!
You survived.
Hey--I did! That means the training actually works!
You didn't die! Does that mean there's a chance that we can actually be successful?
Can we get the Kismet Core?

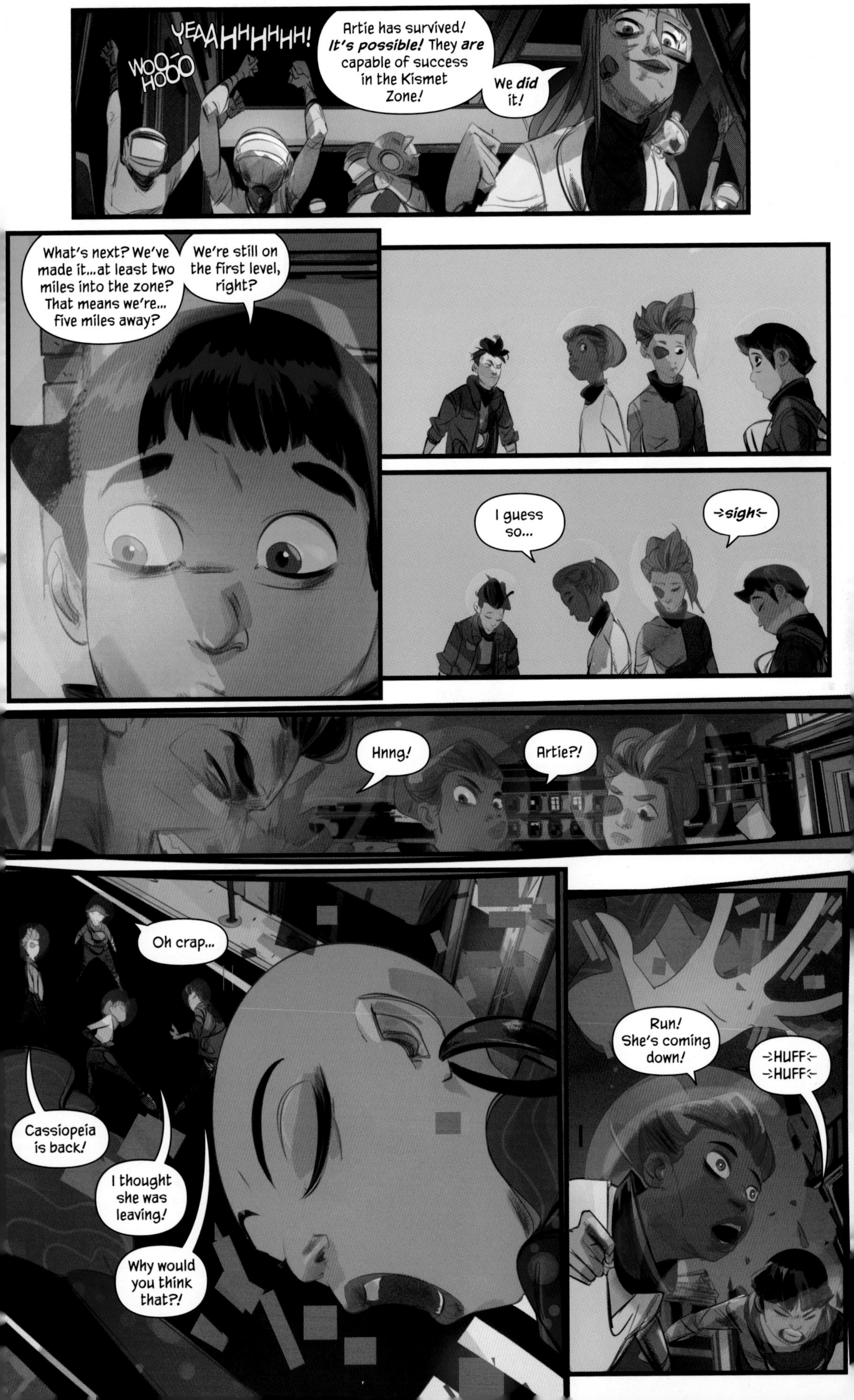
WOO-HOOO
YEAAHHHHHH!
Artie has survived! It's possible! They are capable of success in the Kismet Zone!
We did it!
What's next? We've made it...at least two miles into the zone? That means we're... five miles away?
We're still on the first level, right?
I guess so...
sigh
Hnng!
Artie?!
Oh crap...
Cassiopeia is back!
I thought she was leaving!
Why would you think that?!
Run! She's coming down!
HUFF
HUFF

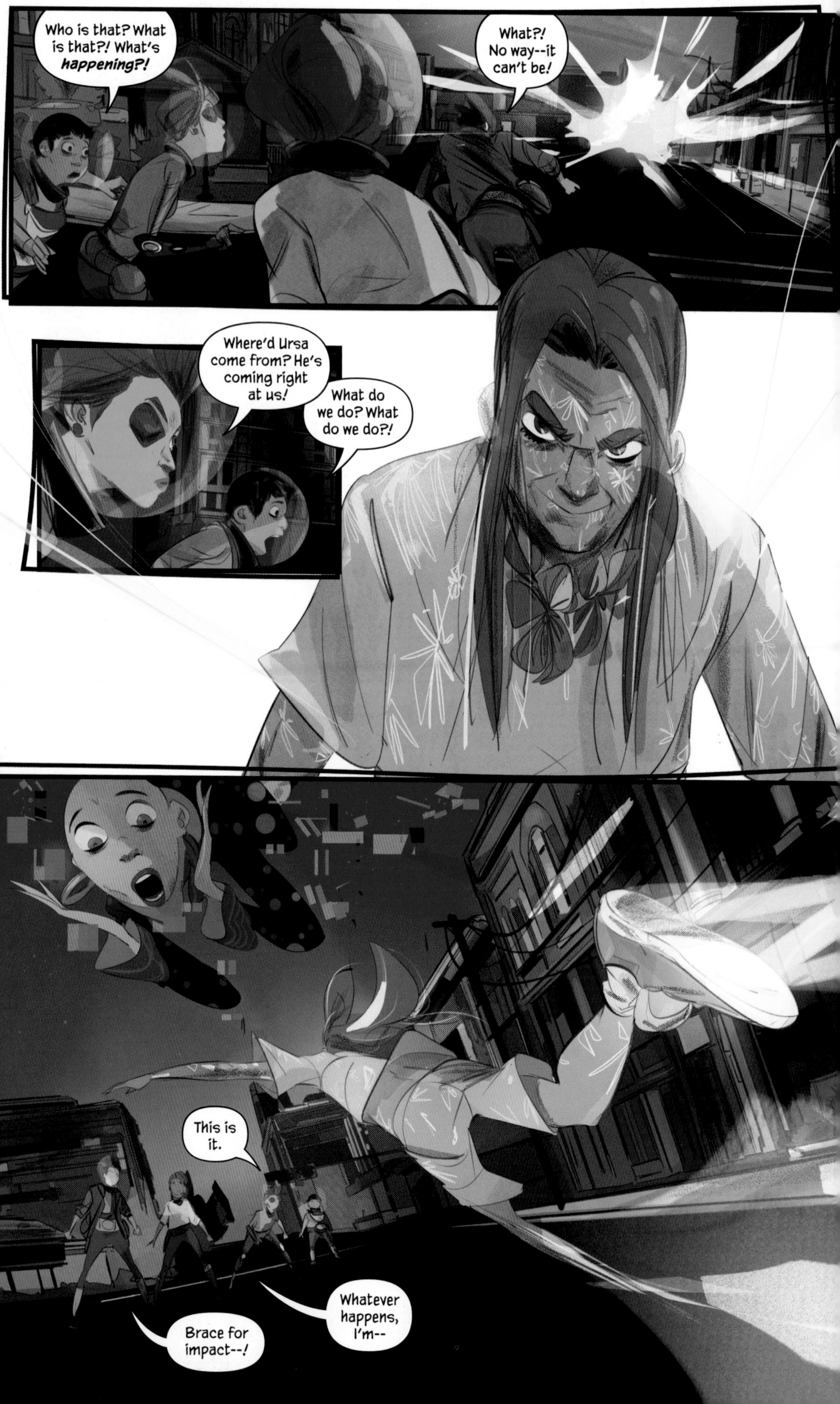
Who is that? What is that?! What's *happening?!*
What?! No way--it can't be!
Where'd Ursa come from? He's coming right at us!
What do we do? What do we do?!
This is it.
Brace for impact--!
Whatever happens, I'm--

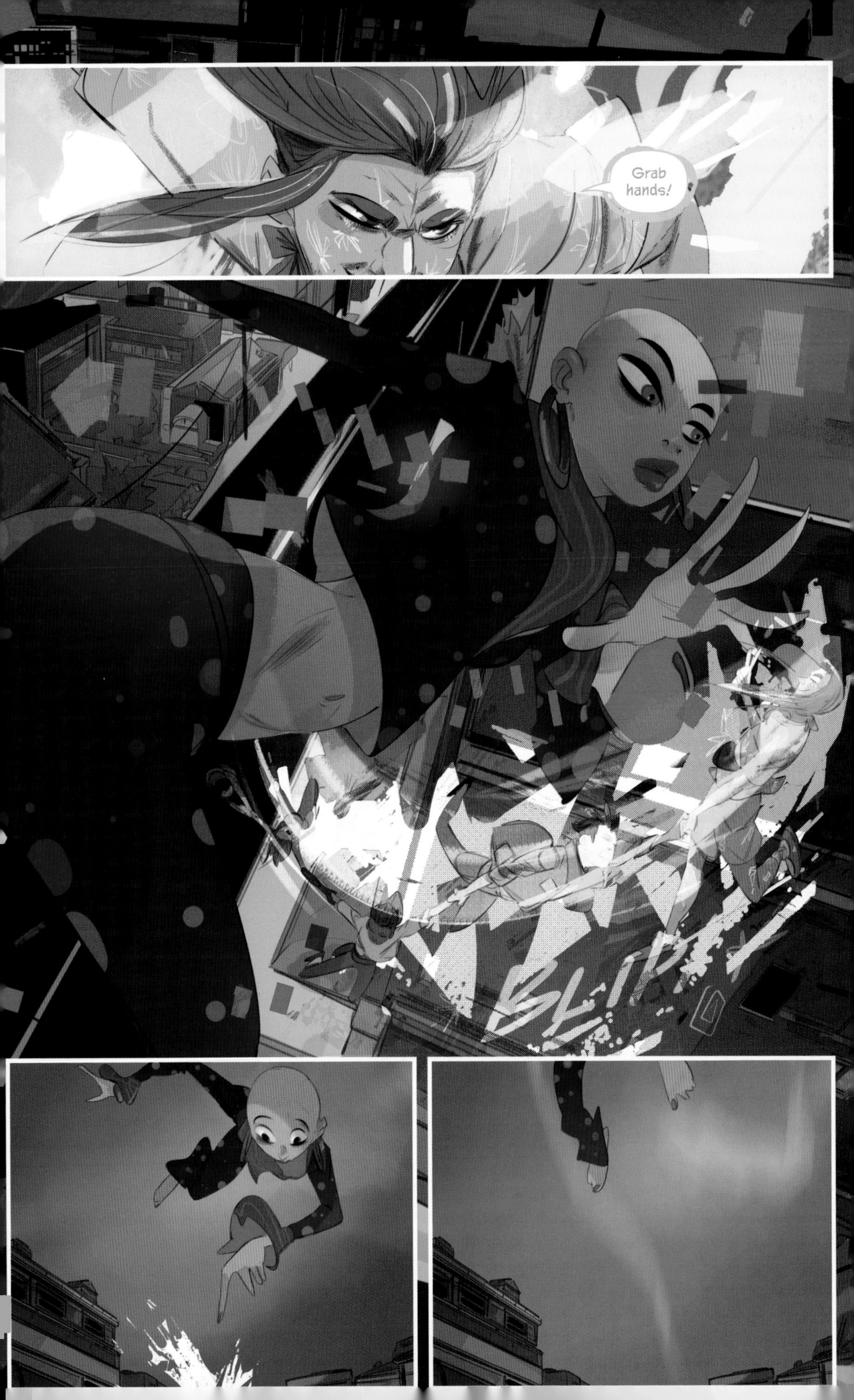
Grab hands!
BLIP

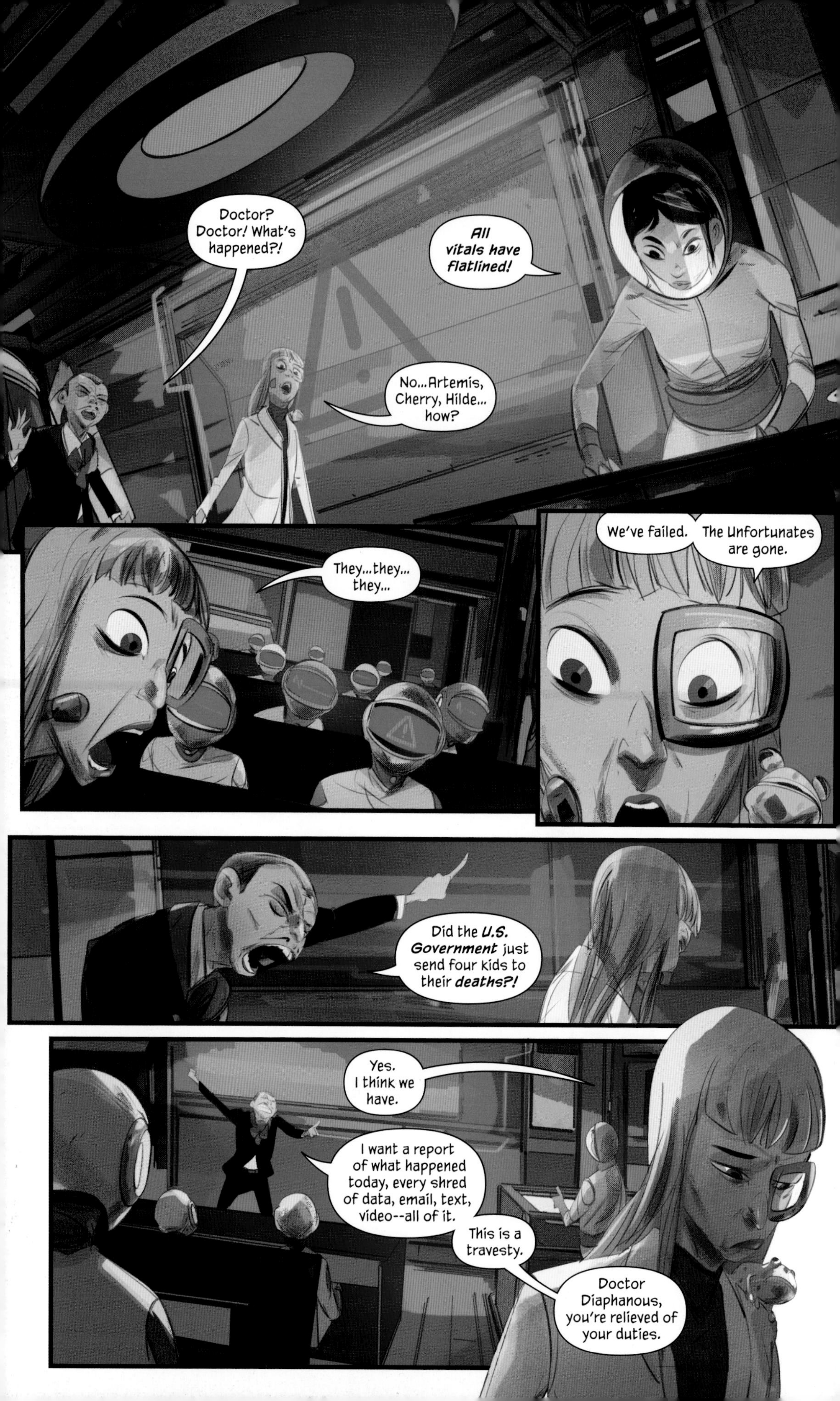

Doctor? Doctor! What's happened?!
All vitals have flatlined!
No...Artemis, Cherry, Hilde... how?
They...they... they...
We've failed.
The Unfortunates are gone.
Did the U.S. Government just send four kids to their deaths?!
Yes. I think we have.
I want a report of what happened today, every shred of data, email, text, video--all of it.
This is a travesty.
Doctor Diaphanous, you're relieved of your duties.

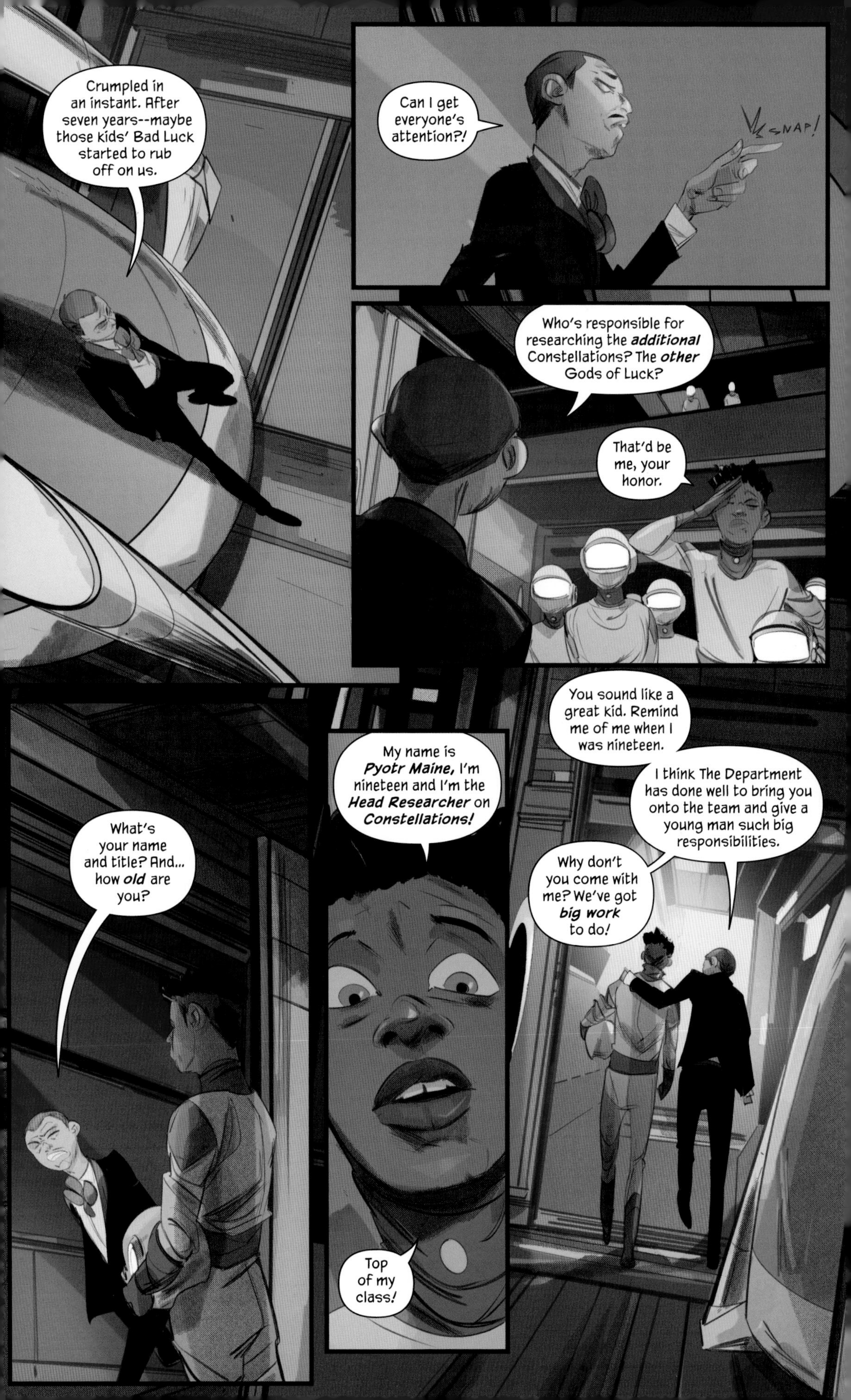
Crumpled in an instant. After seven years--maybe those kids' Bad Luck started to rub off on us.
Can I get everyone's attention?!
SNAP!
Who's responsible for researching the *additional* Constellations? The *other* Gods of Luck?
That'd be me, your honor.
What's your name and title? And... how *old* are you?
My name is *Pyotr Maine,* I'm nineteen and I'm the *Head Researcher* on *Constellations!*
Top of my class!
You sound like a great kid. Remind me of me when I was nineteen.
I think The Department has done well to bring you onto the team and give a young man such big responsibilities.
Why don't you come with me? We've got *big work* to do!

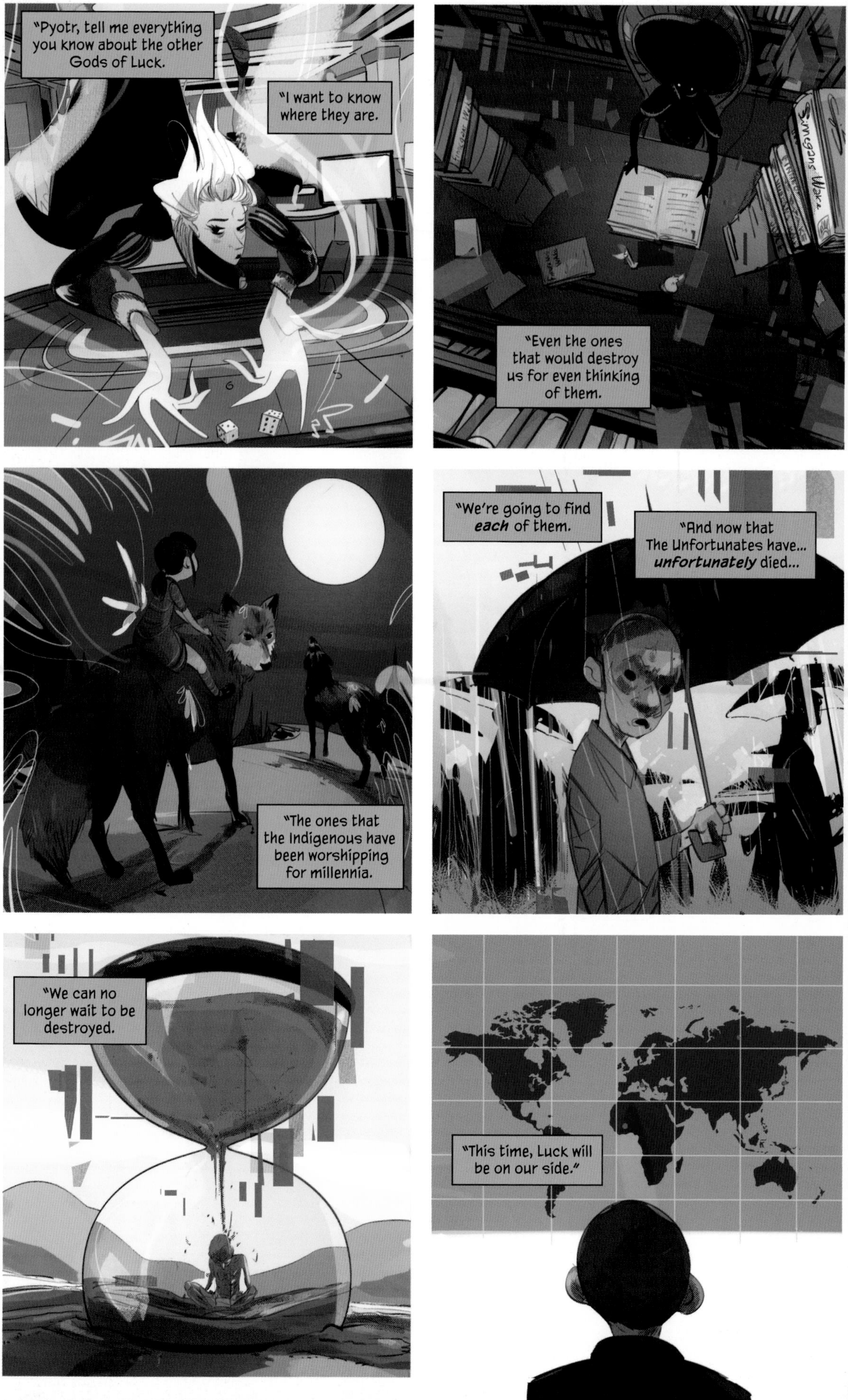
"Pyotr, tell me everything you know about the other Gods of Luck.
"I want to know where they are.
"Even the ones that would destroy us for even thinking of them.
"The ones that the Indigenous have been worshipping for millennia.
"We're going to find ***each*** of them.
"And now that The Unfortunates have... ***unfortunately*** died...
"We can no longer wait to be destroyed.
"This time, Luck will be on our side."

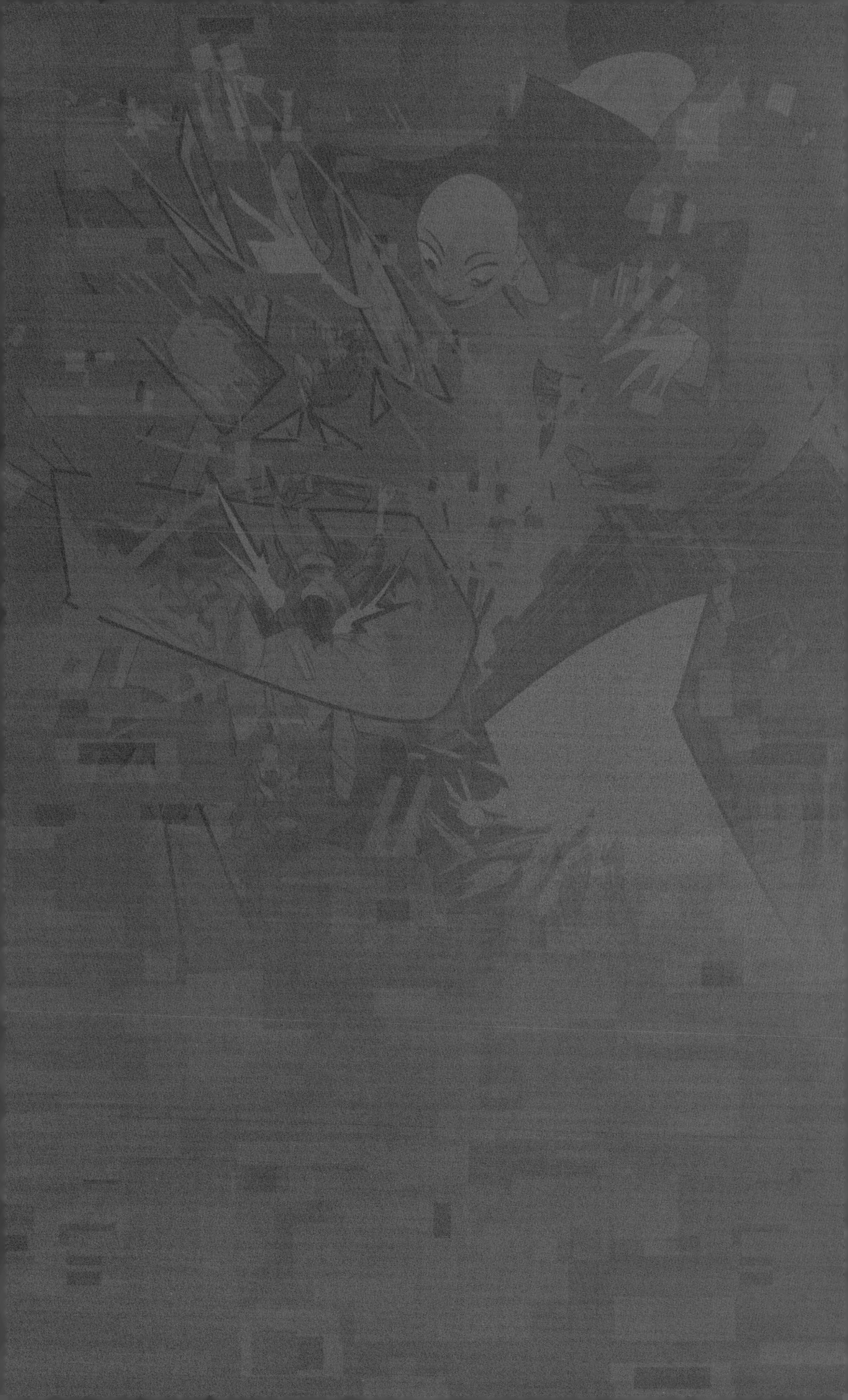

CHAPTER

3

HEAVEN OR LAS VEGAS

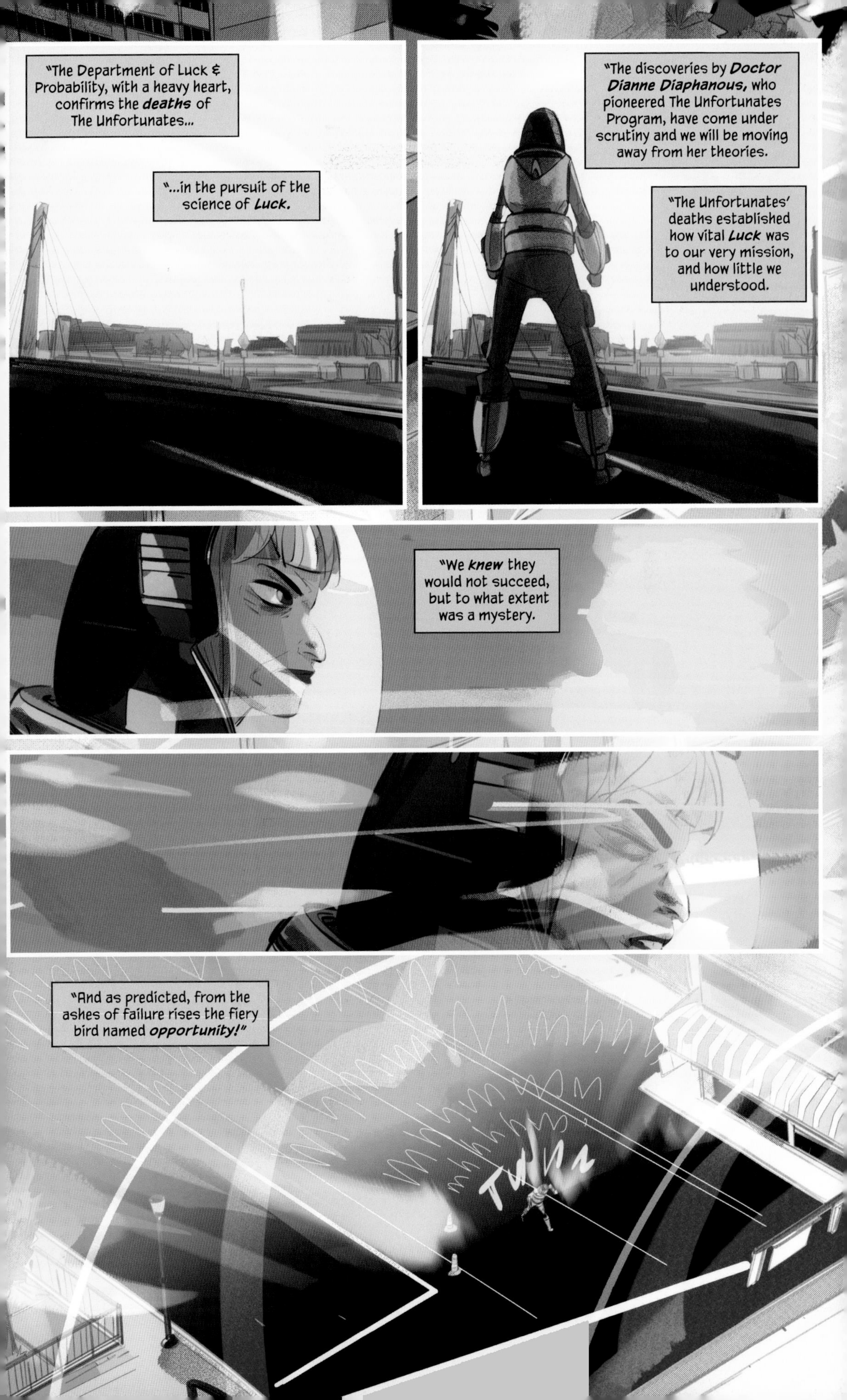
"The Department of Luck & Probability, with a heavy heart, confirms the deaths of The Unfortunates...
"...in the pursuit of the science of Luck.
"The discoveries by Doctor Dianne Diaphanous, who pioneered The Unfortunates Program, have come under scrutiny and we will be moving away from her theories.
"The Unfortunates' deaths established how vital Luck was to our very mission, and how little we understood.
"We knew they would not succeed, but to what extent was a mystery.
"And as predicted, from the ashes of failure rises the fiery bird named opportunity!"

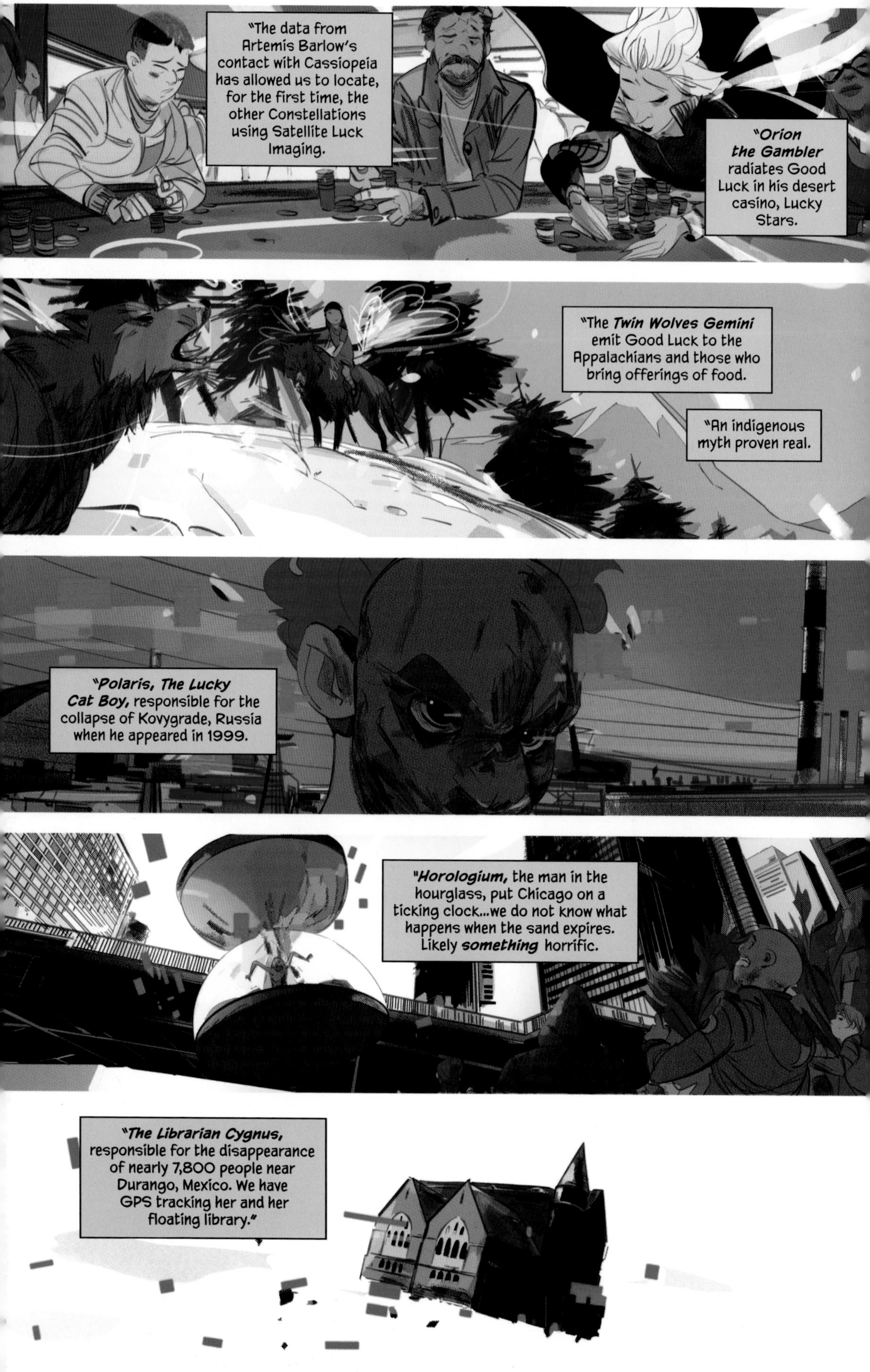
"The data from Artemis Barlow's contact with Cassiopeia has allowed us to locate, for the first time, the other Constellations using Satellite Luck Imaging.
"*Orion the Gambler* radiates Good Luck in his desert casino, Lucky Stars.
"The *Twin Wolves Gemini* emit Good Luck to the Appalachians and those who bring offerings of food.
"An indigenous myth proven real.
"*Polaris, The Lucky Cat Boy,* responsible for the collapse of Kovygrade, Russia when he appeared in 1999.
"*Horologium,* the man in the hourglass, put Chicago on a ticking clock...we do not know what happens when the sand expires. Likely *something* horrific.
"*The Librarian Cygnus,* responsible for the disappearance of nearly 7,800 people near Durango, Mexico. We have GPS tracking her and her floating library."

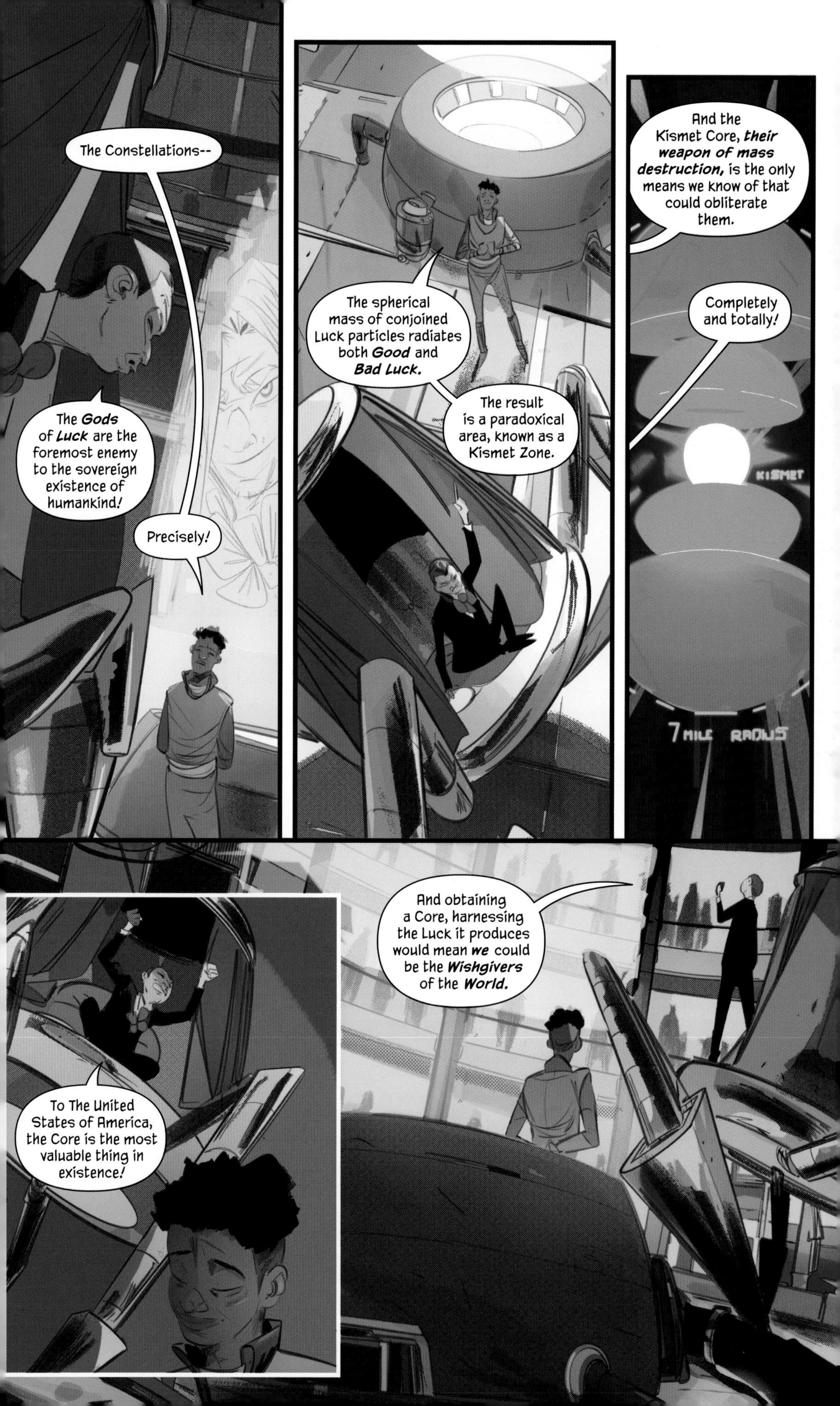
The Constellations--
The Gods of Luck are the foremost enemy to the sovereign existence of humankind!
Precisely!
The spherical mass of conjoined Luck particles radiates both Good and Bad Luck.
The result is a paradoxical area, known as a Kismet Zone.
And the Kismet Core, their weapon of mass destruction, is the only means we know of that could obliterate them.
Completely and totally!
KISMET
7 MILE RADIUS
To The United States of America, the Core is the most valuable thing in existence!
And obtaining a Core, harnessing the Luck it produces would mean we could be the Wishgivers of the World.

Creating *additional* Zones on American soil is of the utmost importance!

Wait, *additional* Zones?! Millions could be lost in perpetual Kismet!

And billions will reap the benefits of their sacrifice! The more Zones there are, the more Cores exist in this great country!

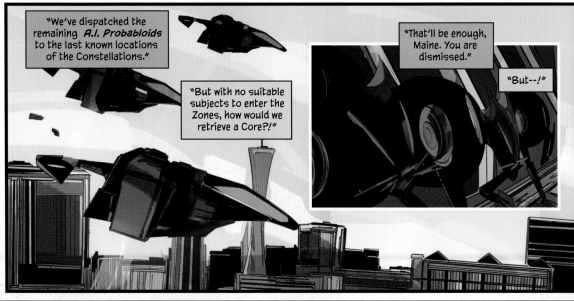

"We've dispatched the remaining *A.I. Probabloids* to the last known locations of the Constellations."

"But with no suitable subjects to enter the Zones, how would we retrieve a Core?!"

"That'll be enough, Maine. You are dismissed."

"But--!"

Enough!

Your work is vital, but you are not. Once we wander into the fog of circumstantial morality there is no way out.

And we are the frontline against the Constellations.

We *must* destroy them!

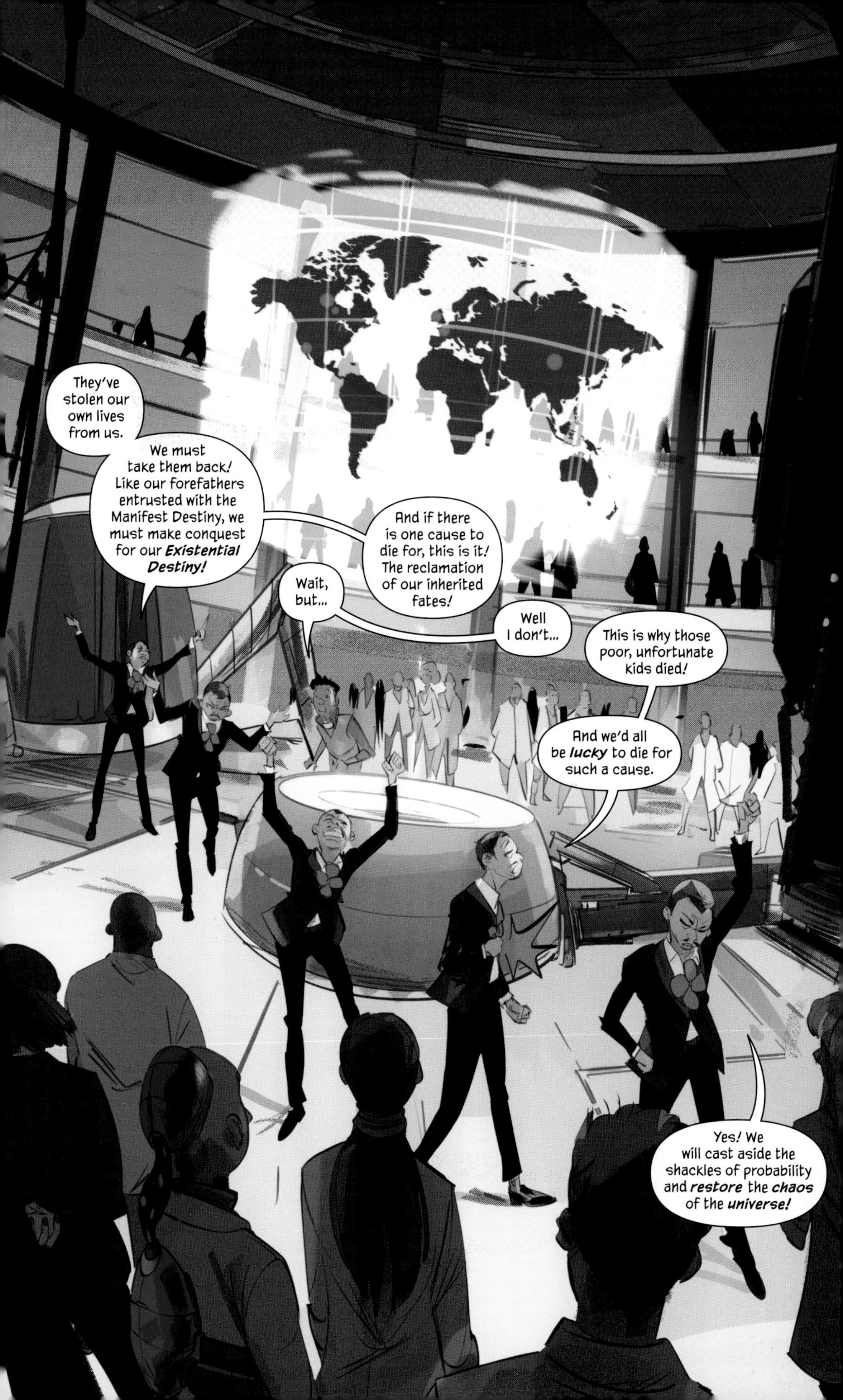
They've stolen our own lives from us.
We must take them back! Like our forefathers entrusted with the Manifest Destiny, we must make conquest for our **Existential Destiny!**
Wait, but...
And if there is one cause to die for, this is it! The reclamation of our inherited fates!
Well I don't...
This is why those poor, unfortunate kids died!
And we'd all be ***lucky*** to die for such a cause.
Yes! We will cast aside the shackles of probability and ***restore*** the ***chaos*** of the ***universe!***

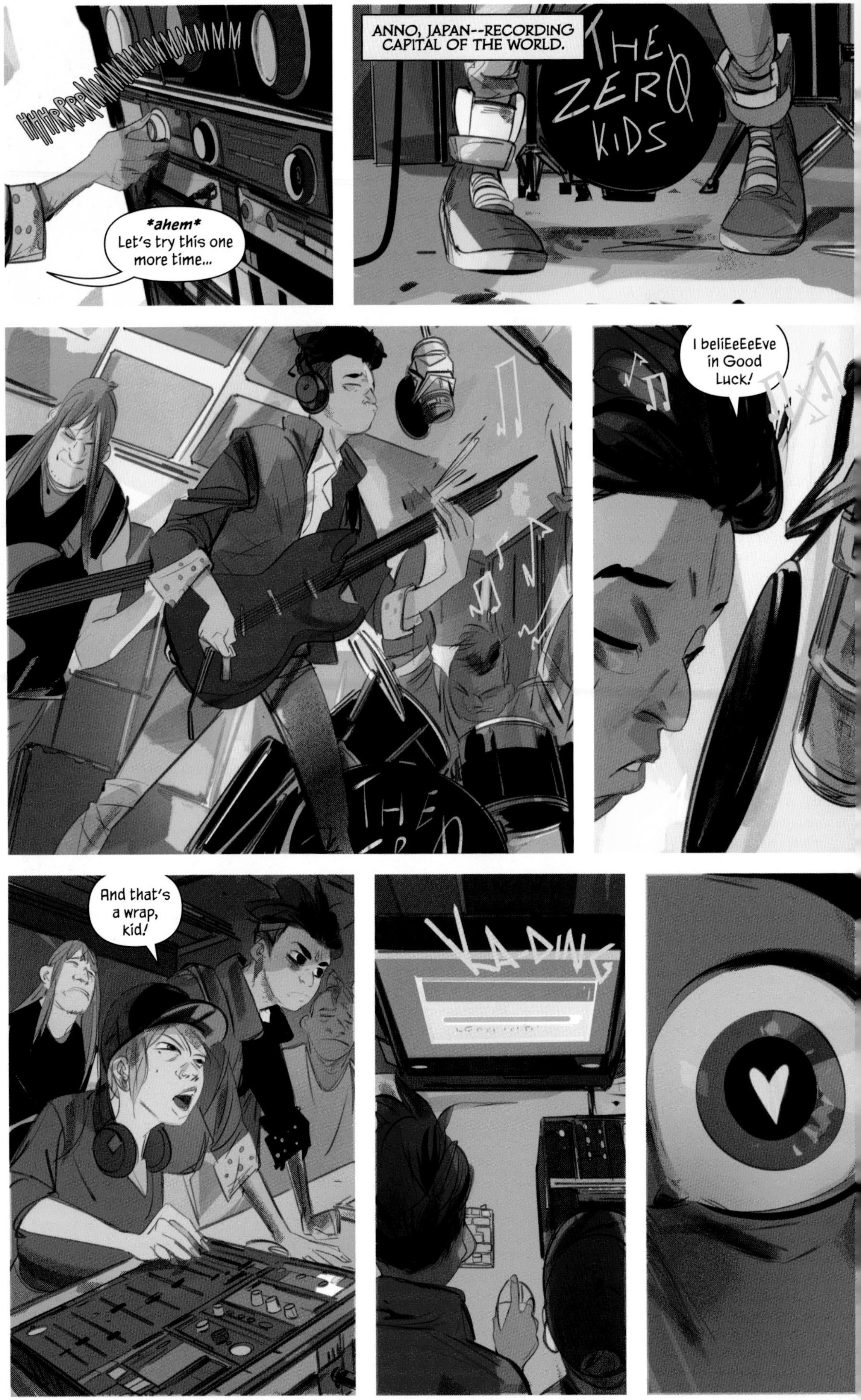
HHHRRRRNNNNNNMMMMMMMM
ahem Let's try this one more time...
ANNO, JAPAN--RECORDING CAPITAL OF THE WORLD.
THE ZERO KIDS
THE
I beliEeEeEve in Good Luck!
And that's a wrap, kid!
KA-DING

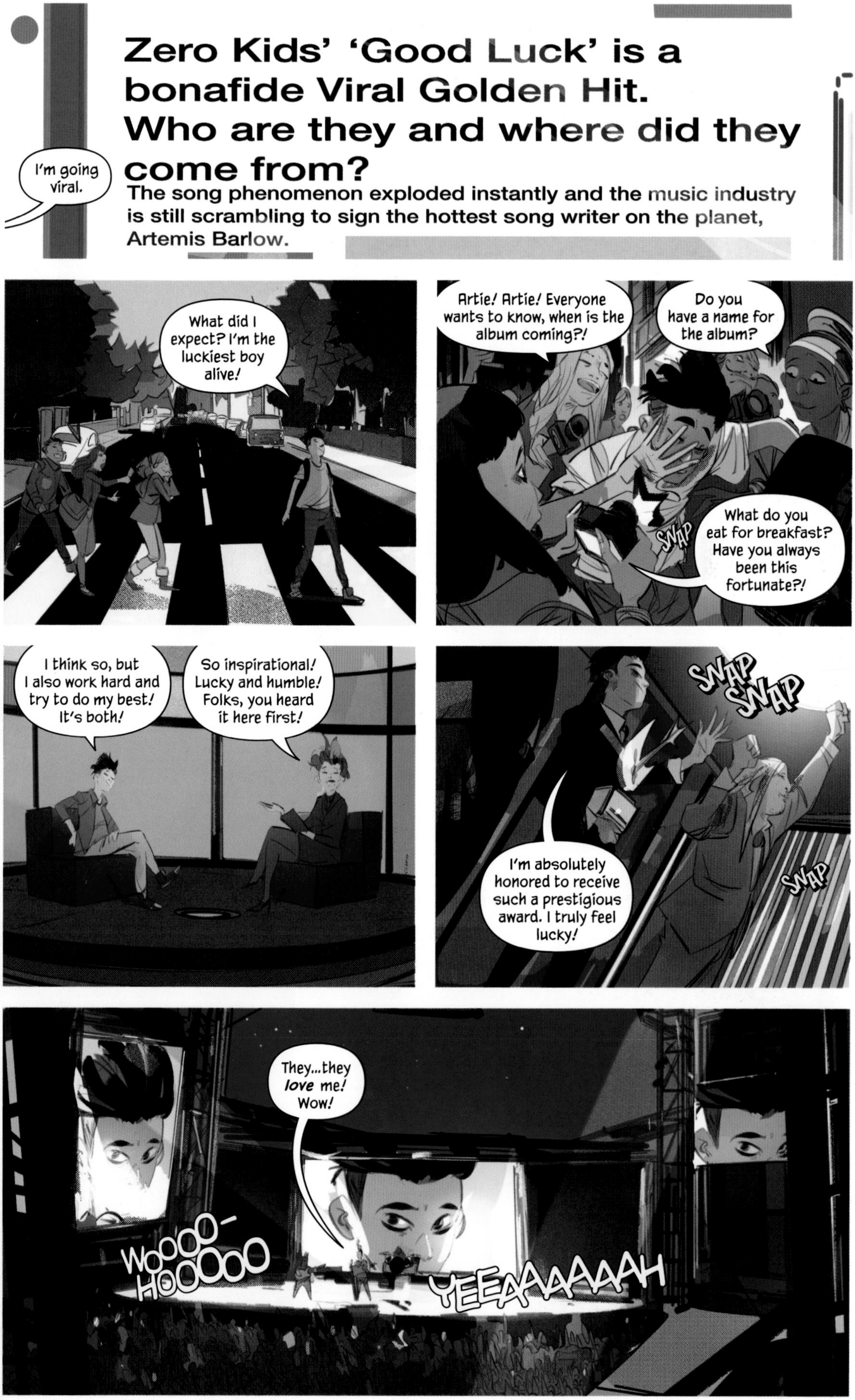
Zero Kids' 'Good Luck' is a bonafide Viral Golden Hit. Who are they and where did they come from?
I'm going viral.
The song phenomenon exploded instantly and the music industry is still scrambling to sign the hottest song writer on the planet, Artemis Barlow.
What did I expect? I'm the luckiest boy alive!
Artie! Artie! Everyone wants to know, when is the album coming?!
Do you have a name for the album?
SNAP
What do you eat for breakfast? Have you always been this fortunate?!
I think so, but I also work hard and try to do my best! It's both!
So inspirational! Lucky and humble! Folks, you heard it here first!
SNAP SNAP
I'm absolutely honored to receive such a prestigious award. I truly feel lucky!
SNAP
They...they *love* me! Wow!
WOOOO-HOOOOO
YEEAAAAAAH

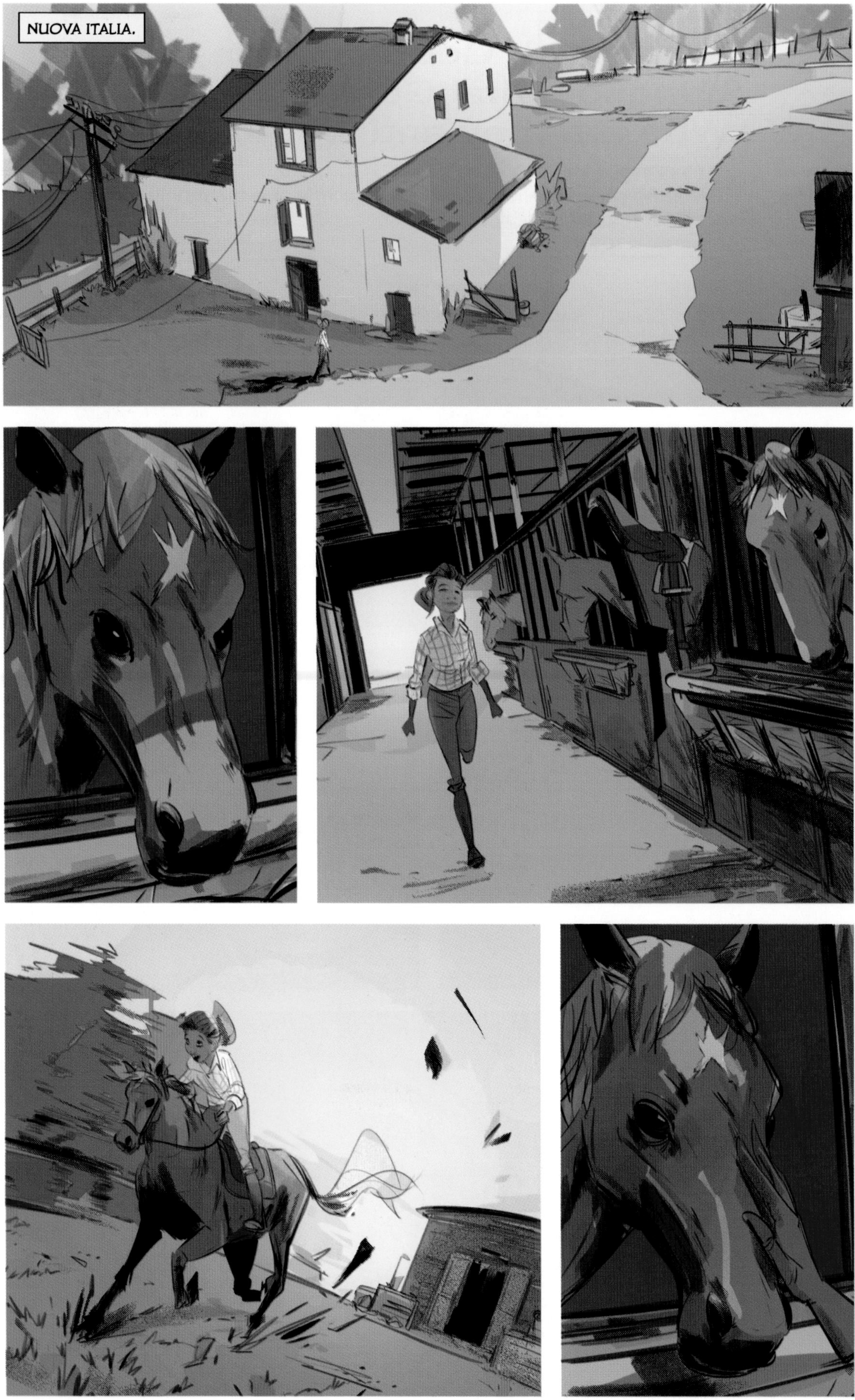
NUOVA ITALIA.

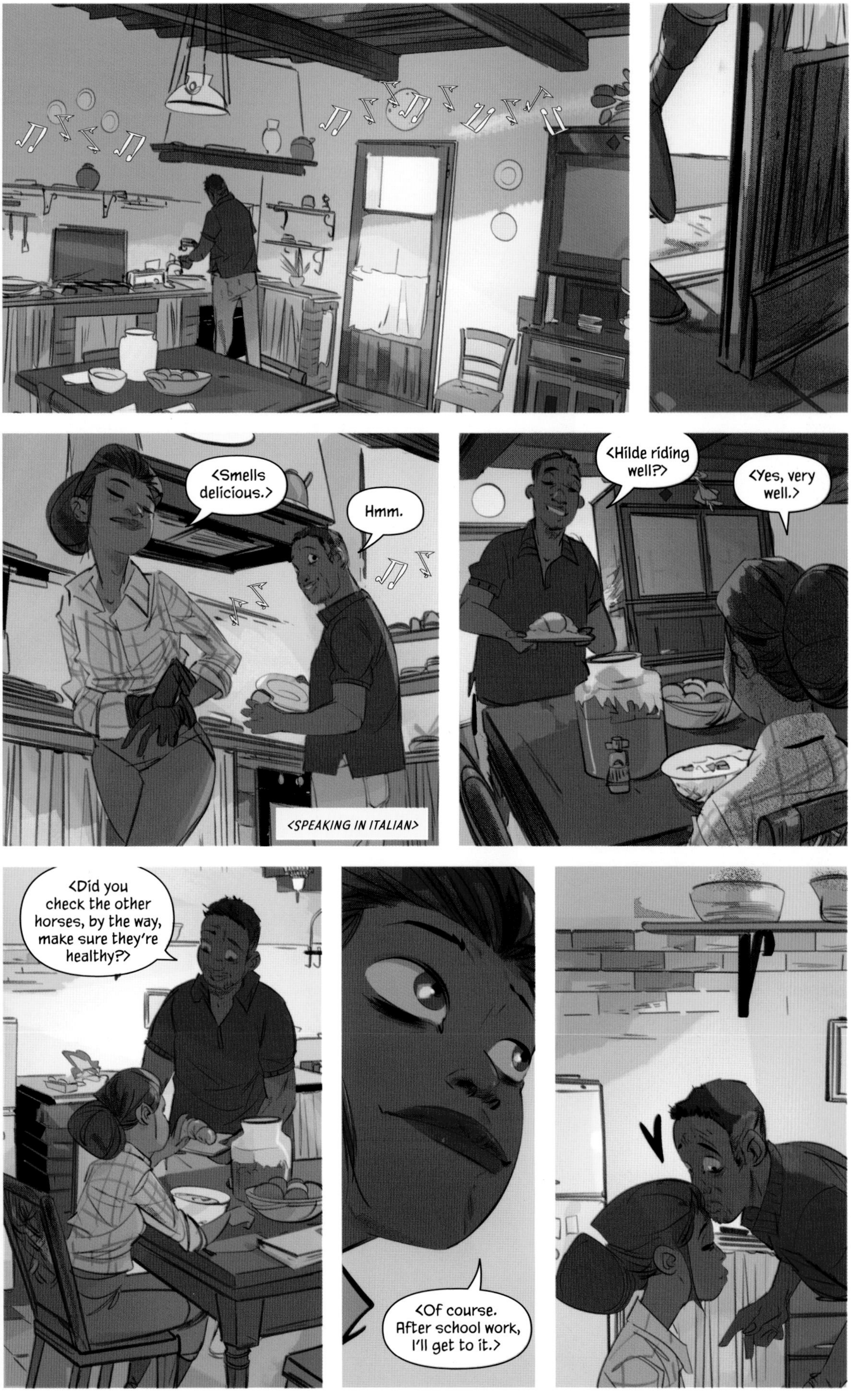
<Smells delicious.>
Hmm.
<SPEAKING IN ITALIAN>
<Hilde riding well?>
<Yes, very well.>
<Did you check the other horses, by the way, make sure they're healthy?>
<Of course. After school work, I'll get to it.>

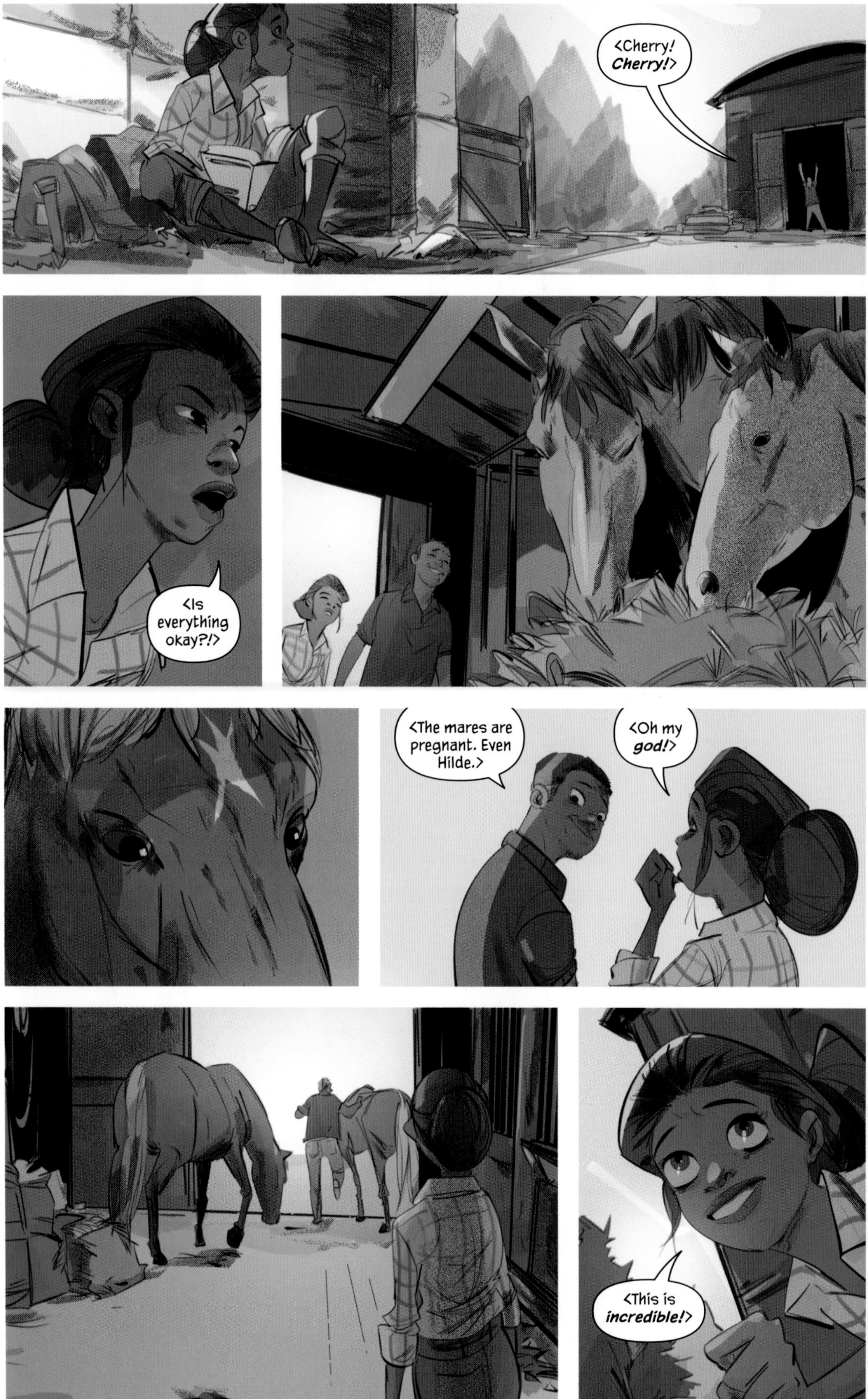
<Cherry! Cherry!>
<Is everything okay?!>
<The mares are pregnant. Even Hilde.>
<Oh my god!>
<This is incredible!>

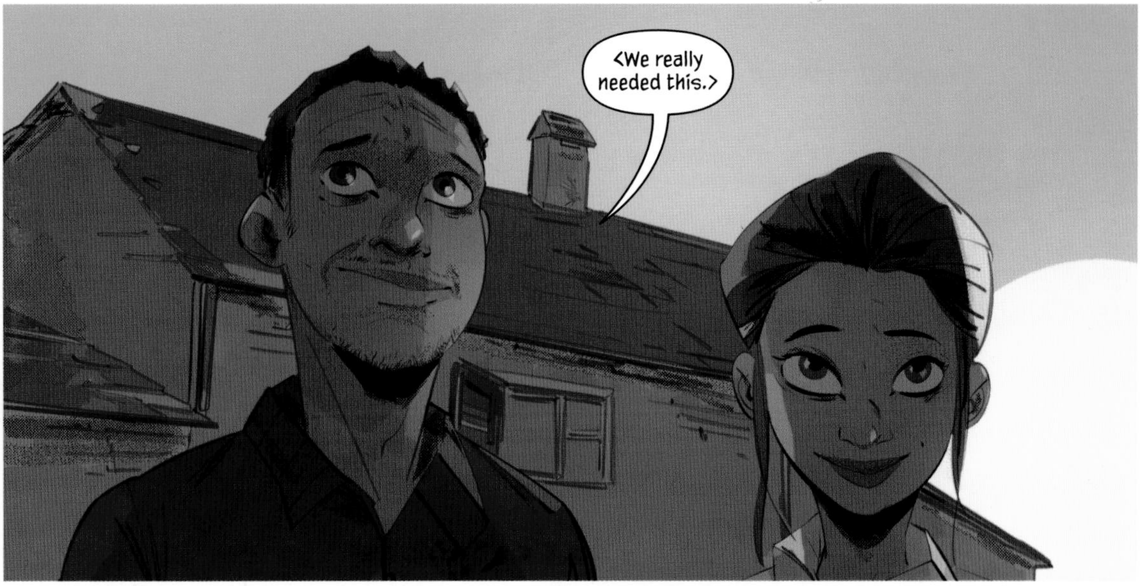
<We really needed this.>

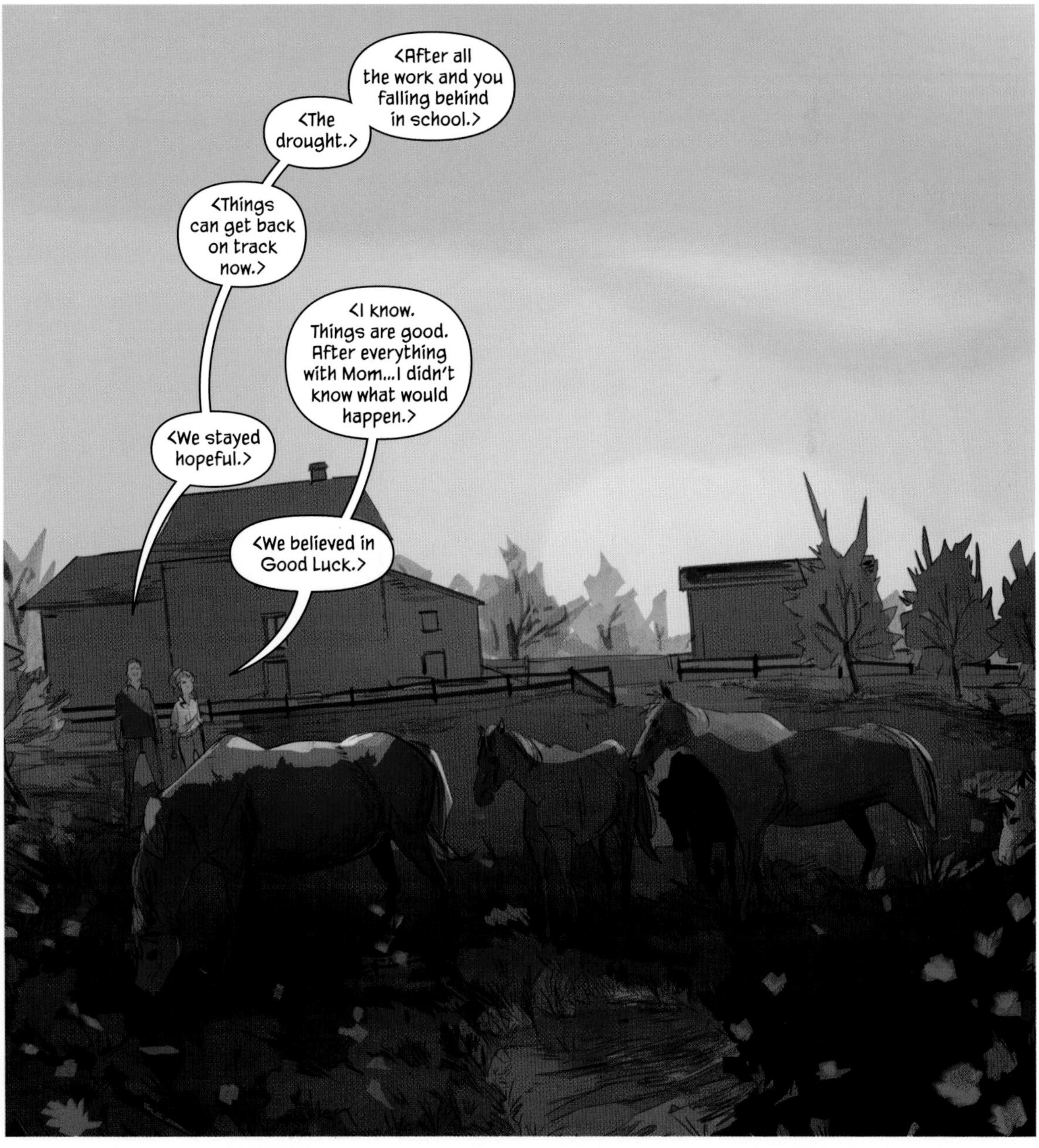
<The drought.>
<After all the work and you falling behind in school.>
<Things can get back on track now.>
<We stayed hopeful.>
<I know. Things are good. After everything with Mom...I didn't know what would happen.>
<We believed in Good Luck.>

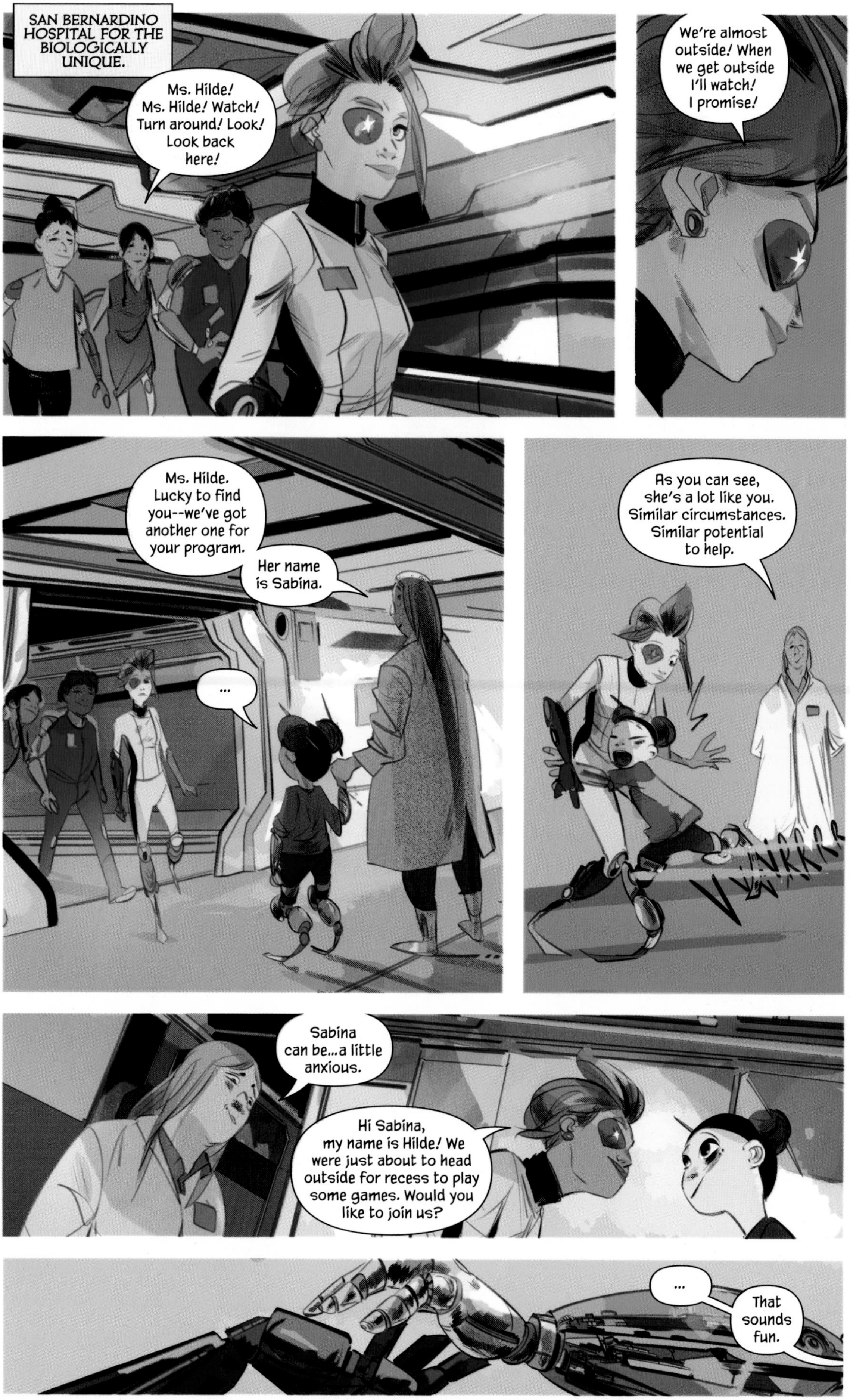
SAN BERNARDINO HOSPITAL FOR THE BIOLOGICALLY UNIQUE.
Ms. Hilde! Ms. Hilde! Watch! Turn around! Look! Look back here!
We're almost outside! When we get outside I'll watch! I promise!
Ms. Hilde. Lucky to find you--we've got another one for your program.
Her name is Sabina.
...
As you can see, she's a lot like you. Similar circumstances. Similar potential to help.
VVVRRRR
Sabina can be...a little anxious.
Hi Sabina, my name is Hilde! We were just about to head outside for recess to play some games. Would you like to join us?
...
That sounds fun.

So...are *you*...

Still human...?

Of course! I'm *just* like you and just like all of us.

We're still us. Nothing can change that.

Do you...still... poop?

Well...uhh-- lots of things are different about each of us!

It's part of our mission here.

So! Do you want to play with the other kids or do you want to talk?

I want to play with you...

Then let's play...

NEON ATTACK GIRLS!

AAAEEEE!!!

POW *POW* POW *POW* AAAEEEE CHUHCUHUCHU!!

MEGA ATTACK! DON'T HOLD BACK, SABINA!!

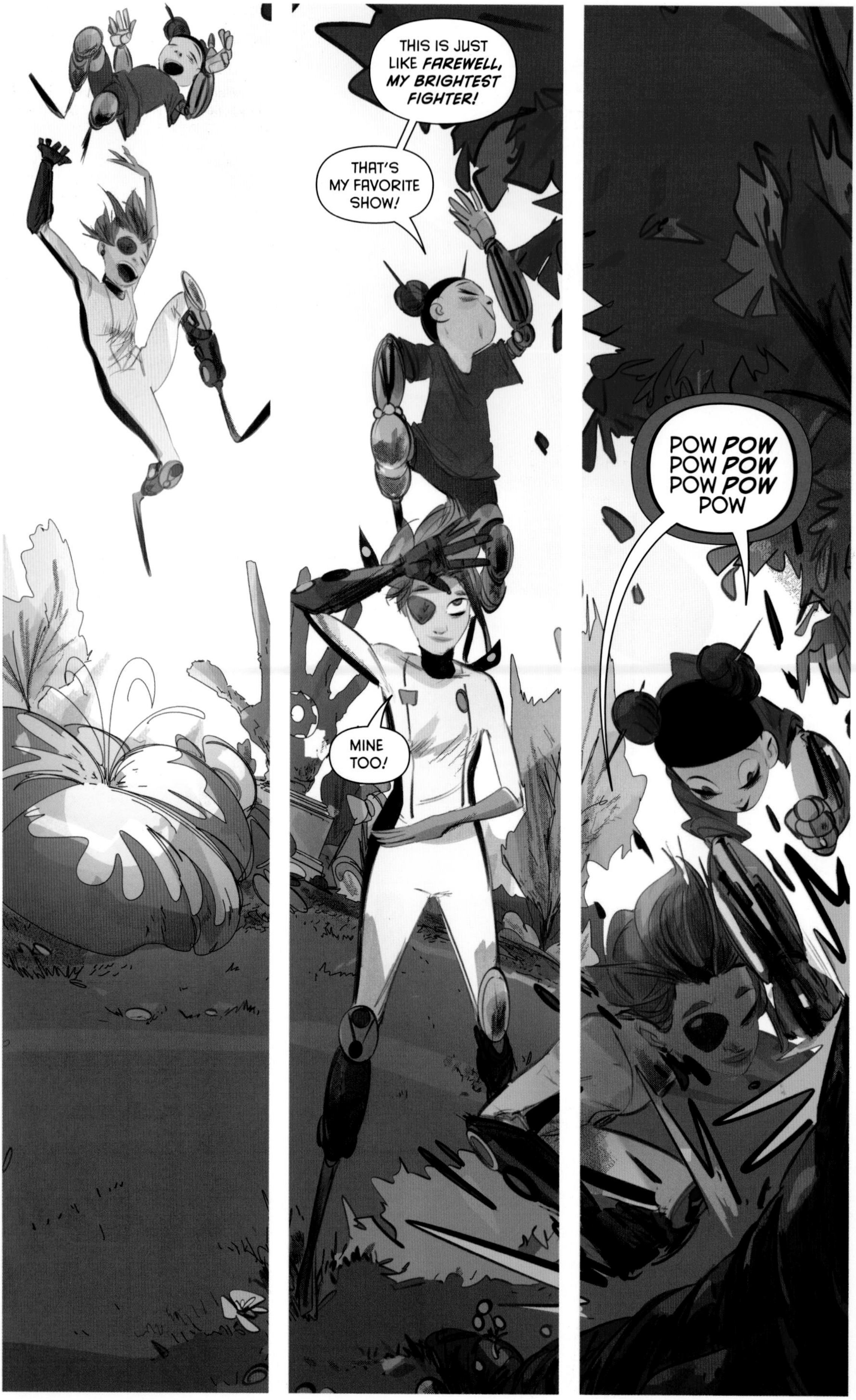
THIS IS JUST LIKE *FAREWELL, MY BRIGHTEST FIGHTER!*
THAT'S MY FAVORITE SHOW!
MINE TOO!
POW **POW** POW **POW** POW **POW** POW

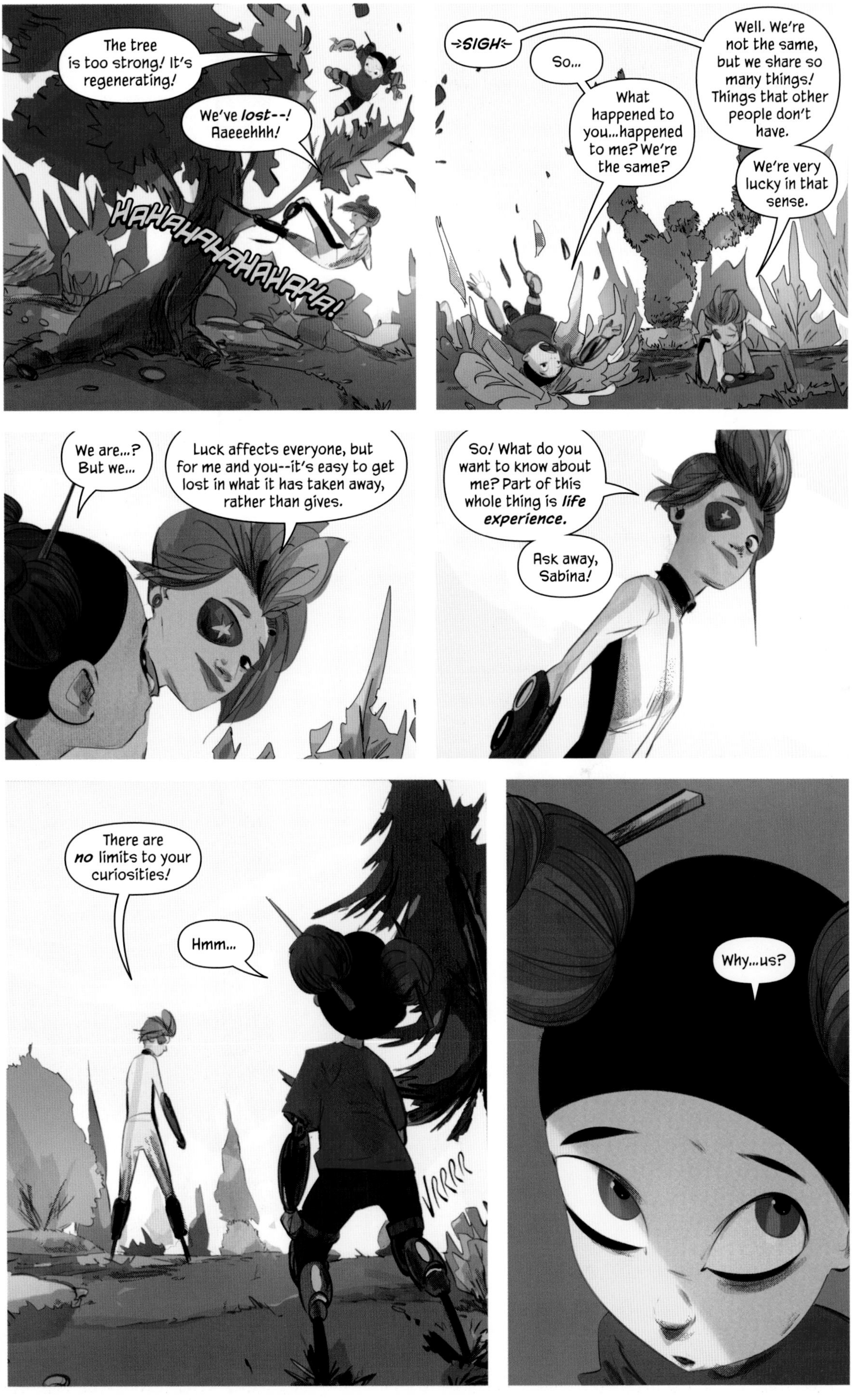

The tree is too strong! It's regenerating!
We've *lost*--! Aaeeehhh!
HAHAHAHAHAHAHAHA!
SIGH
So...
What happened to you...happened to me? We're the same?
Well. We're not the same, but we share so many things! Things that other people don't have.
We're very lucky in that sense.
We are...? But we...
Luck affects everyone, but for me and you--it's easy to get lost in what it has taken away, rather than gives.
So! What do you want to know about me? Part of this whole thing is *life experience.*
Ask away, Sabina!
There are *no* limits to your curiosities!
Hmm...
VRRRR
Why...us?

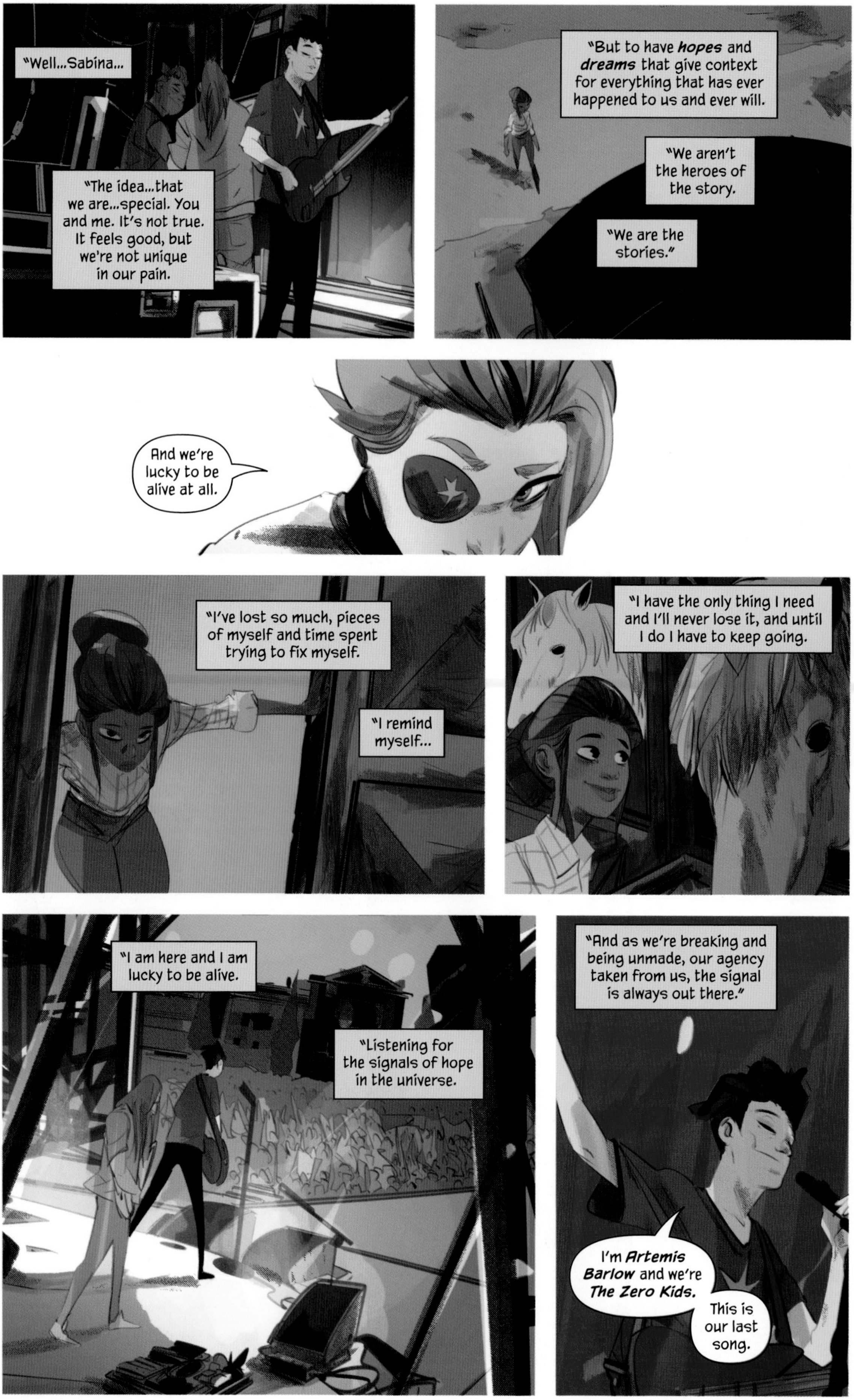
"Well...Sabina...
"The idea...that we are...special. You and me. It's not true. It feels good, but we're not unique in our pain.
"But to have ***hopes*** and ***dreams*** that give context for everything that has ever happened to us and ever will.
"We aren't the heroes of the story.
"We are the stories."
And we're lucky to be alive at all.
"I've lost so much, pieces of myself and time spent trying to fix myself.
"I remind myself...
"I have the only thing I need and I'll never lose it, and until I do I have to keep going.
"I am here and I am lucky to be alive.
"Listening for the signals of hope in the universe.
"And as we're breaking and being unmade, our agency taken from us, the signal is always out there."
I'm ***Artemis Barlow*** and we're ***The Zero Kids.***
This is our last song.

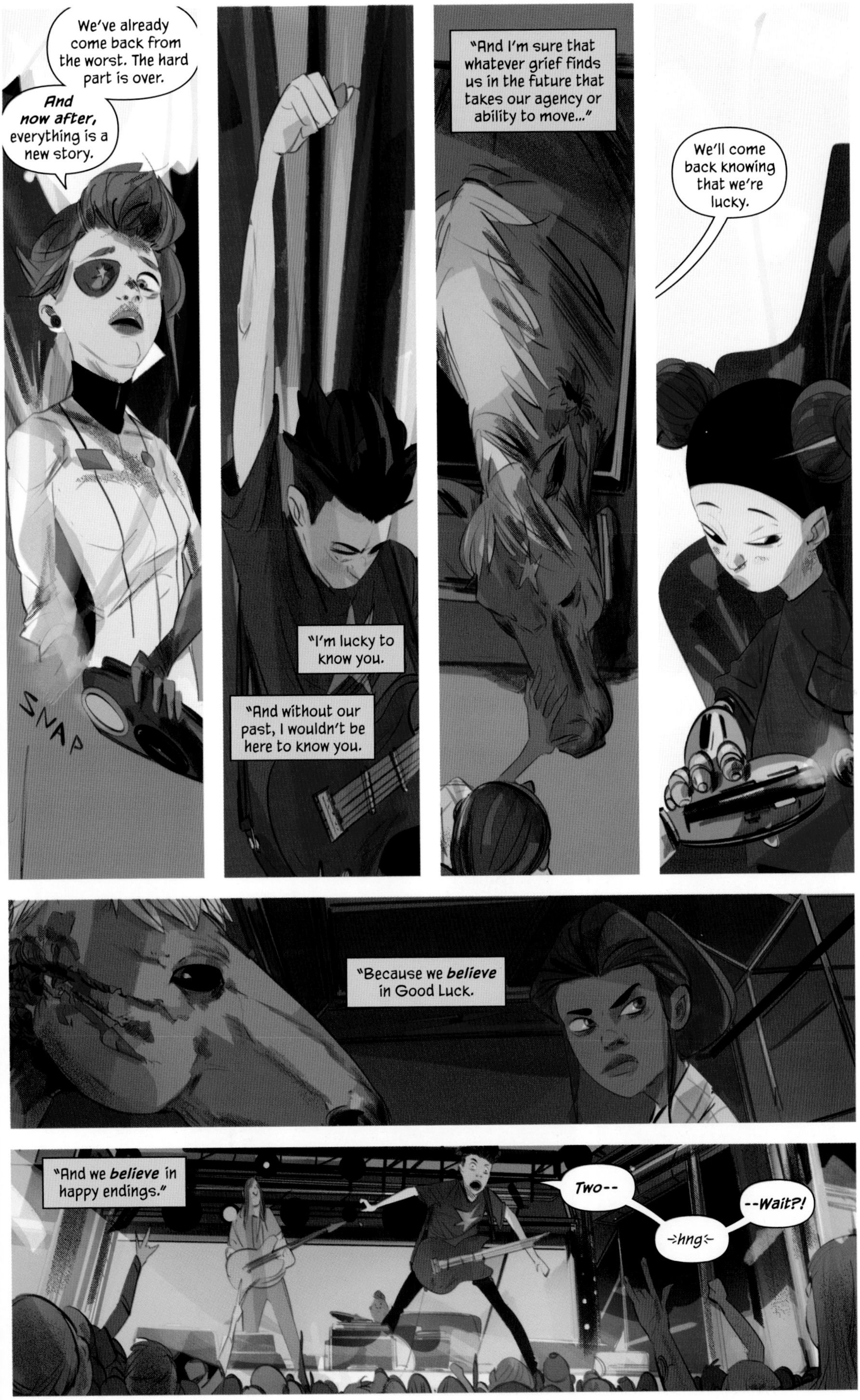
We've already come back from the worst. The hard part is over.
And now after, everything is a new story.
SNAP
"I'm lucky to know you.
"And without our past, I wouldn't be here to know you.
"And I'm sure that whatever grief finds us in the future that takes our agency or ability to move..."
We'll come back knowing that we're lucky.
"Because we *believe* in Good Luck.
"And we *believe* in happy endings."
Two--
-hng-
--Wait?!

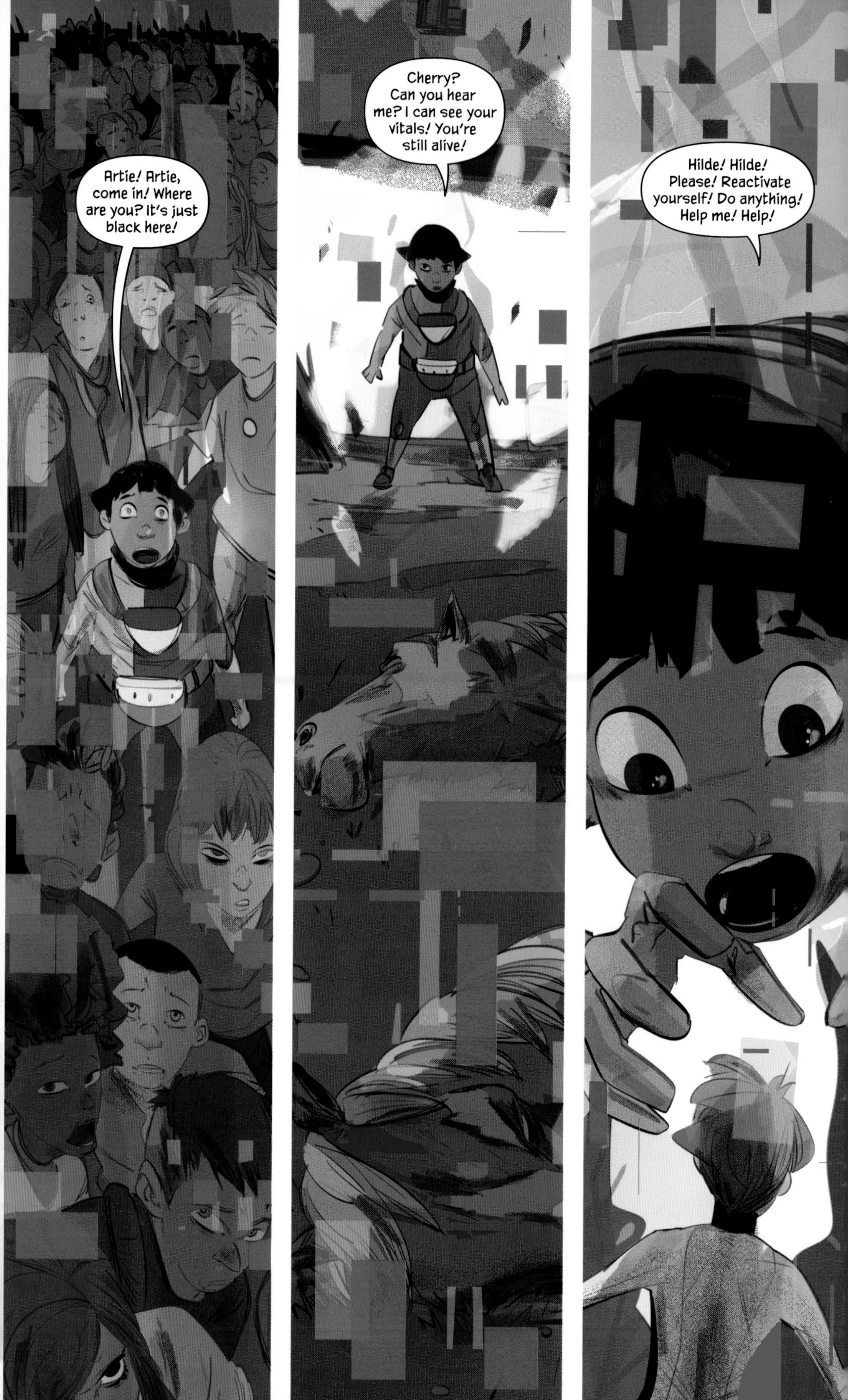
Artie! Artie, come in! Where are you? It's just black here!
Cherry? Can you hear me? I can see your vitals! You're still alive!
Hilde! Hilde! Please! Reactivate yourself! Do anything! Help me! Help!

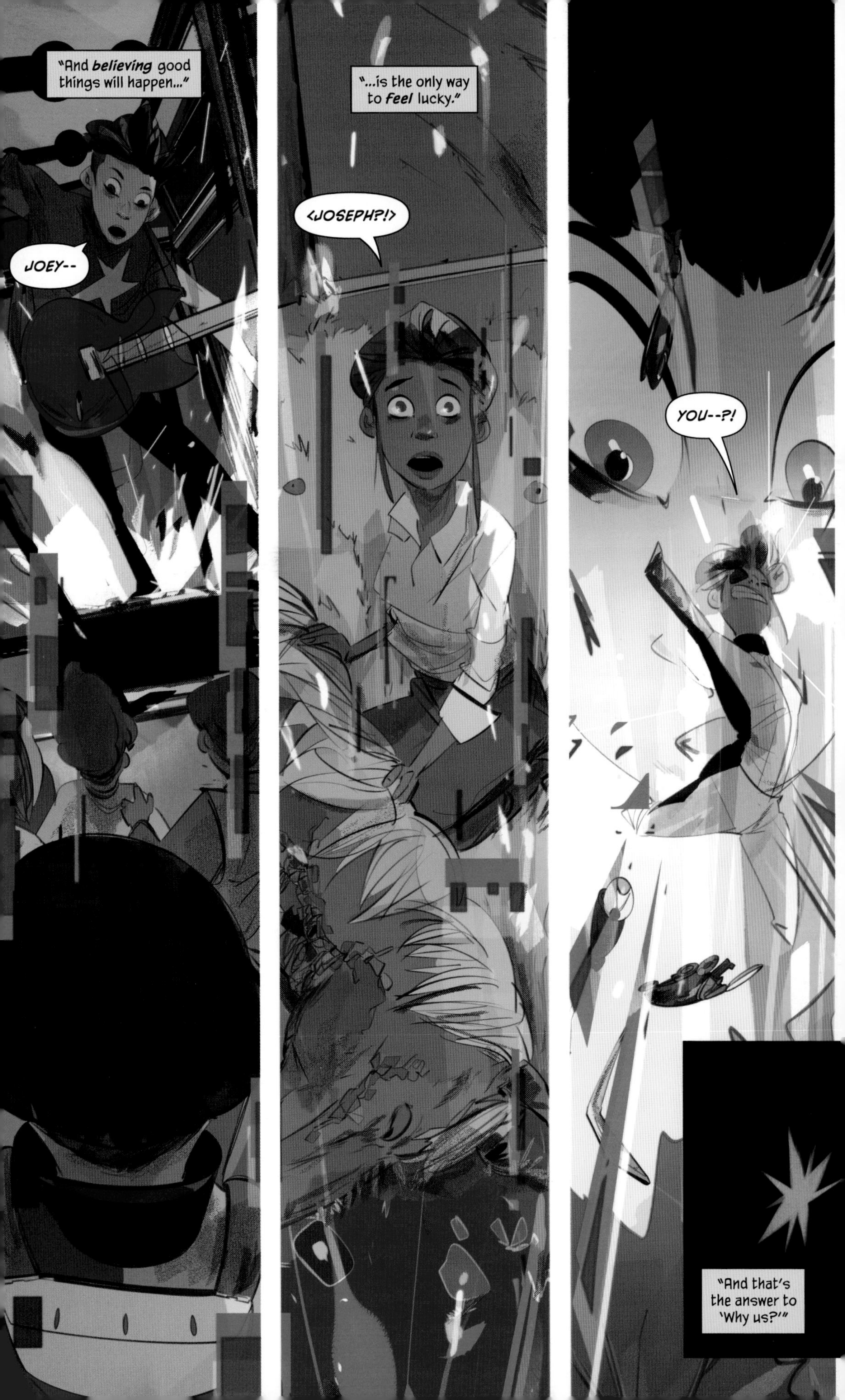

"And *believing* good things will happen..."
JOEY--
"...is the only way to *feel* lucky."
<JOSEPH?!>
YOU--?!
"And that's the answer to 'Why us?'"

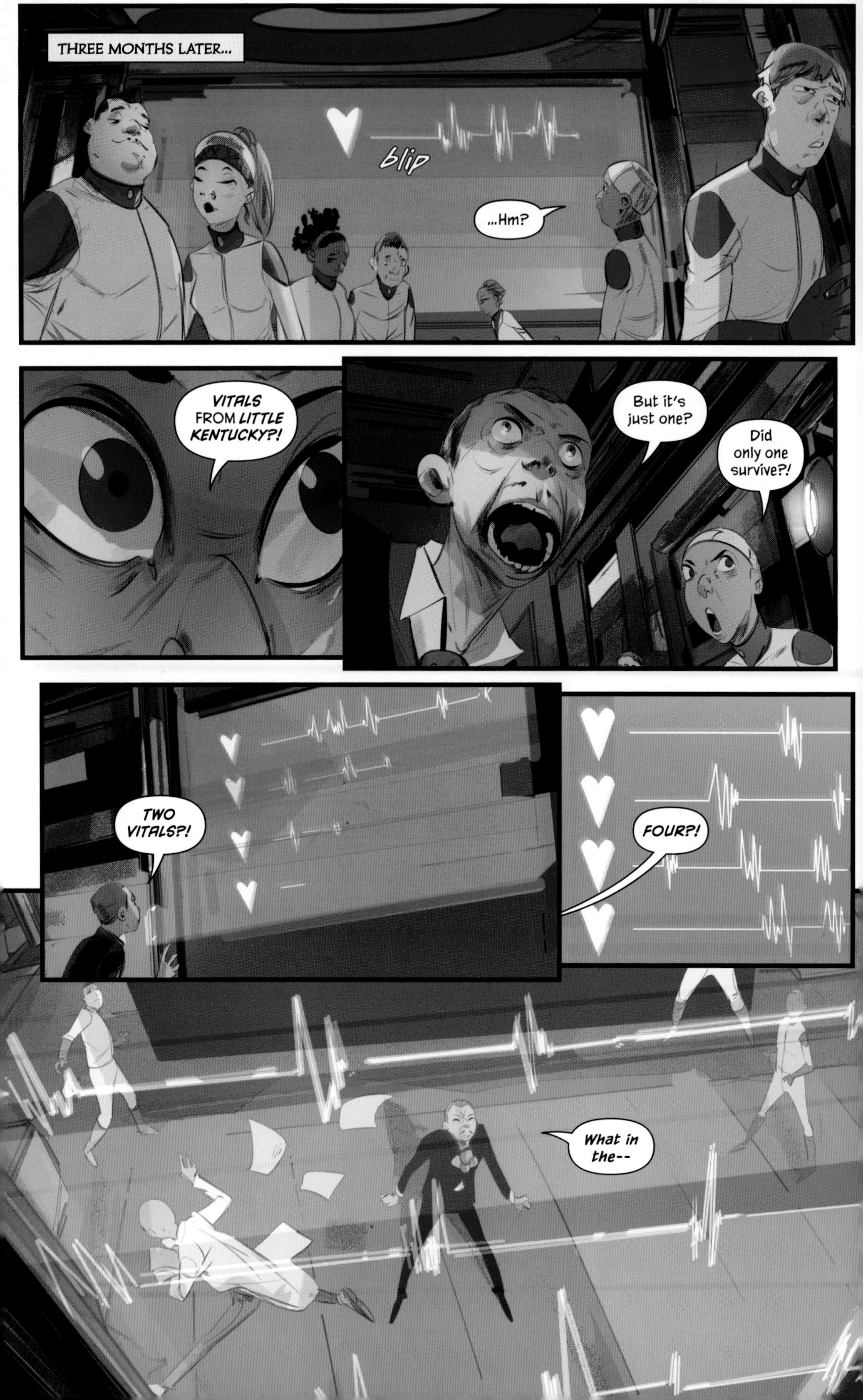
THREE MONTHS LATER...
blip
...Hm?
VITALS FROM LITTLE KENTUCKY?!
But it's just one?
Did only one survive?!
TWO VITALS?!
FOUR?!
What in the--

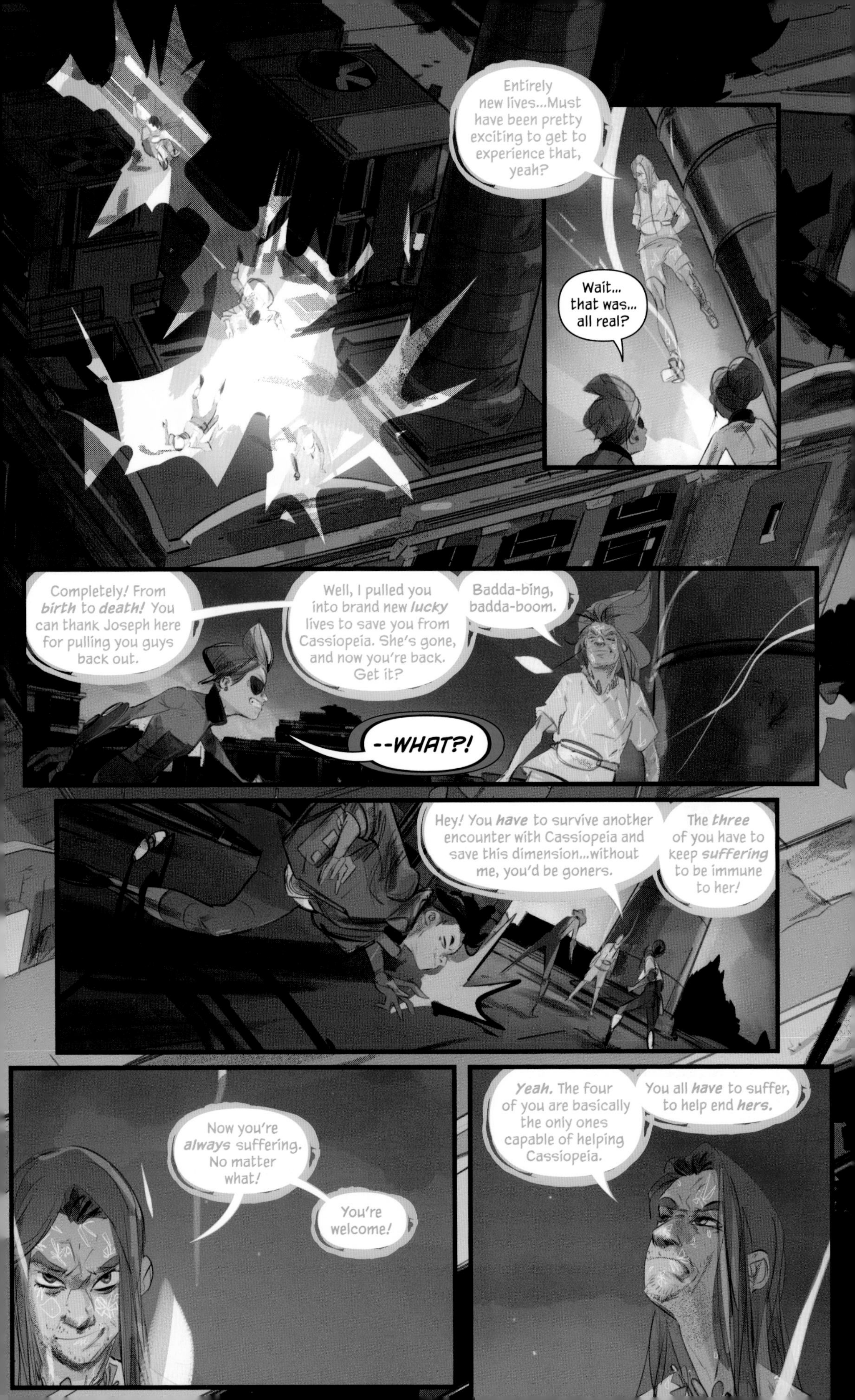

Entirely new lives...Must have been pretty exciting to get to experience that, yeah?
Wait... that was... all real?
Completely! From *birth* to *death!* You can thank Joseph here for pulling you guys back out.
Well, I pulled you into brand new *lucky* lives to save you from Cassiopeia. She's gone, and now you're back. Get it?
Badda-bing, badda-boom.
--WHAT?!
Hey! You *have* to survive another encounter with Cassiopeia and save this dimension...without me, you'd be goners.
The *three* of you have to keep *suffering* to be immune to her!
Now you're *always* suffering. No matter what!
You're welcome!
Yeah. The four of you are basically the only ones capable of helping Cassiopeia.
You all *have* to suffer, to help end *hers.*

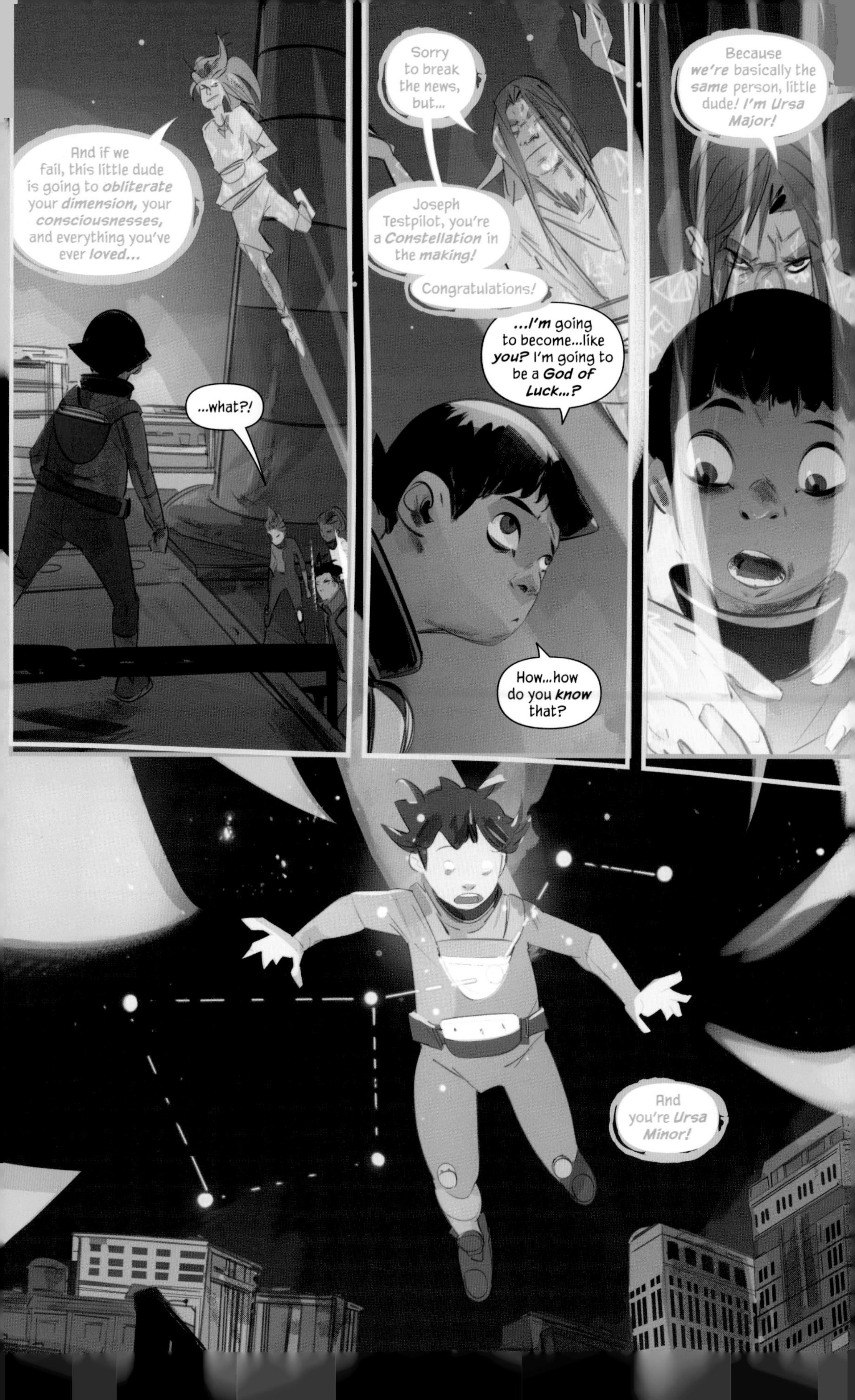
And if we fail, this little dude is going to *obliterate* your *dimension,* your *consciousnesses,* and everything you've ever *loved...*
...what?!
Sorry to break the news, but...
Joseph Testpilot, you're a *Constellation* in the *making!*
Congratulations!
...I'm going to become...like *you?* I'm going to be a *God of Luck...?*
How...how do you *know* that?
Because *we're* basically the *same* person, little dude! *I'm Ursa Major!*
And you're *Ursa Minor!*

CHAPTER

4

TWO-HEADED BOY

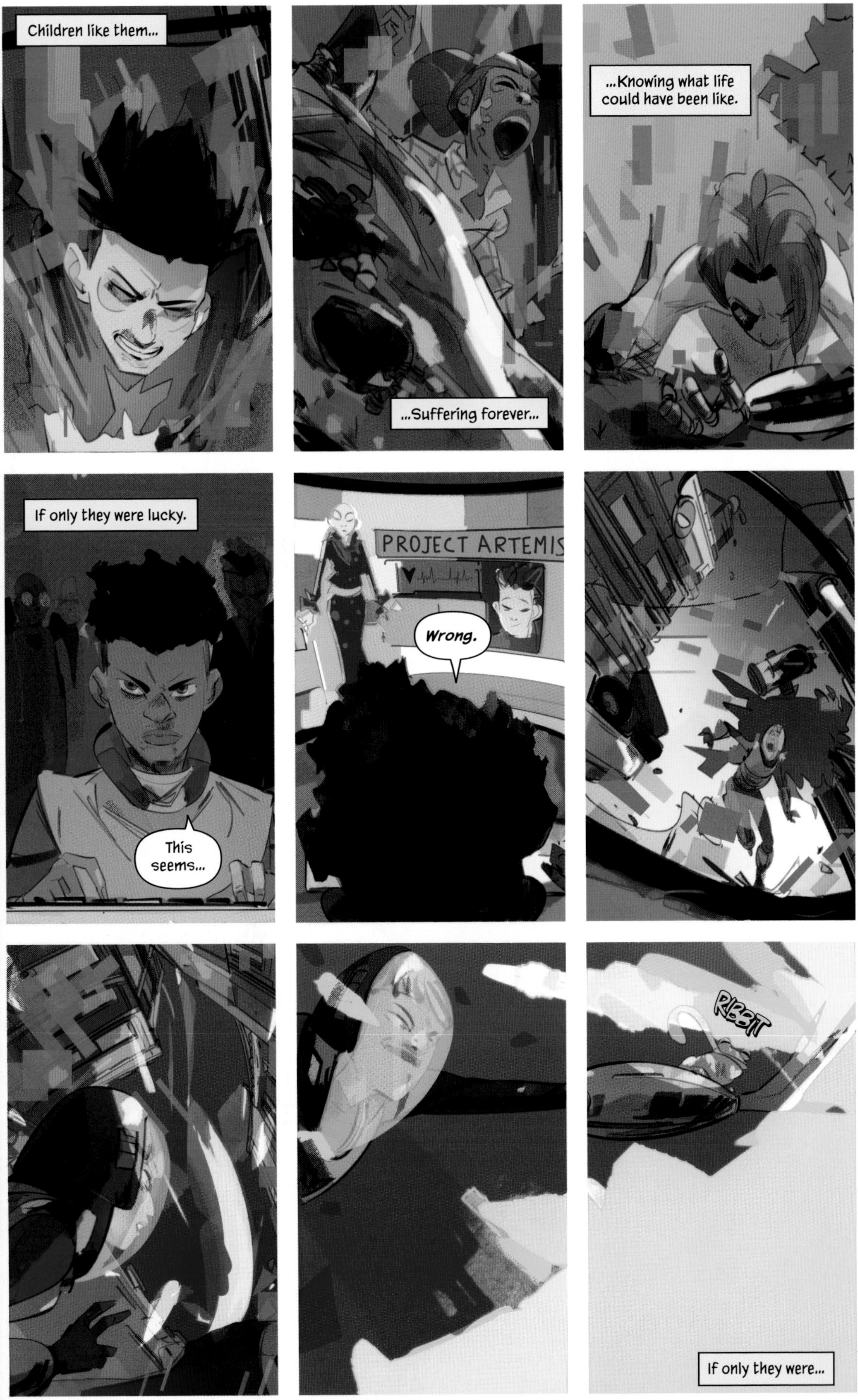
Children like them...
...Suffering forever...
...Knowing what life could have been like.
If only they were lucky.
This seems...
PROJECT ARTEMIS
Wrong.
RIBBIT
If only they were...

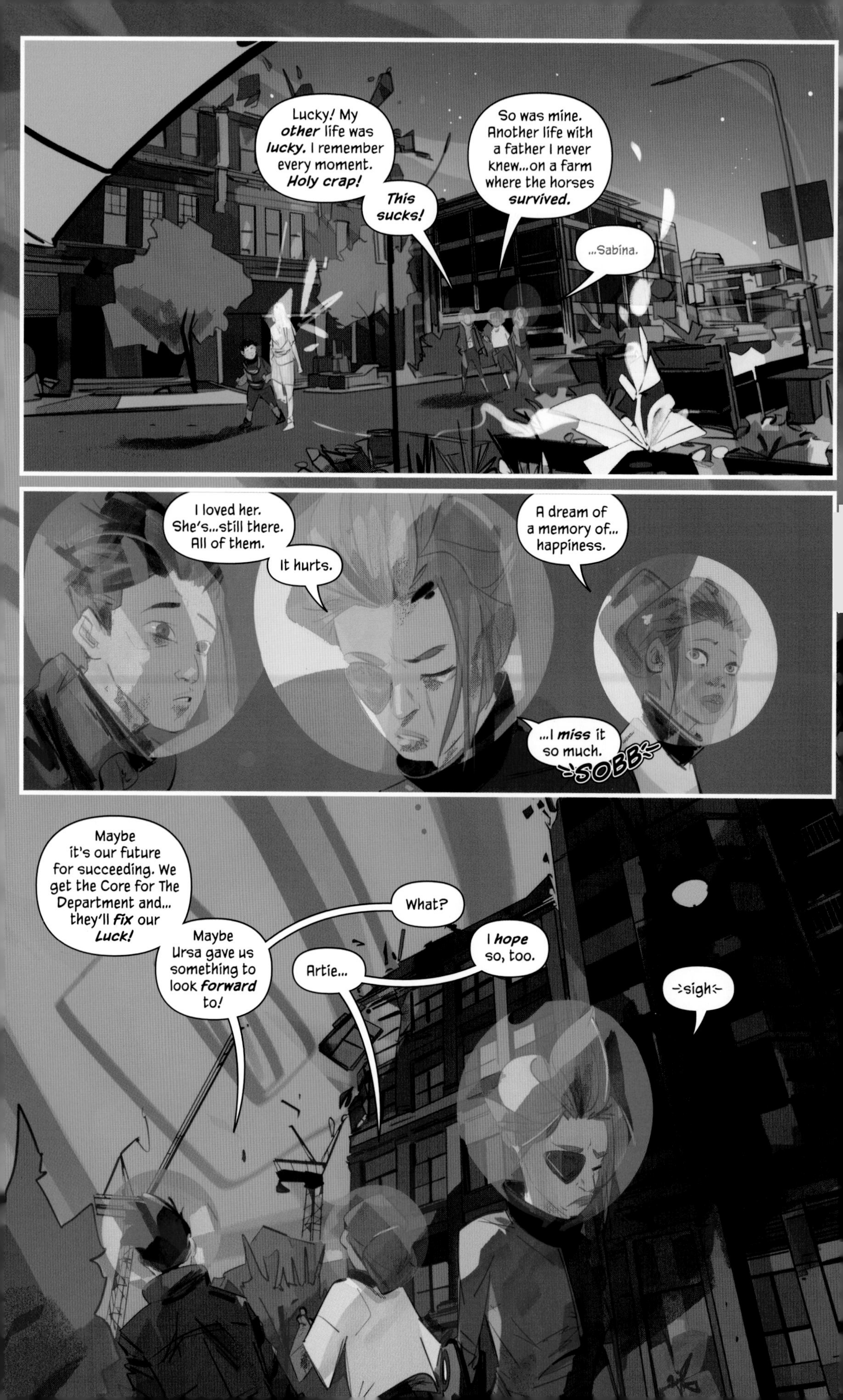
Lucky! My *other* life was *lucky.* I remember every moment. *Holy crap!*
This sucks!
So was mine. Another life with a father I never knew...on a farm where the horses *survived.*
...Sabina.
I loved her. She's...still there. All of them.
It hurts.
A dream of a memory of... happiness.
...I *miss* it so much.
SOBB
Maybe it's our future for succeeding. We get the Core for The Department and... they'll *fix* our *Luck!*
Maybe Ursa gave us something to look *forward* to!
What?
Artie...
I *hope* so, too.
sigh

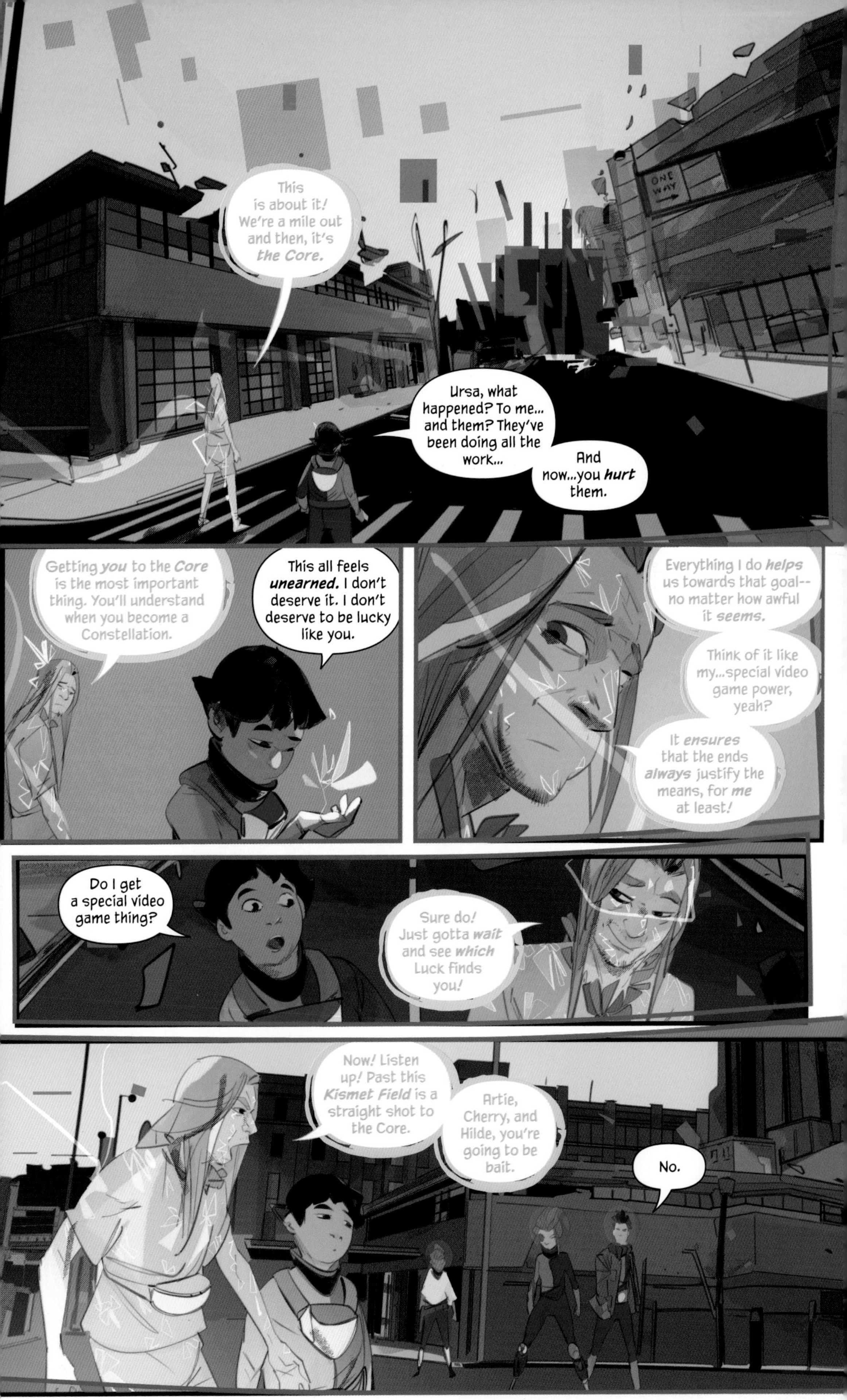
This is about it! We're a mile out and then, it's *the Core.*
ONE WAY
Ursa, what happened? To me... and them? They've been doing all the work...
And now...you ***hurt*** them.
Getting *you* to the *Core* is the most important thing. You'll understand when you become a Constellation.
This all feels ***unearned.*** I don't deserve it. I don't deserve to be lucky like you.
Everything I do ***helps*** us towards that goal--no matter how awful it ***seems.***
Think of it like my...special video game power, yeah?
It ***ensures*** that the ends ***always*** justify the means, for ***me*** at least!
Do I get a special video game thing?
Sure do! Just gotta ***wait*** and see ***which*** Luck finds you!
Now! Listen up! Past this ***Kismet Field*** is a straight shot to the Core.
Artie, Cherry, and Hilde, you're going to be bait.
No.

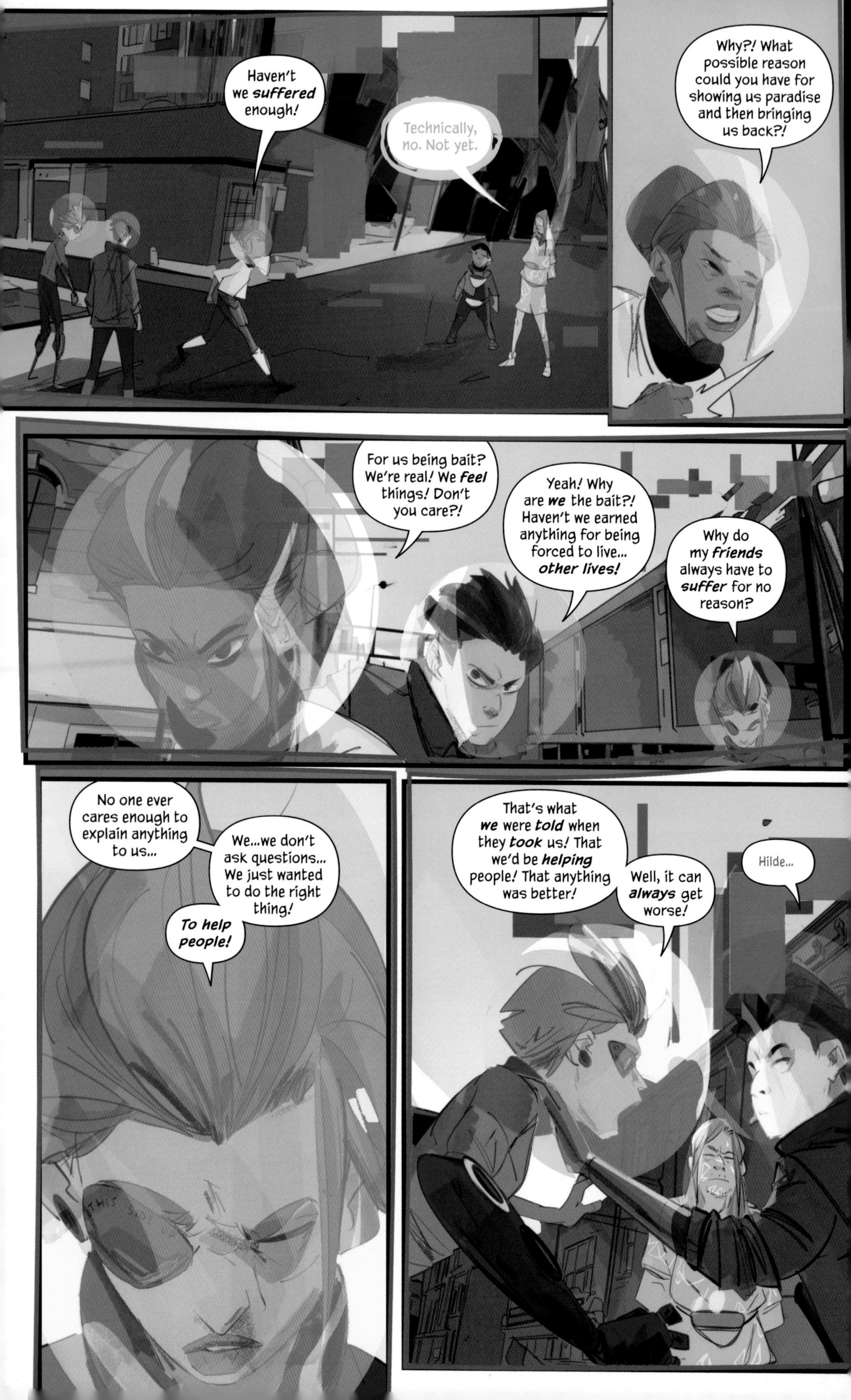
Haven't we suffered enough!
Technically, no. Not yet.
Why?! What possible reason could you have for showing us paradise and then bringing us back?!
For us being bait? We're real! We feel things! Don't you care?!
Yeah! Why are we the bait?! Haven't we earned anything for being forced to live... other lives!
Why do my friends always have to suffer for no reason?
No one ever cares enough to explain anything to us...
We...we don't ask questions... We just wanted to do the right thing!
To help people!
That's what we were told when they took us! That we'd be helping people! That anything was better!
Well, it can always get worse!
Hilde...

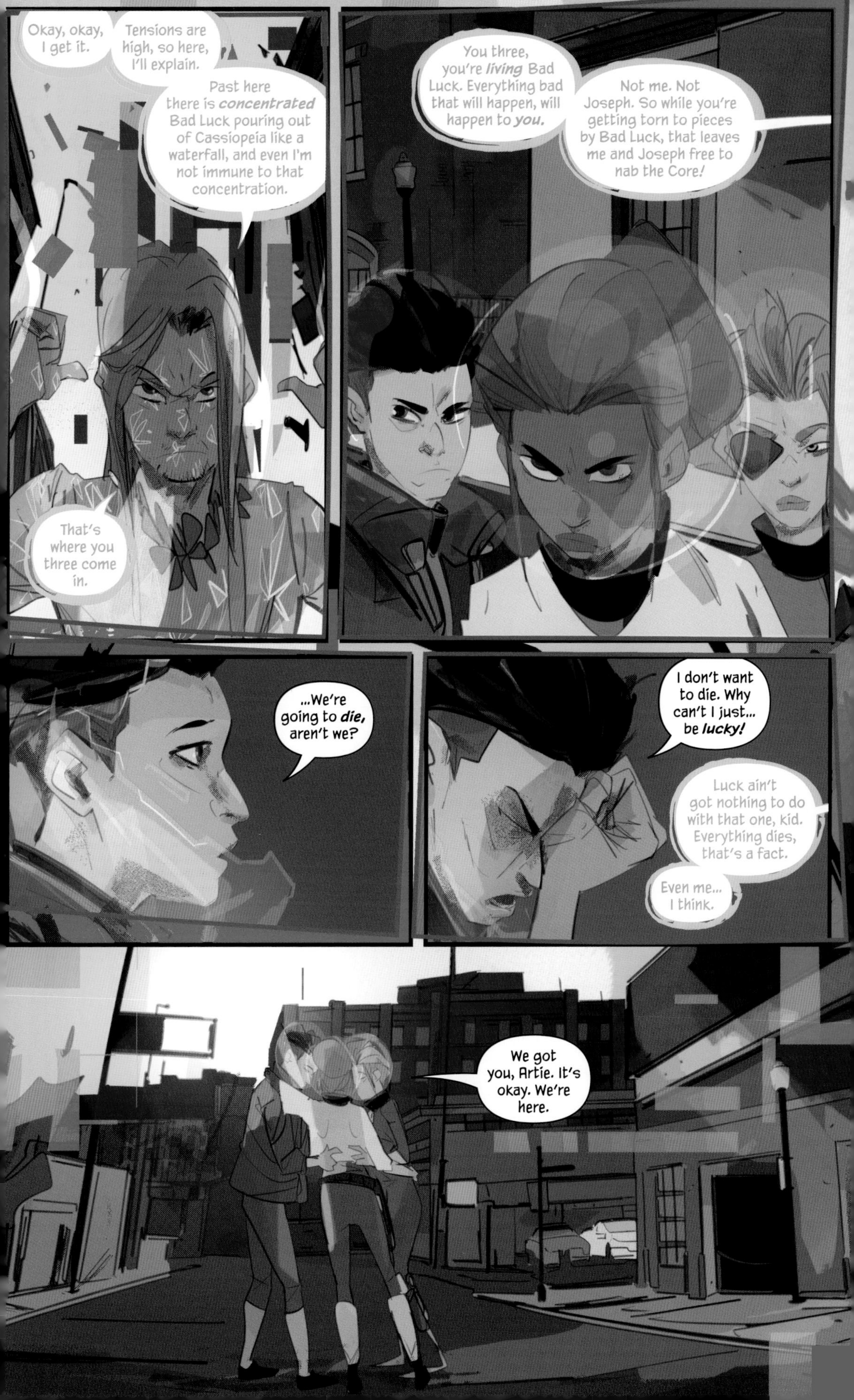
Okay, okay, I get it.
Tensions are high, so here, I'll explain.
Past here there is *concentrated* Bad Luck pouring out of Cassiopeia like a waterfall, and even I'm not immune to that concentration.
That's where you three come in.
You three, you're *living* Bad Luck. Everything bad that will happen, will happen to *you.*
Not me. Not Joseph. So while you're getting torn to pieces by Bad Luck, that leaves me and Joseph free to nab the Core!
...We're going to *die,* aren't we?
I don't want to die. Why can't I just... be *lucky!*
Luck ain't got nothing to do with that one, kid. Everything dies, that's a fact.
Even me... I think.
We got you, Artie. It's okay. We're here.

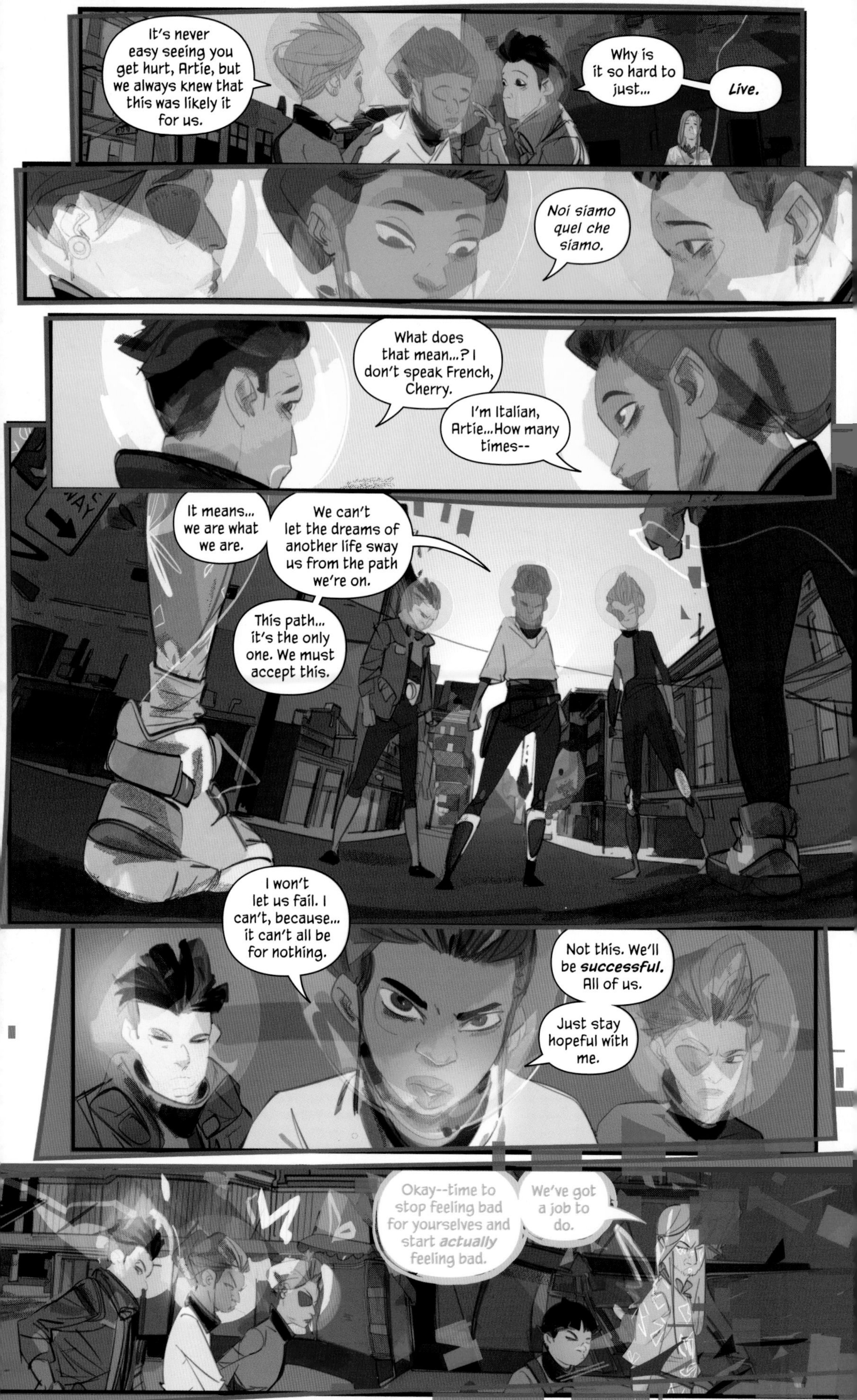

It's never easy seeing you get hurt, Artie, but we always knew that this was likely it for us.
Why is it so hard to just...
Live.
Noi siamo quel che siamo.
What does that mean...? I don't speak French, Cherry.
I'm Italian, Artie...How many times--
It means... we are what we are.
We can't let the dreams of another life sway us from the path we're on.
This path... it's the only one. We must accept this.
I won't let us fail. I can't, because... it can't all be for nothing.
Not this. We'll be ***successful.*** All of us.
Just stay hopeful with me.
Okay--time to stop feeling bad for yourselves and start *actually* feeling bad.
We've got a job to do.

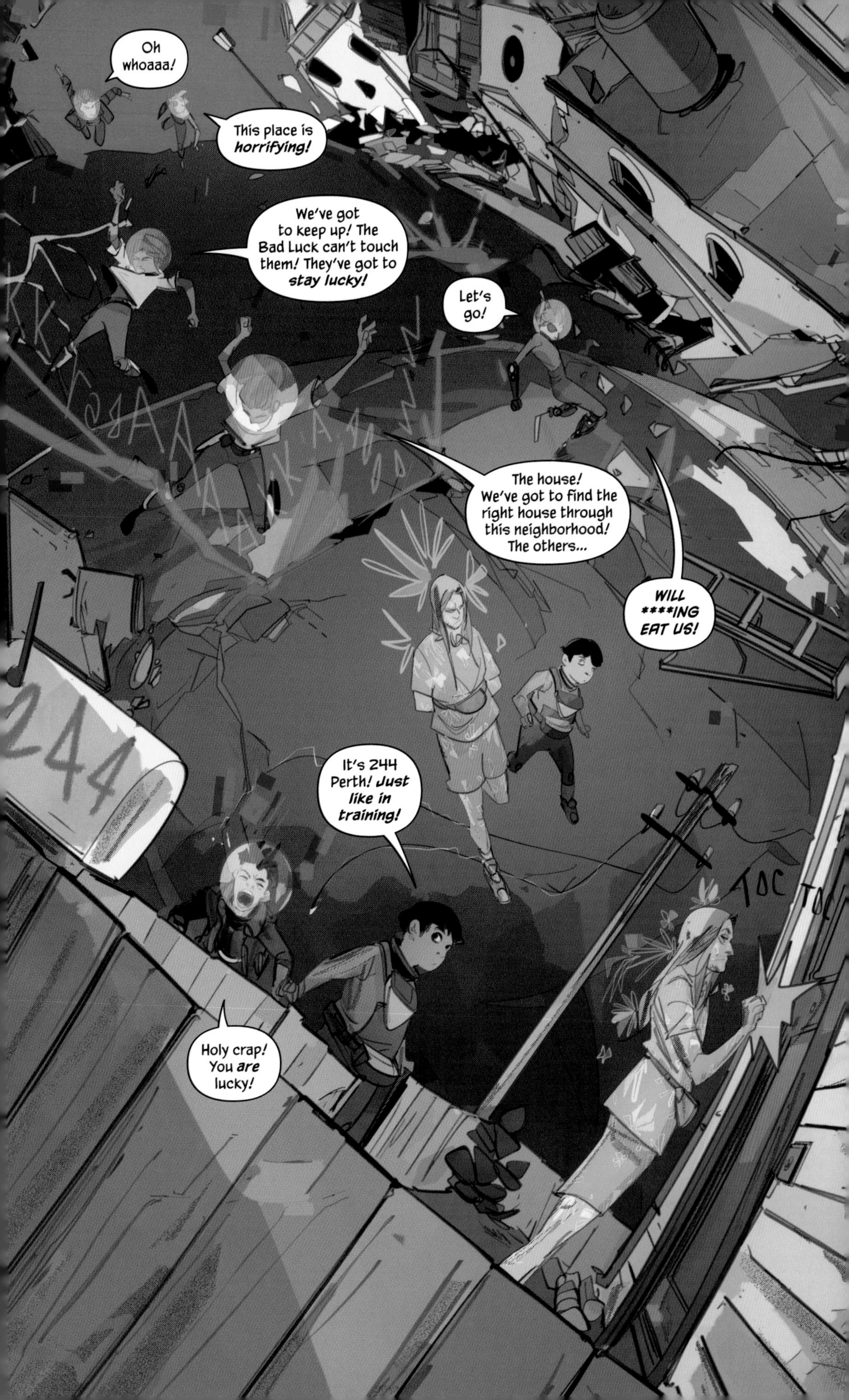
Oh whoaaa!
This place is *horrifying!*
We've got to keep up! The Bad Luck can't touch them! They've got to ***stay lucky!***
Let's go!
The house! We've got to find the right house through this neighborhood! The others...
WILL ****ING EAT US!
244
It's 244 Perth! ***Just like in training!***
Holy crap! You *are* lucky!
TOC TOC

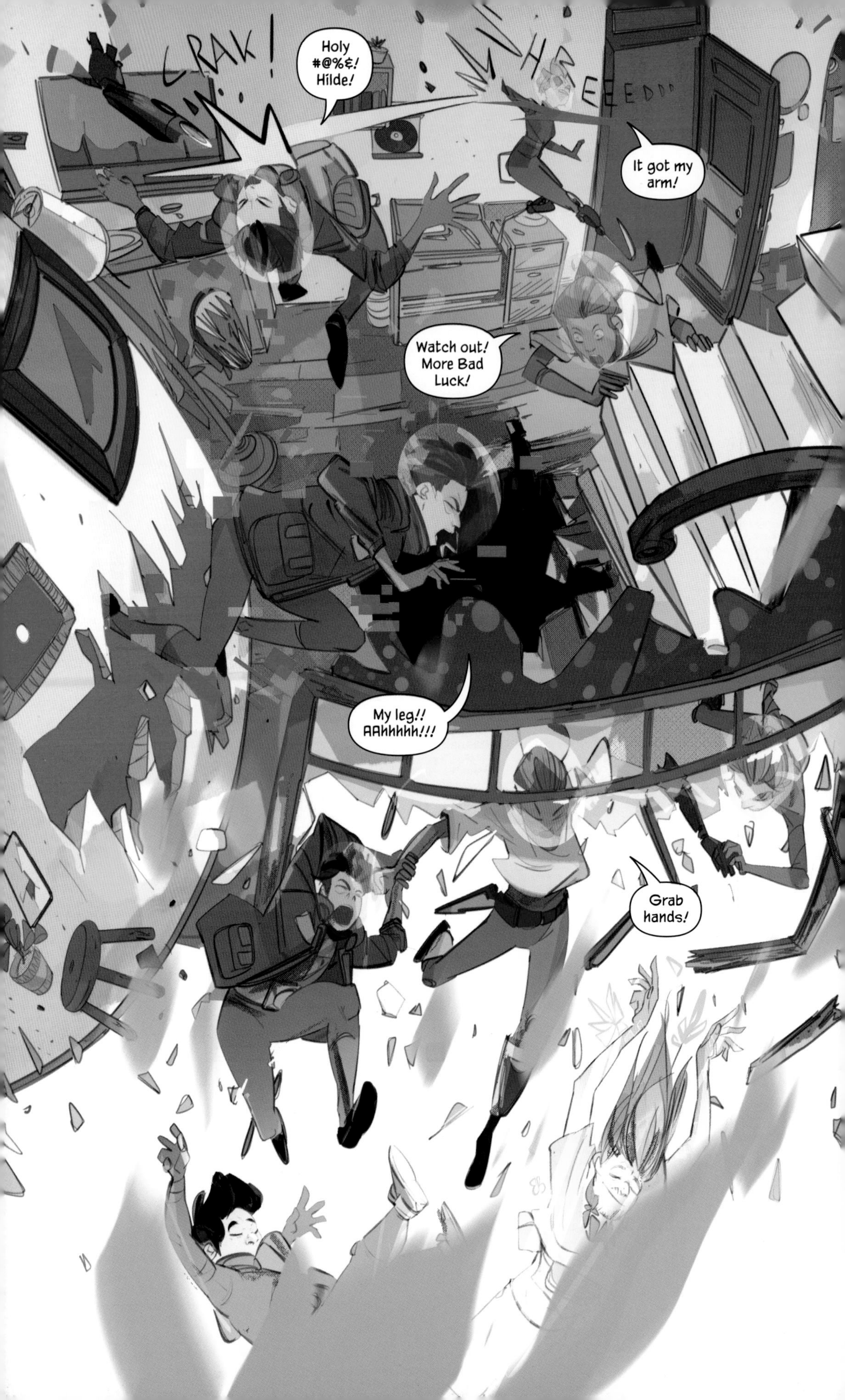
CRAK!
Holy #@%&! Hilde!
SHREEEDDD
It got my arm!
Watch out! More Bad Luck!
My leg!! AAhhhhh!!!
Grab hands!

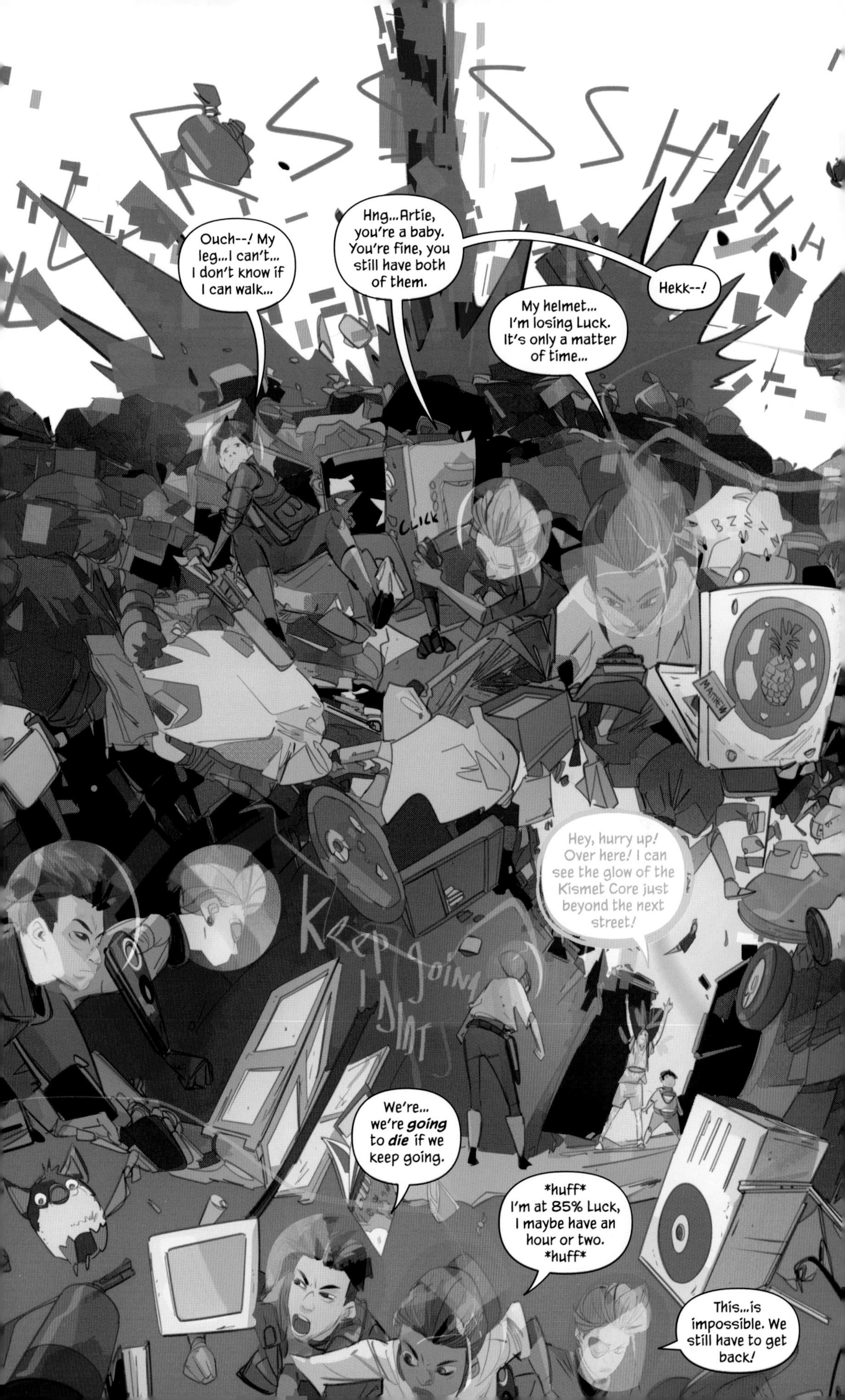
Ouch--! My leg...I can't... I don't know if I can walk...
Hng...Artie, you're a baby. You're fine, you still have both of them.
Hekk--!
My helmet... I'm losing Luck. It's only a matter of time...
CLICK
BZZZ
Hey, hurry up! Over here! I can see the glow of the Kismet Core just beyond the next street!
We're... we're ***going*** to ***die*** if we keep going.
huff I'm at 85% Luck, I maybe have an hour or two. *huff*
This...is impossible. We still have to get back!

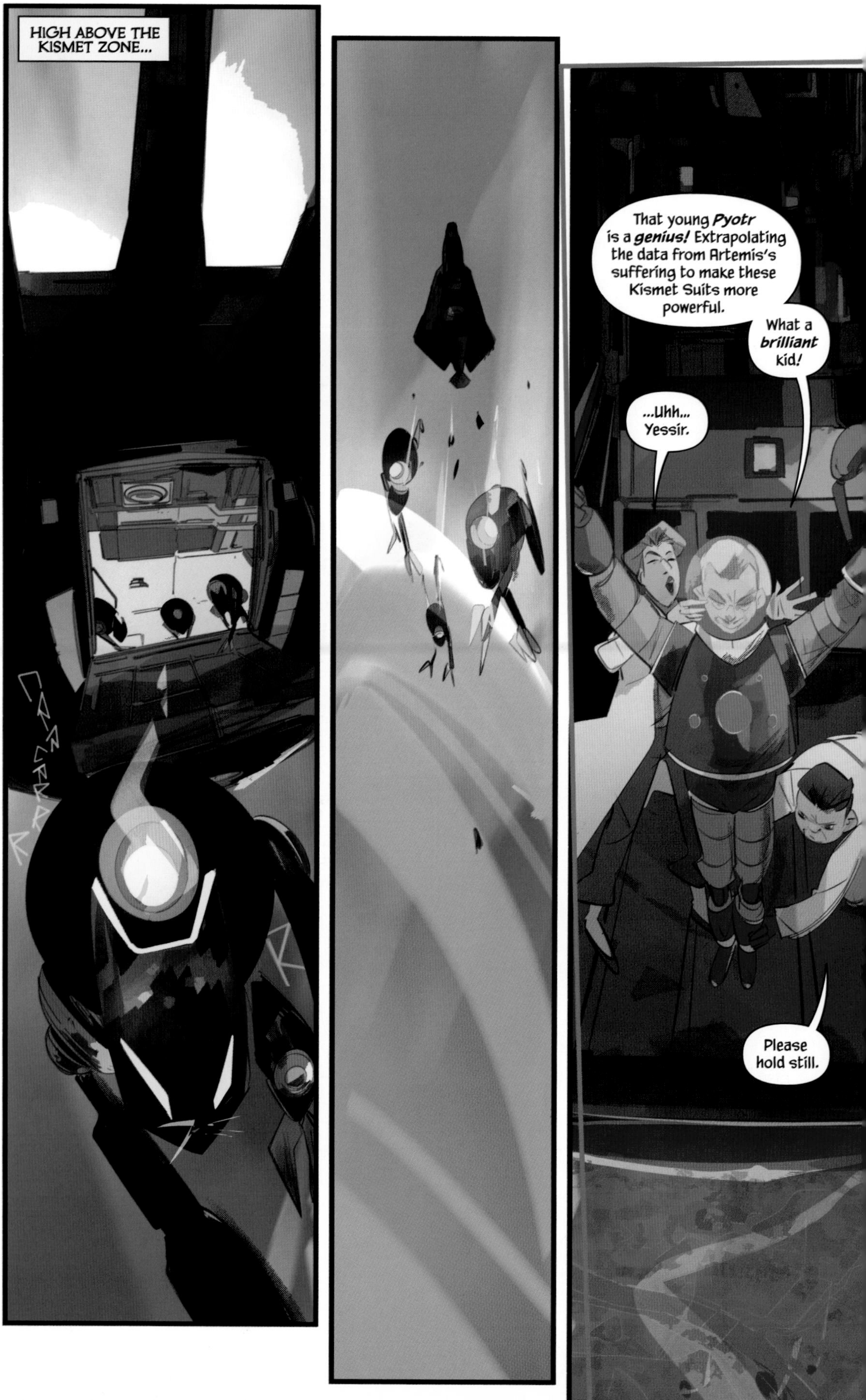
HIGH ABOVE THE KISMET ZONE...
That young *Pyotr* is a ***genius!*** Extrapolating the data from Artemis's suffering to make these Kismet Suits more powerful.
What a ***brilliant*** kid!
...Uhh... Yessir.
Please hold still.

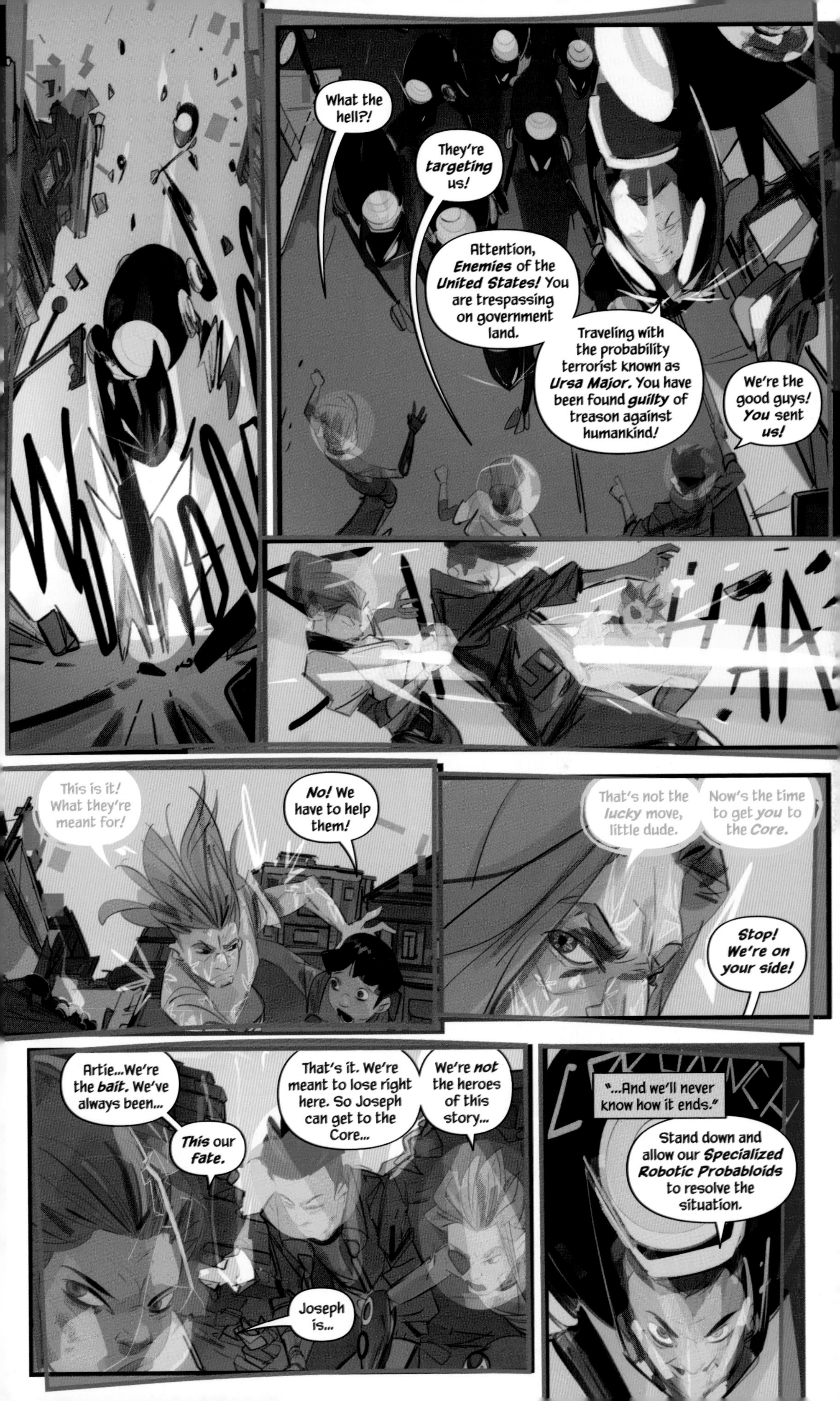

What the hell?!
They're *targeting* us!
Attention, *Enemies* of the *United States!* You are trespassing on government land.
Traveling with the probability terrorist known as *Ursa Major.* You have been found *guilty* of treason against humankind!
We're the good guys! *You* sent *us!*
This is it! What they're meant for!
No! We have to help them!
That's not the *lucky* move, little dude.
Now's the time to get *you* to the *Core.*
Stop! We're on your side!
Artie...We're the *bait.* We've always been...
This our *fate.*
That's it. We're meant to lose right here. So Joseph can get to the Core...
We're *not* the heroes of this story...
Joseph is...
"...And we'll never know how it ends."
Stand down and allow our *Specialized Robotic Probabloids* to resolve the situation.

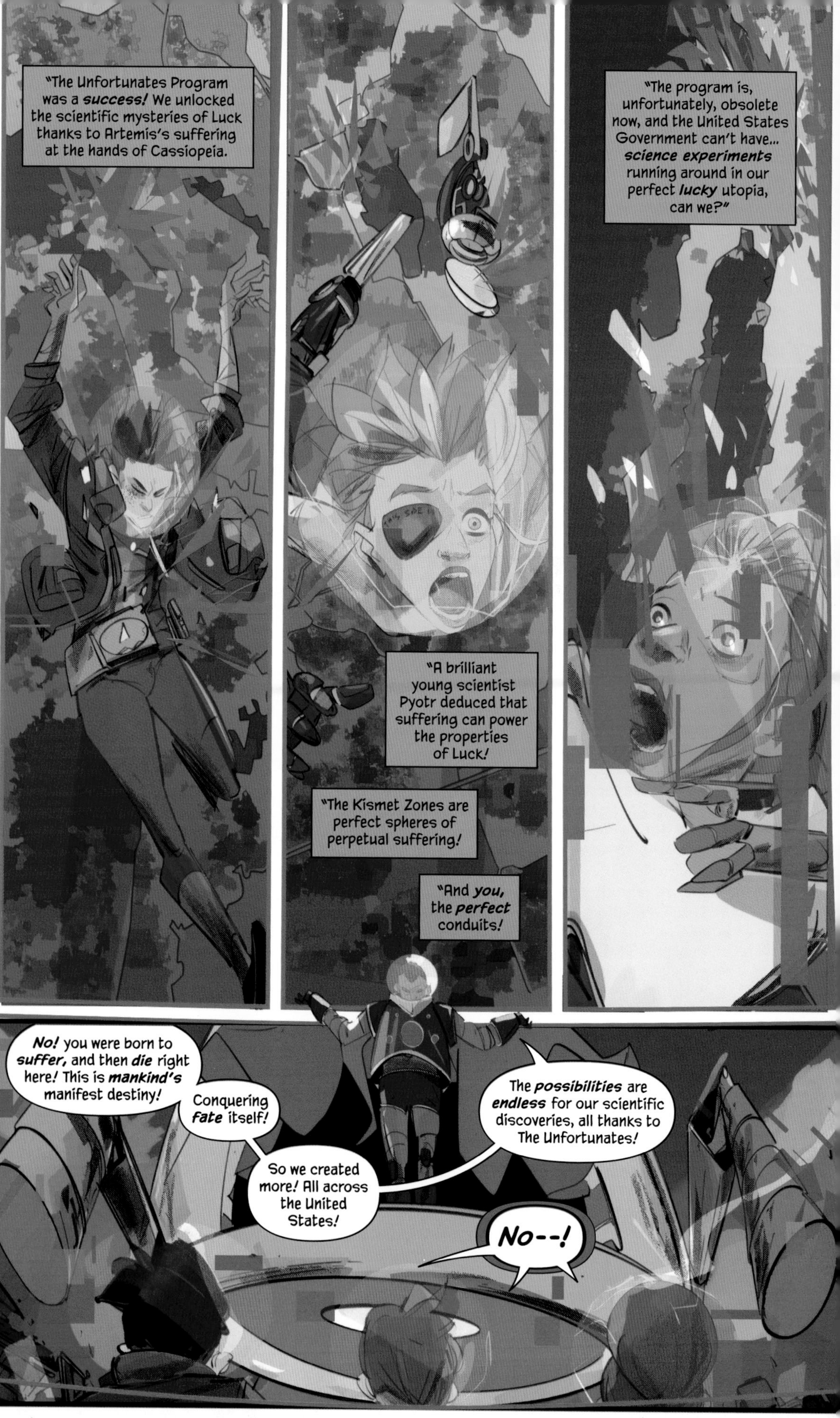
"The Unfortunates Program was a *success!* We unlocked the scientific mysteries of Luck thanks to Artemis's suffering at the hands of Cassiopeia.
"A brilliant young scientist Pyotr deduced that suffering can power the properties of Luck!
"The Kismet Zones are perfect spheres of perpetual suffering!
"And *you*, the *perfect* conduits!
"The program is, unfortunately, obsolete now, and the United States Government can't have... *science experiments* running around in our perfect *lucky* utopia, can we?"
No! you were born to *suffer,* and then *die* right here! This is *mankind's* manifest destiny!
Conquering *fate* itself!
So we created more! All across the United States!
The *possibilities* are *endless* for our scientific discoveries, all thanks to The Unfortunates!
No--!

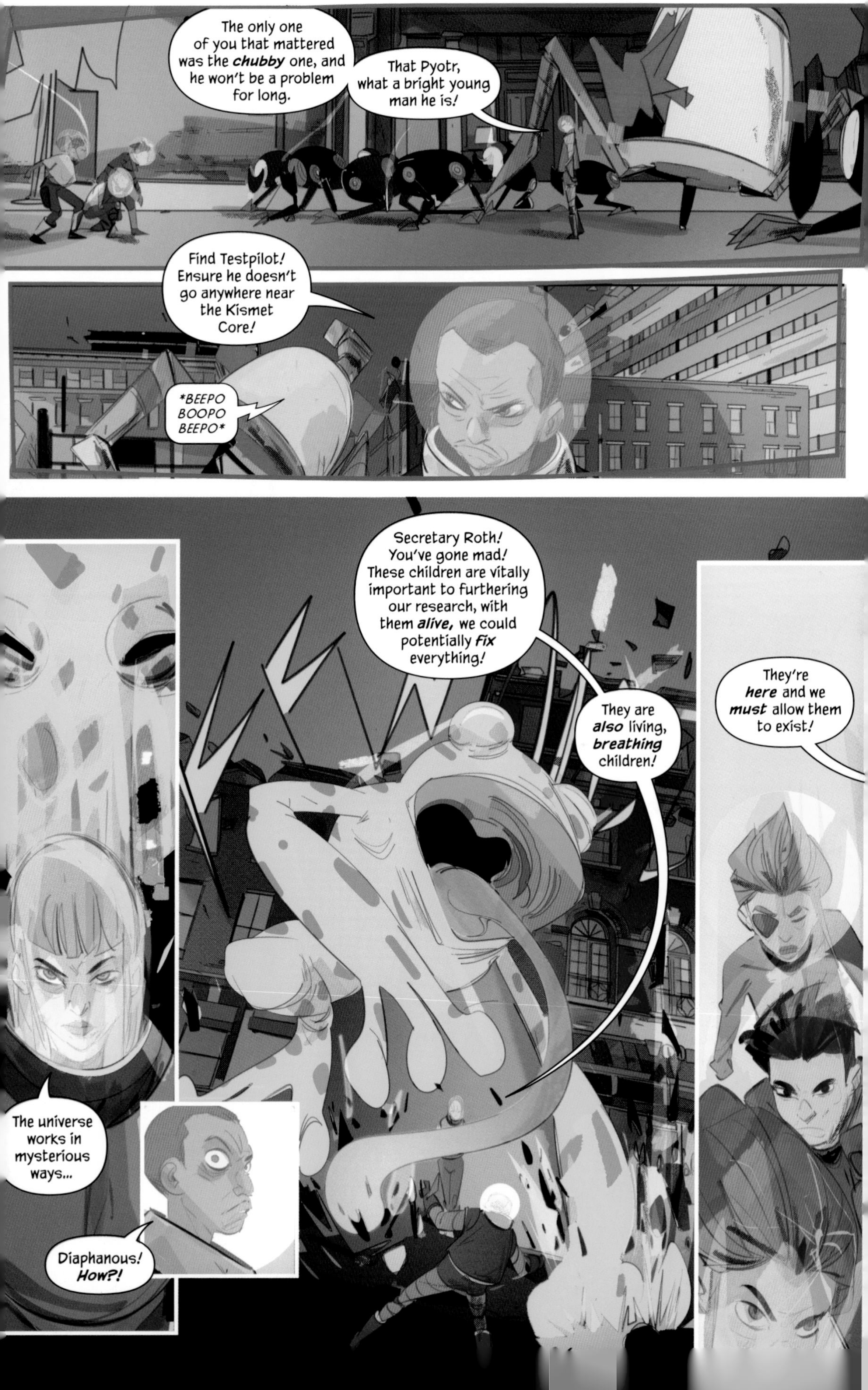
The only one of you that mattered was the ***chubby*** one, and he won't be a problem for long.
That Pyotr, what a bright young man he is!
Find Testpilot! Ensure he doesn't go anywhere near the Kismet Core!
BEEPO BOOPO BEEPO
The universe works in mysterious ways...
Diaphanous! ***How?!***
Secretary Roth! You've gone mad! These children are vitally important to furthering our research, with them ***alive,*** we could potentially ***fix*** everything!
They are ***also*** living, ***breathing*** children!
They're ***here*** and we ***must*** allow them to exist!

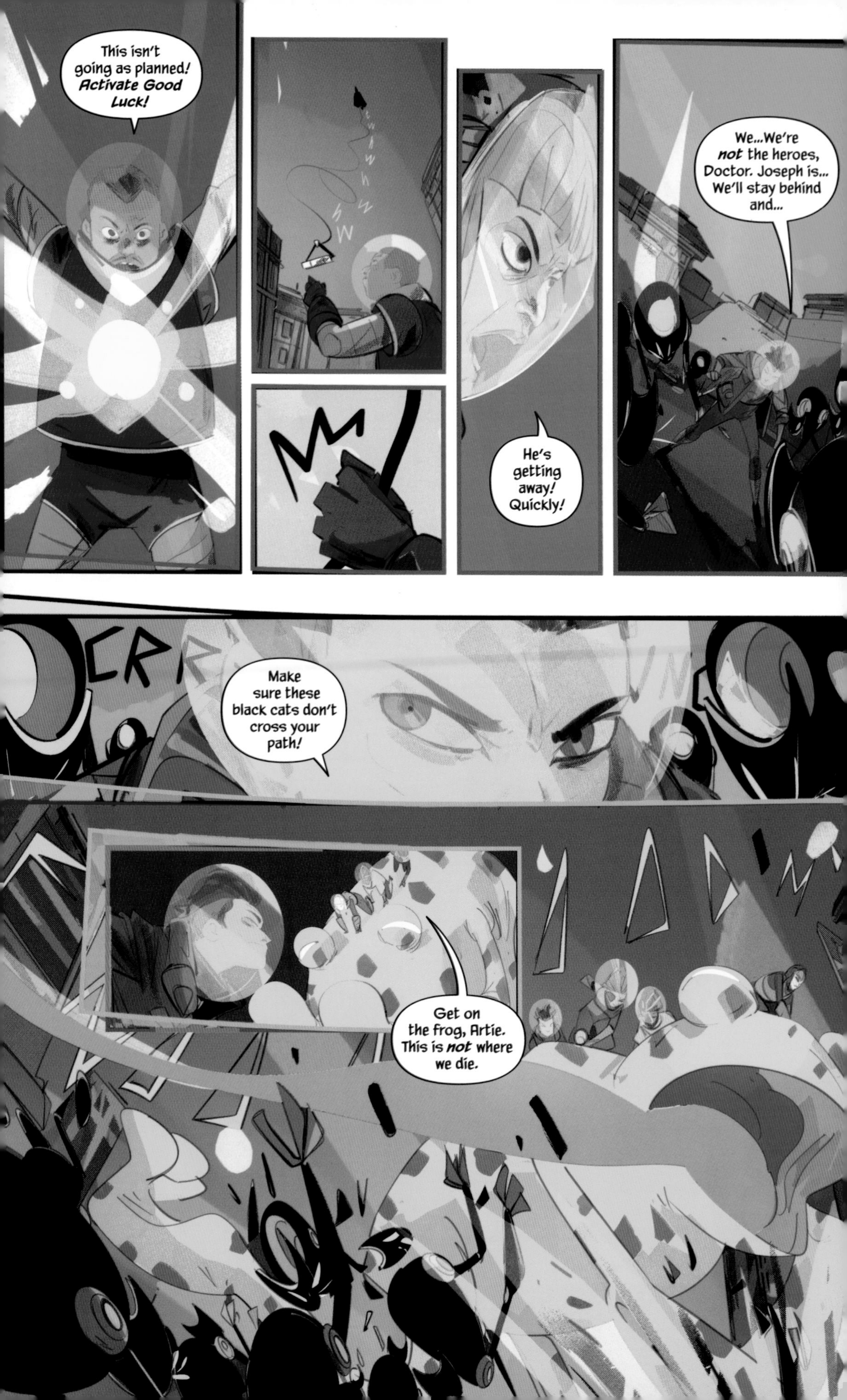
This isn't going as planned! *Activate Good Luck!*
He's getting away! Quickly!
We...We're *not* the heroes, Doctor. Joseph is... We'll stay behind and...
CR
Make sure these black cats don't cross your path!
Get on the frog, Artie. This is *not* where we die.

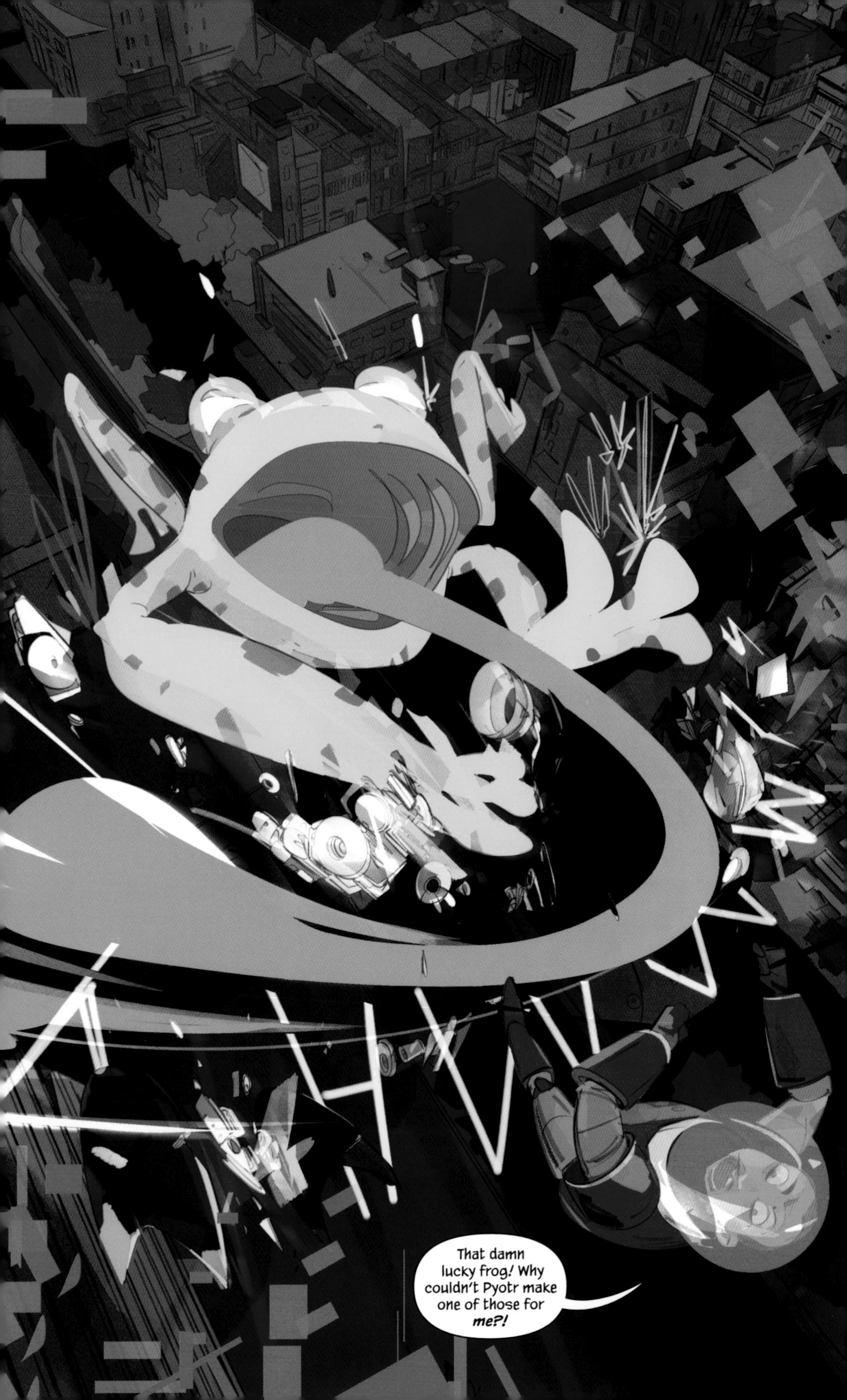
That damn lucky frog! Why couldn't Pyotr make one of those for *me?!*

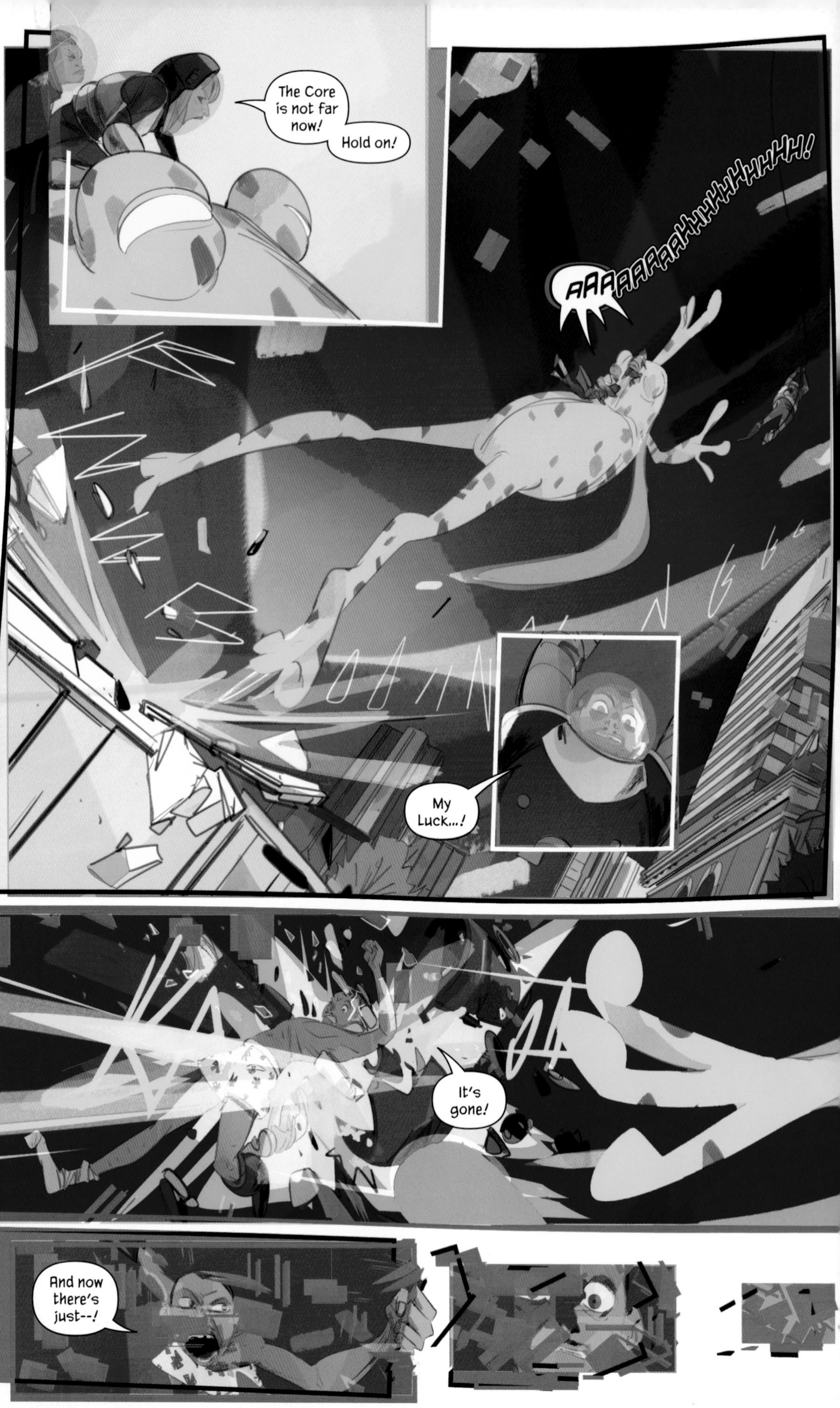
The Core is not far now!
Hold on!
AAAAAAAAHHHHHHHHHH!
My Luck...!
It's gone!
And now there's just--!

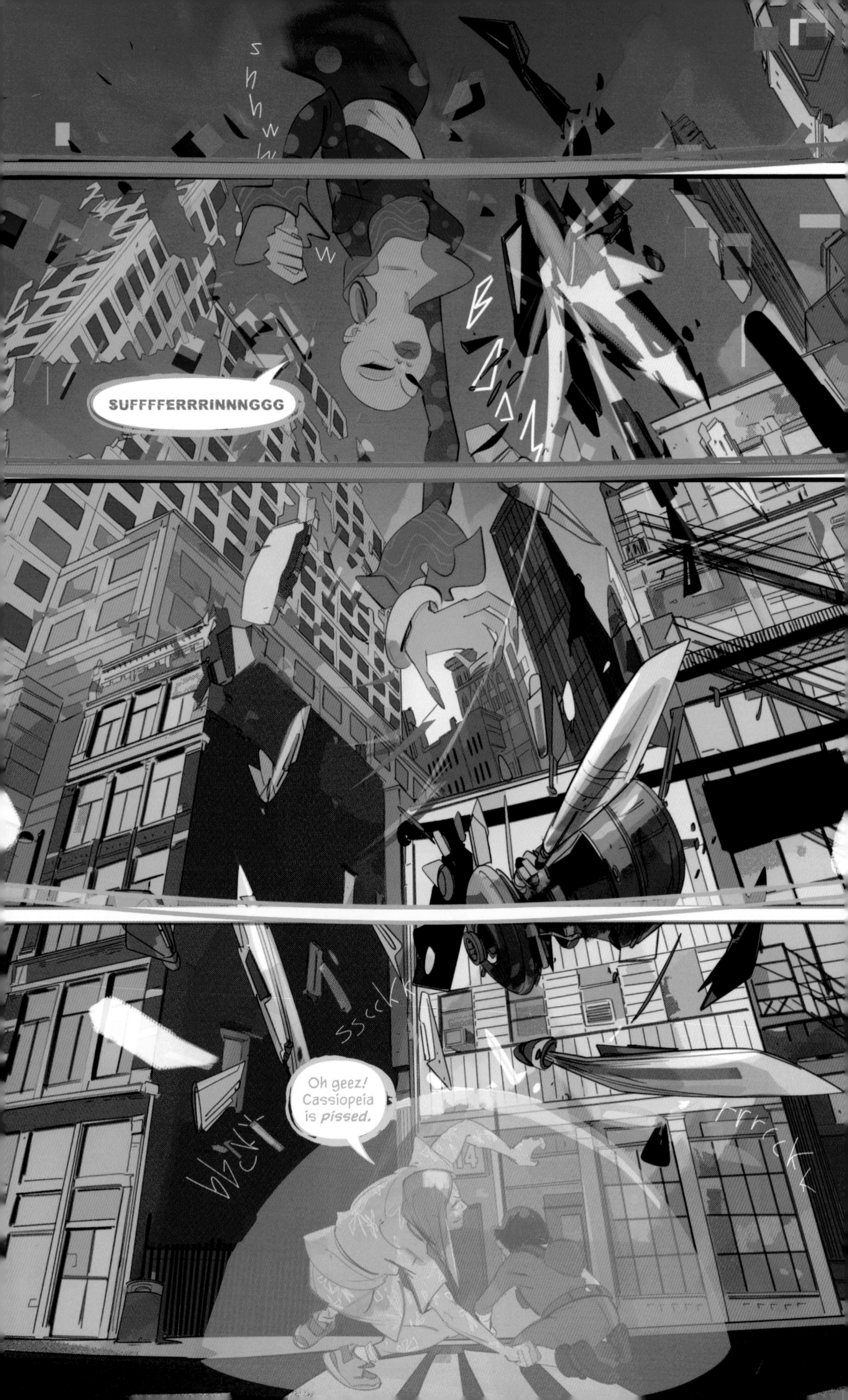
shhwww
BAAM
SUFFFFERRRINNNGGG
ssckk
Oh geez! Cassiopeia is *pissed.*
rrrckk

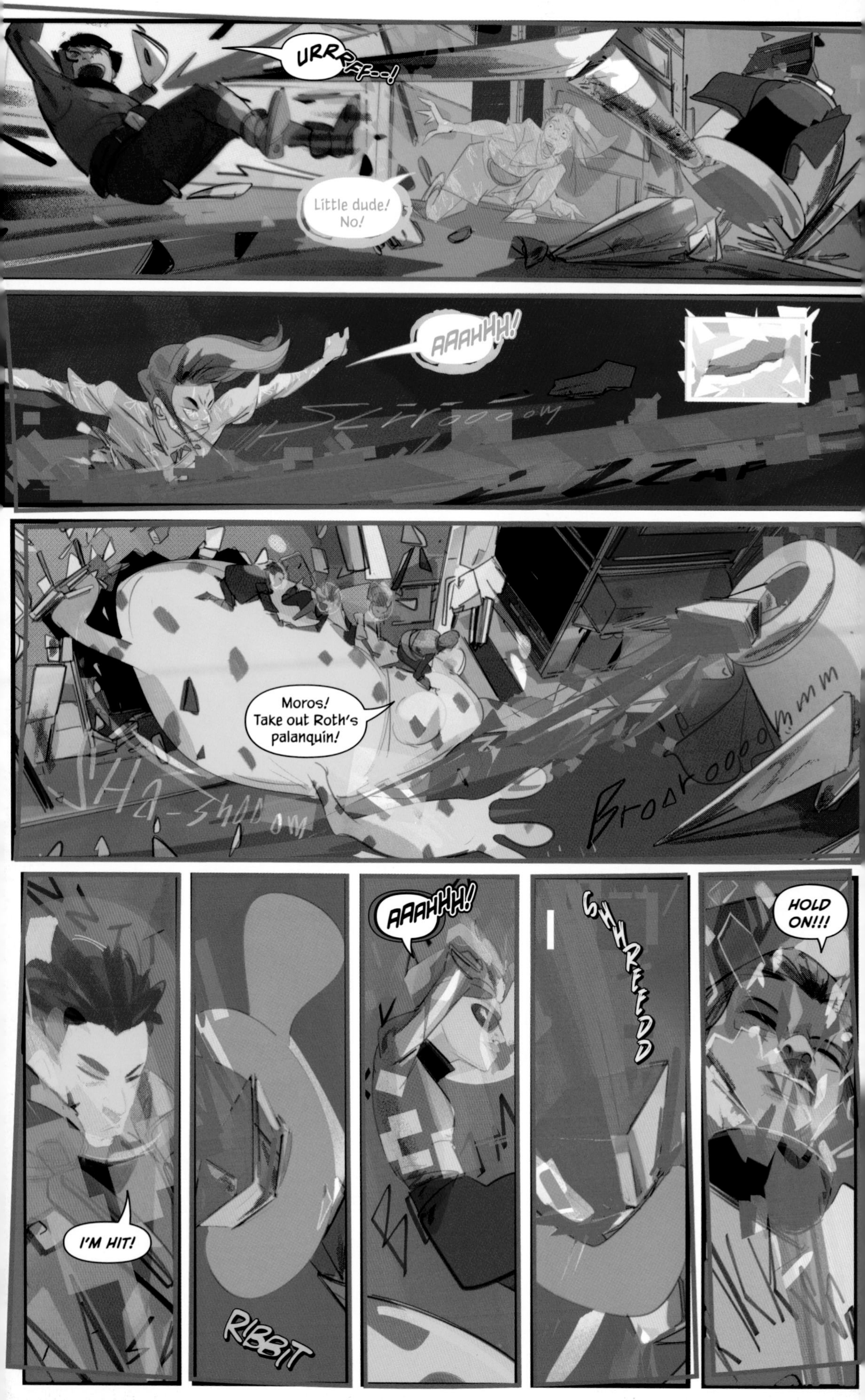
URRRFF--!
Little dude! No!
AAAHHH!
Scrroooom
ZZAP
Moros! Take out Roth's palanquin!
Ha-shooom
Brookooooommm
I'M HIT!
RIBBIT
AAAHHH!
SHHREEDD
HOLD ON!!!

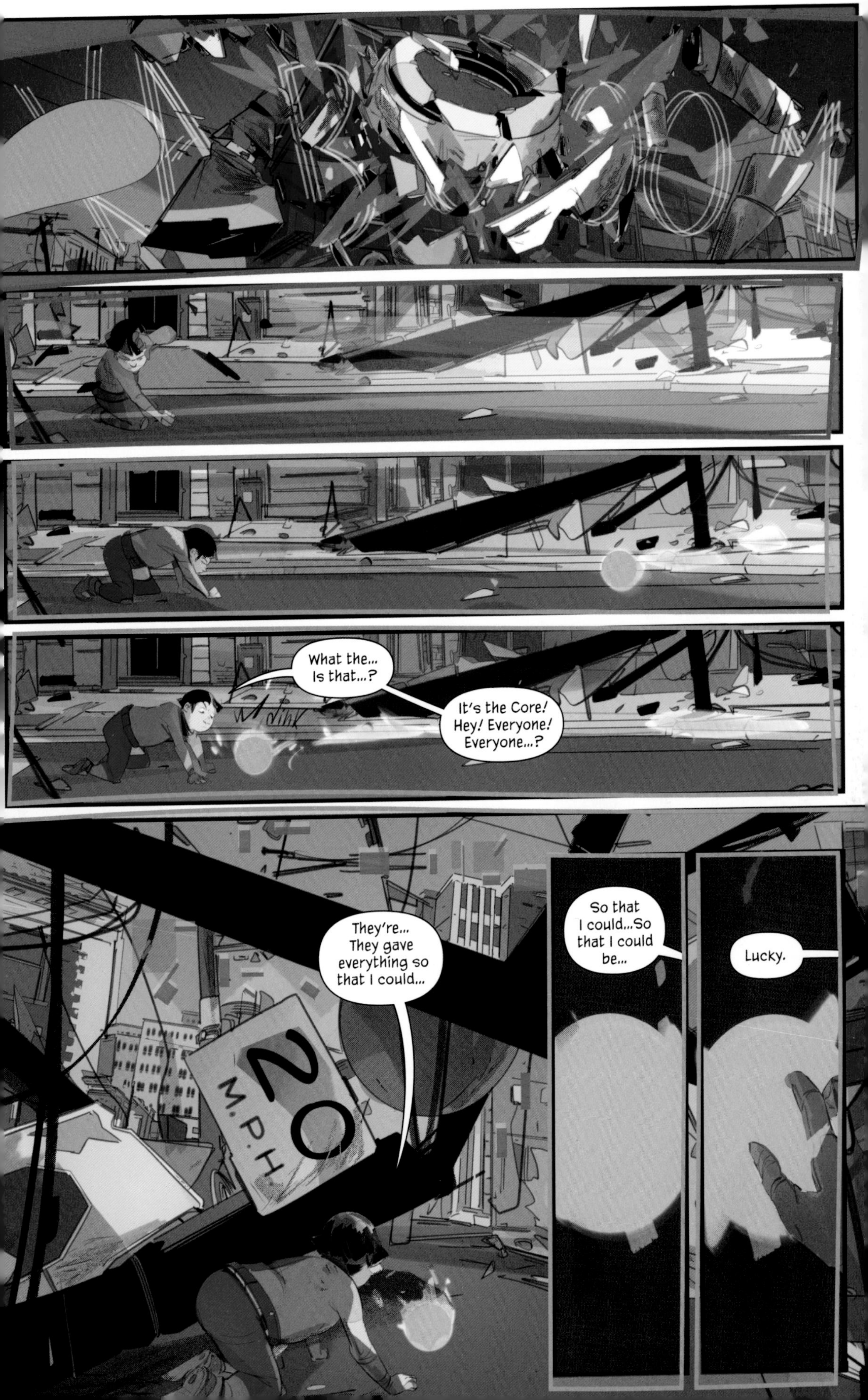
What the... Is that...?
It's the Core! Hey! Everyone! Everyone...?
They're... They gave everything so that I could...
20 M.P.H
So that I could...So that I could be...
Lucky.

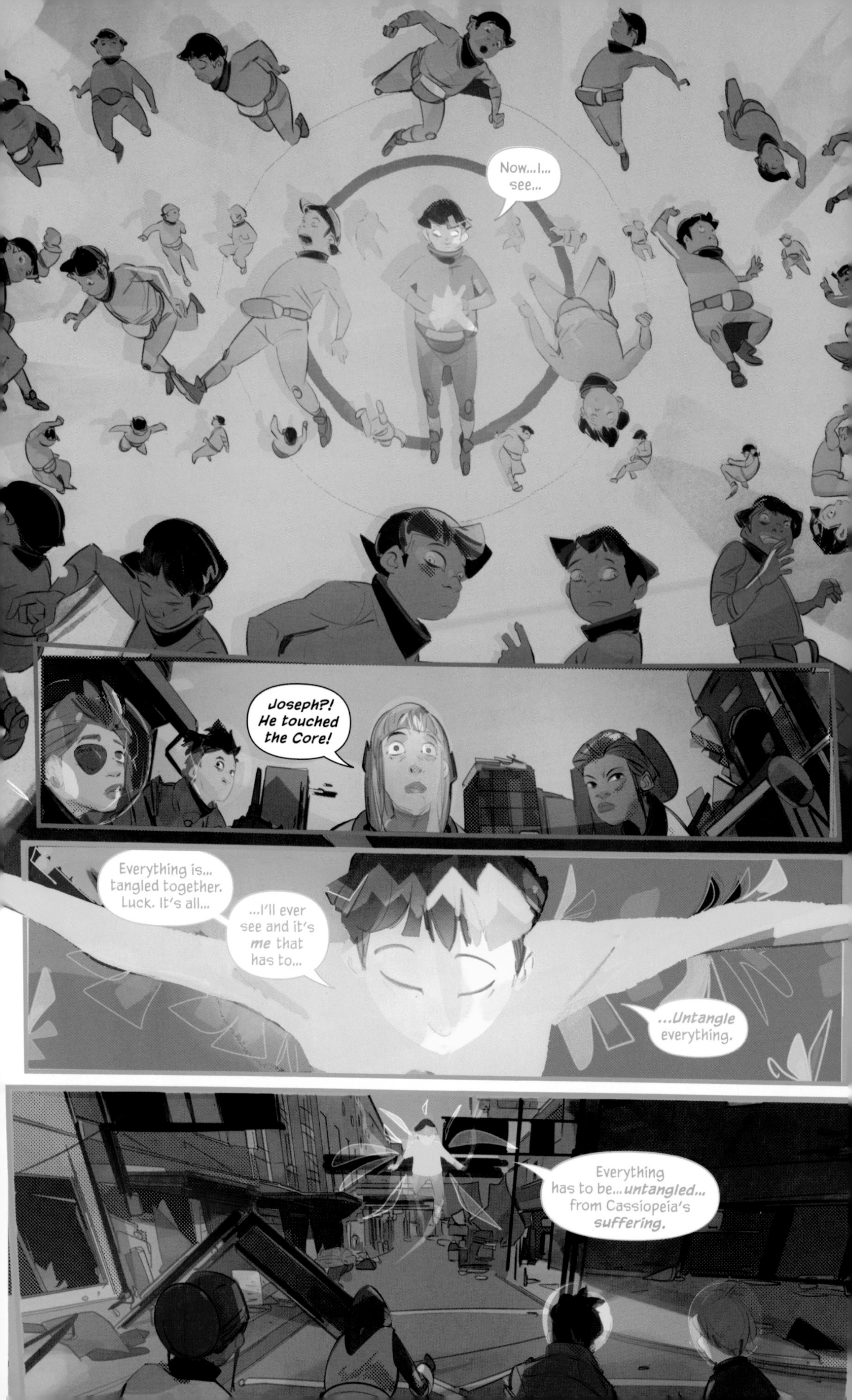
Now...I... see...
Joseph?! He touched the Core!
Everything is... tangled together. Luck. It's all...
...I'll ever see and it's *me* that has to...
...Untangle everything.
Everything has to be...***untangled...*** from Cassiopeia's ***suffering.***

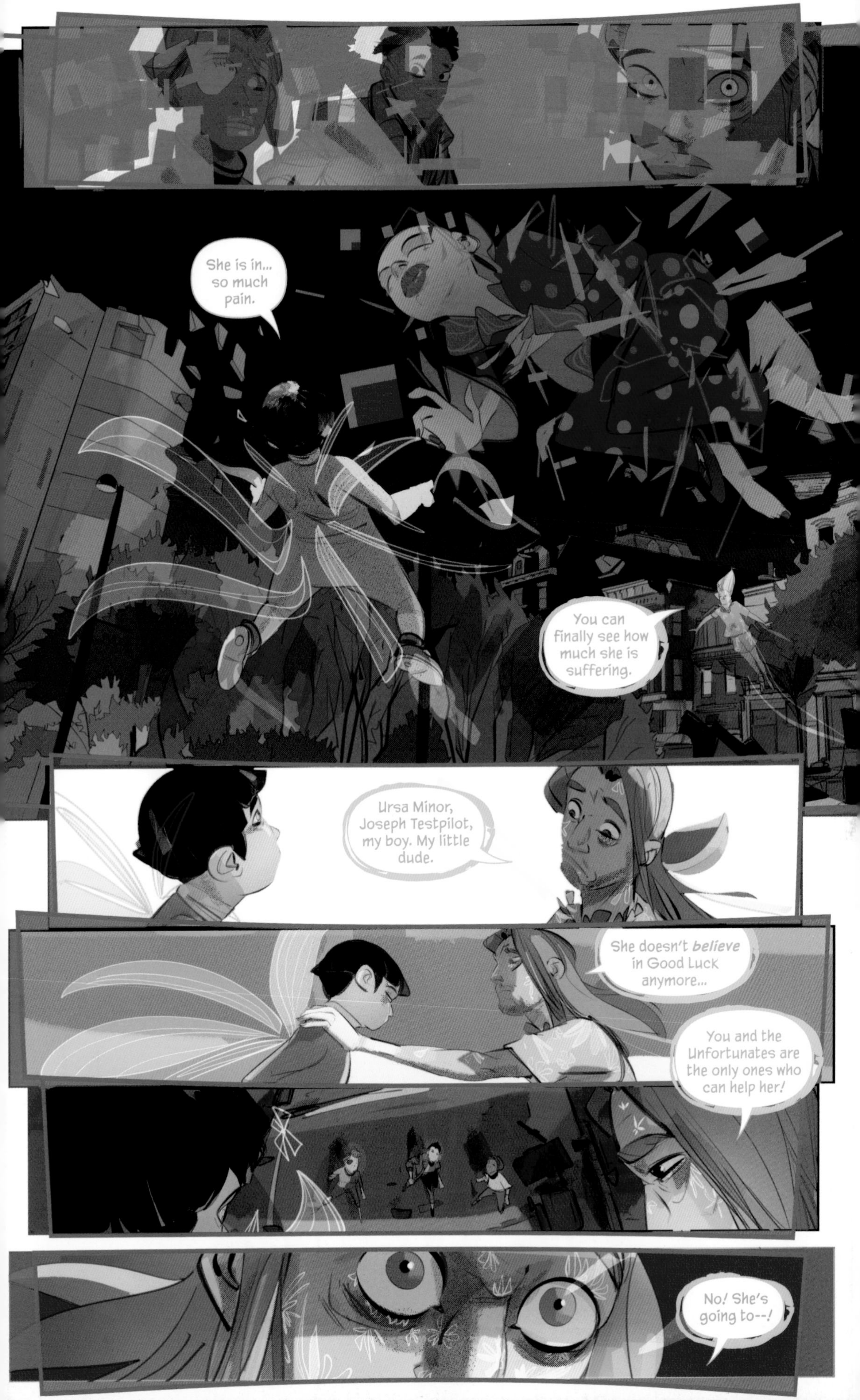
She is in... so much pain.
You can finally see how much she is suffering.
Ursa Minor, Joseph Testpilot, my boy. My little dude.
She doesn't *believe* in Good Luck anymore...
You and the Unfortunates are the only ones who can help her!
No! She's going to--!

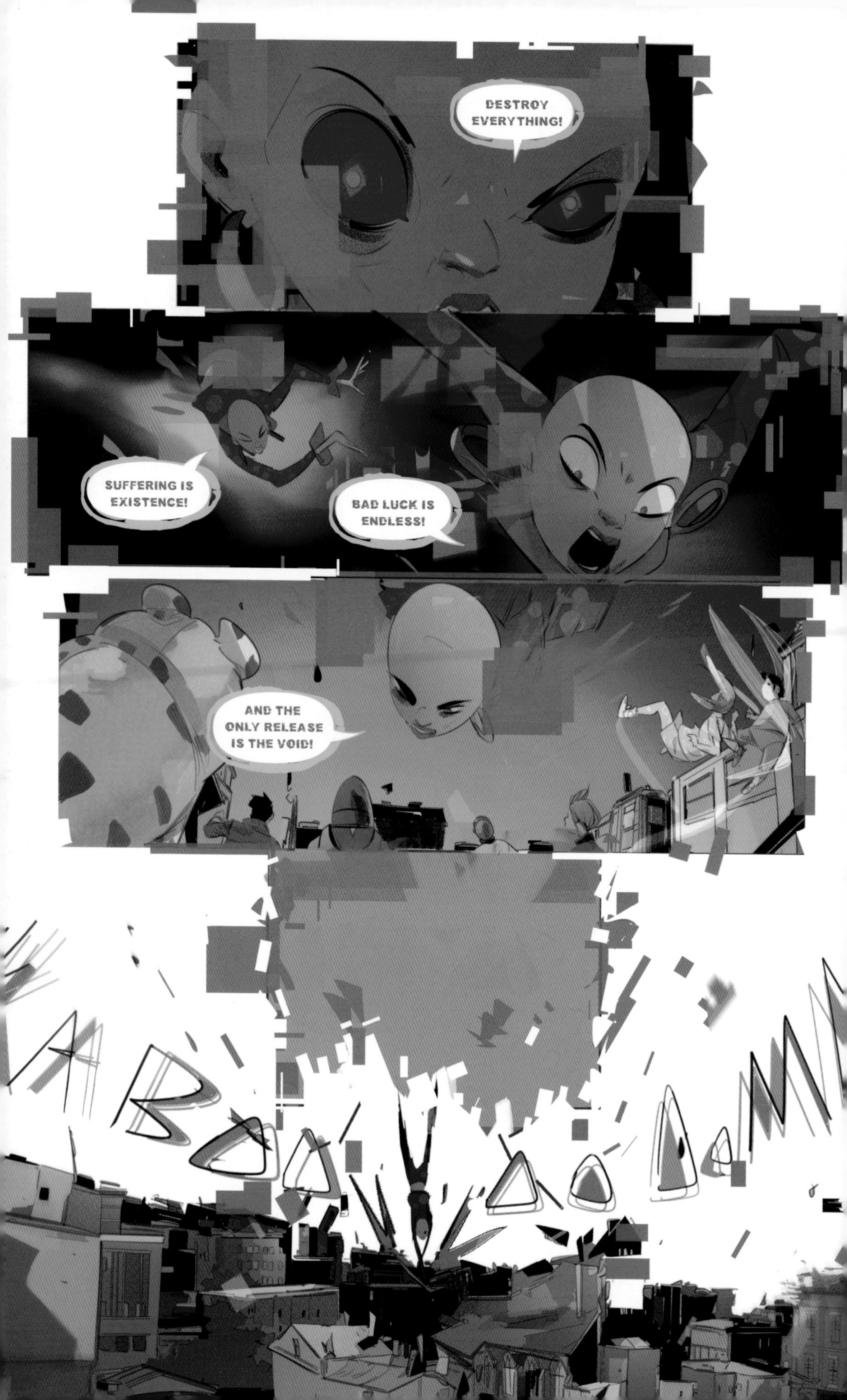
DESTROY EVERYTHING!
SUFFERING IS EXISTENCE!
BAD LUCK IS ENDLESS!
AND THE ONLY RELEASE IS THE VOID!
ABOOOOOM

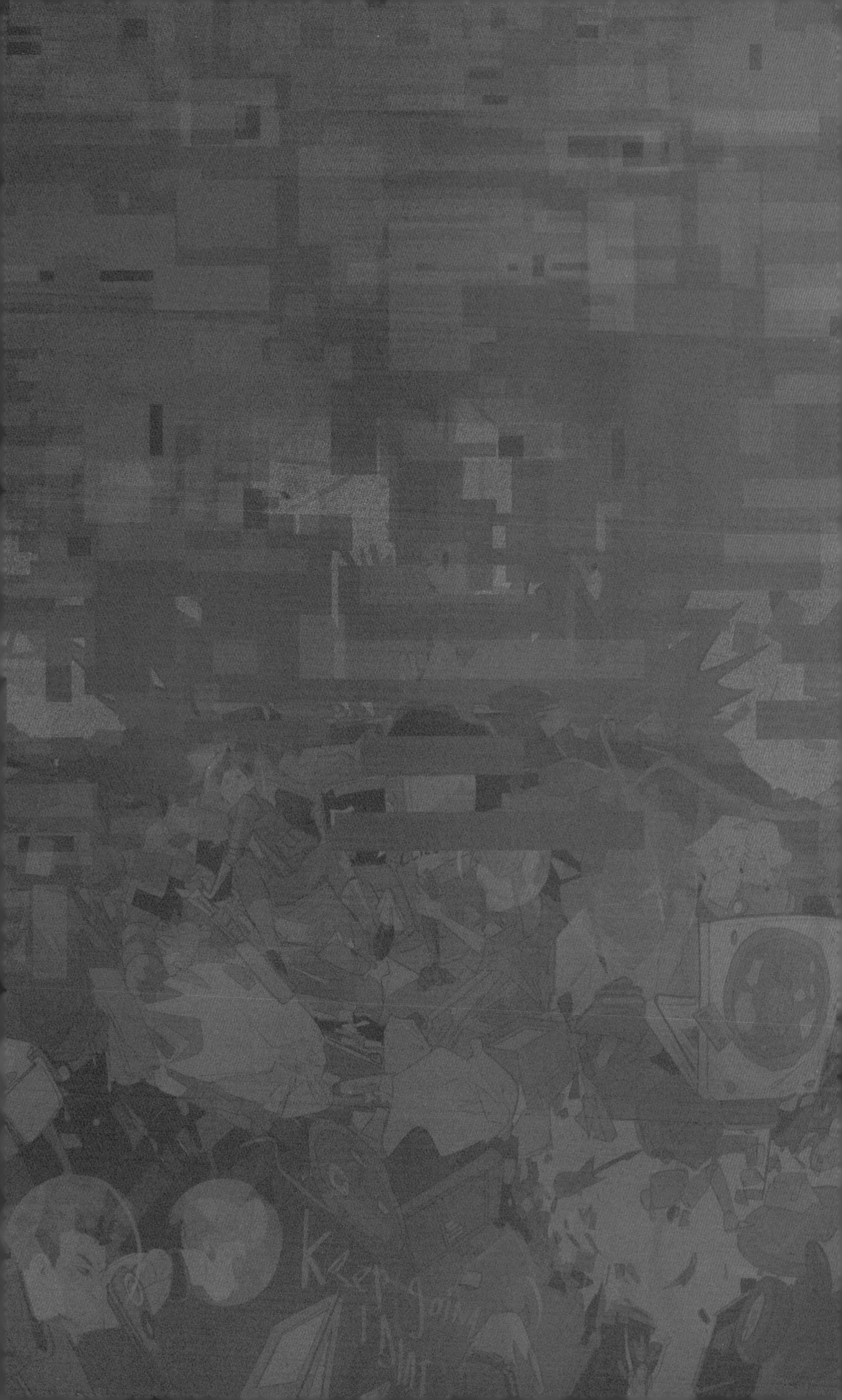

CHAPTER

5

CONGRATULATIONS!

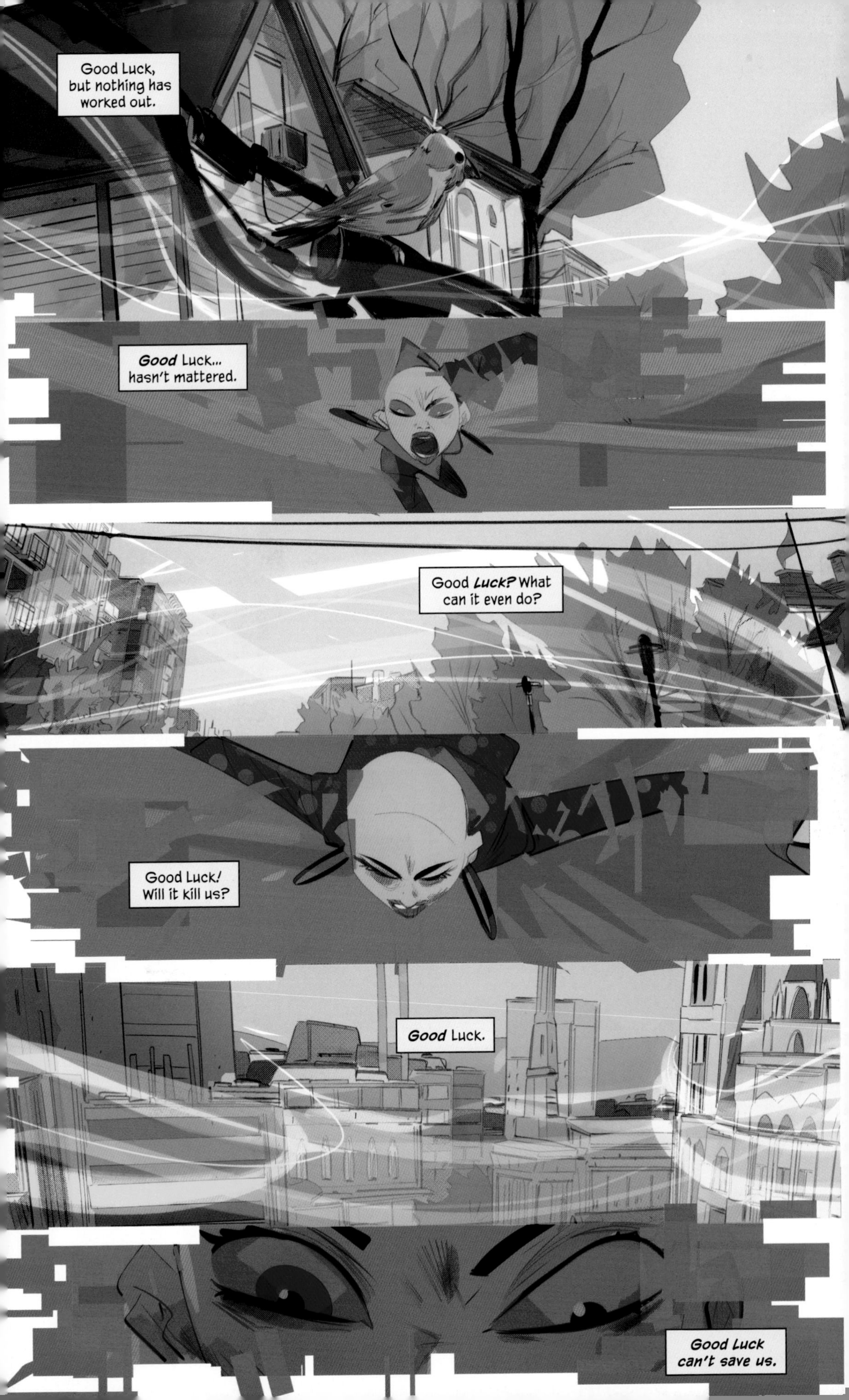

Good Luck, but nothing has worked out.
Good Luck... hasn't mattered.
Good **Luck?** What can it even do?
Good Luck! Will it kill us?
Good Luck.
Good Luck can't save us.

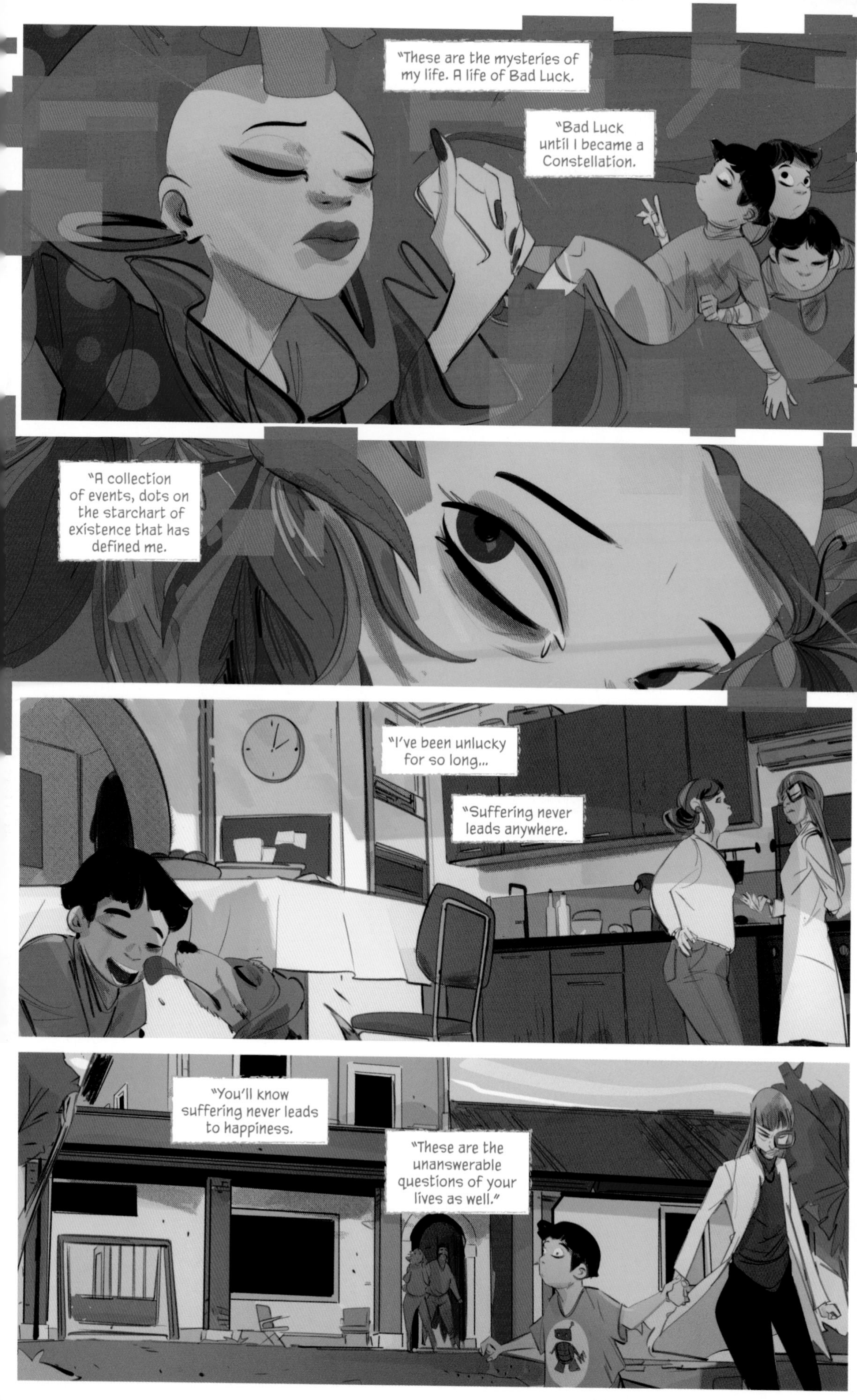
"These are the mysteries of my life. A life of Bad Luck.
"Bad Luck until I became a Constellation.
"A collection of events, dots on the starchart of existence that has defined me.
"I've been unlucky for so long...
"Suffering never leads anywhere.
"You'll know suffering never leads to happiness.
"These are the unanswerable questions of your lives as well."

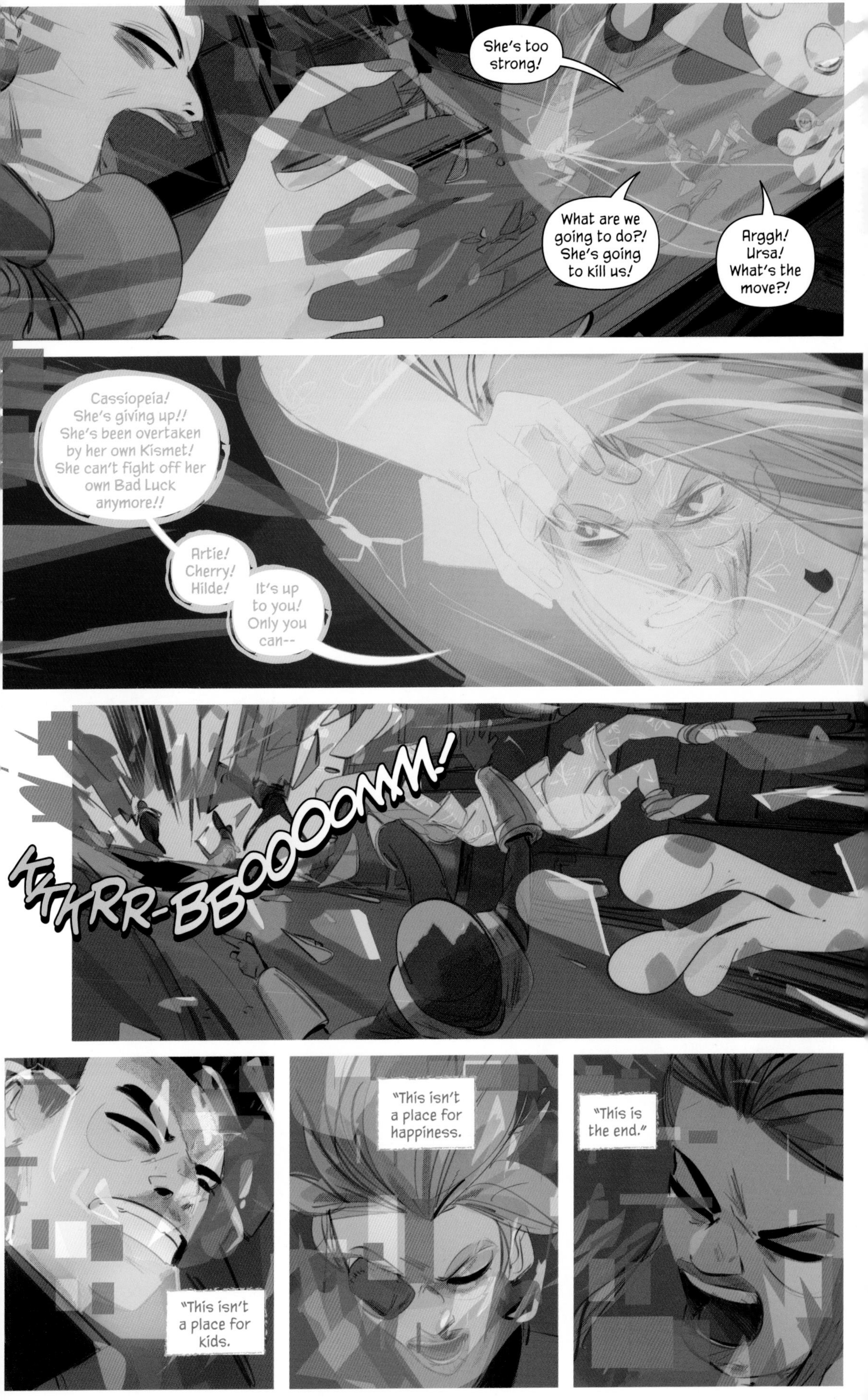
She's too strong!
What are we going to do?! She's going to kill us!
Arggh! Ursa! What's the move?!
Cassiopeia! She's giving up!! She's been overtaken by her own Kismet! She can't fight off her own Bad Luck anymore!!
Artie! Cherry! Hilde!
It's up to you! Only you can--
KKKRR-BBOOOOMM!
"This isn't a place for kids.
"This isn't a place for happiness.
"This is the end."

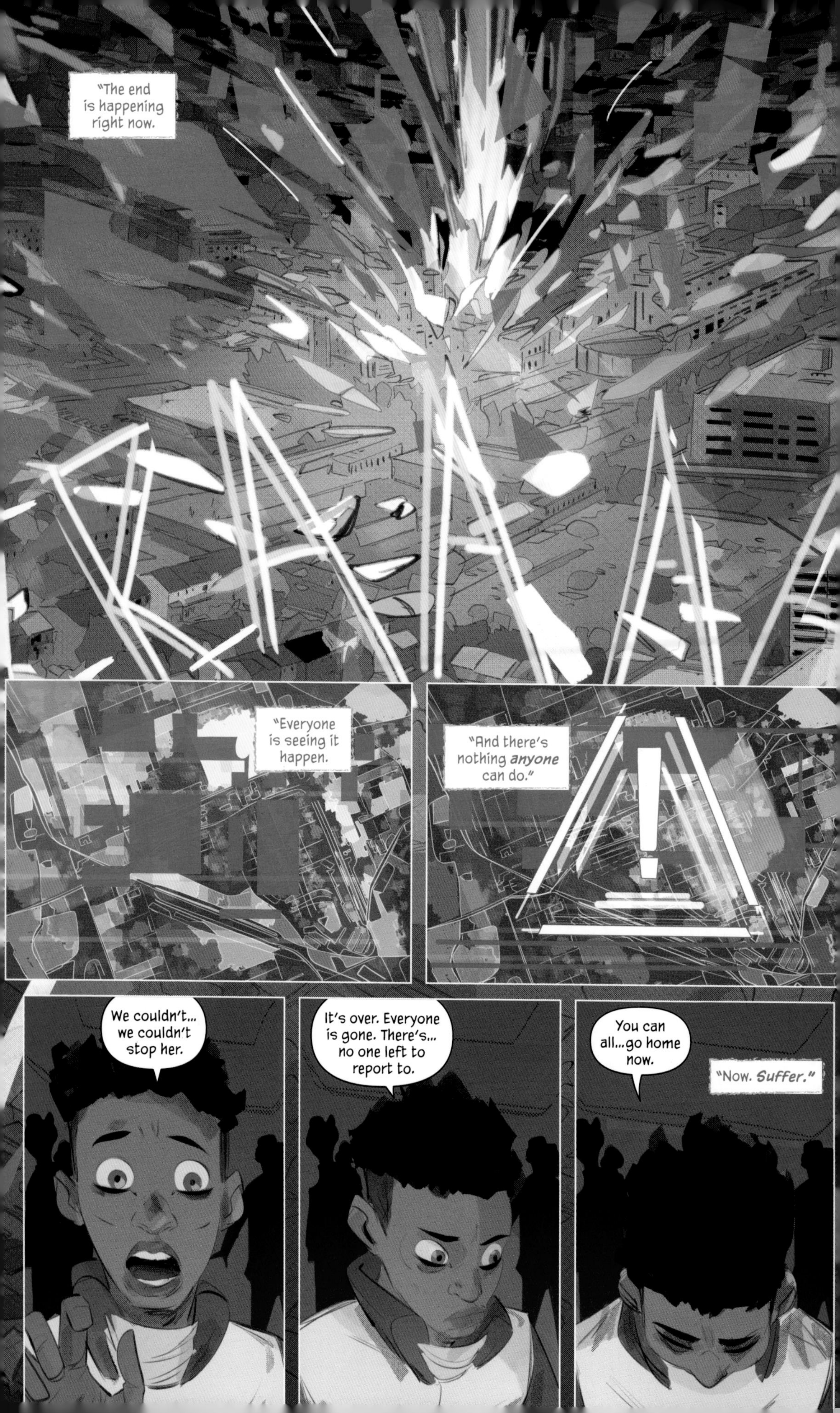
"The end is happening right now.
"Everyone is seeing it happen.
"And there's nothing *anyone* can do."
We couldn't... we couldn't stop her.
It's over. Everyone is gone. There's... no one left to report to.
You can all...go home now.
"Now. *Suffer.*"

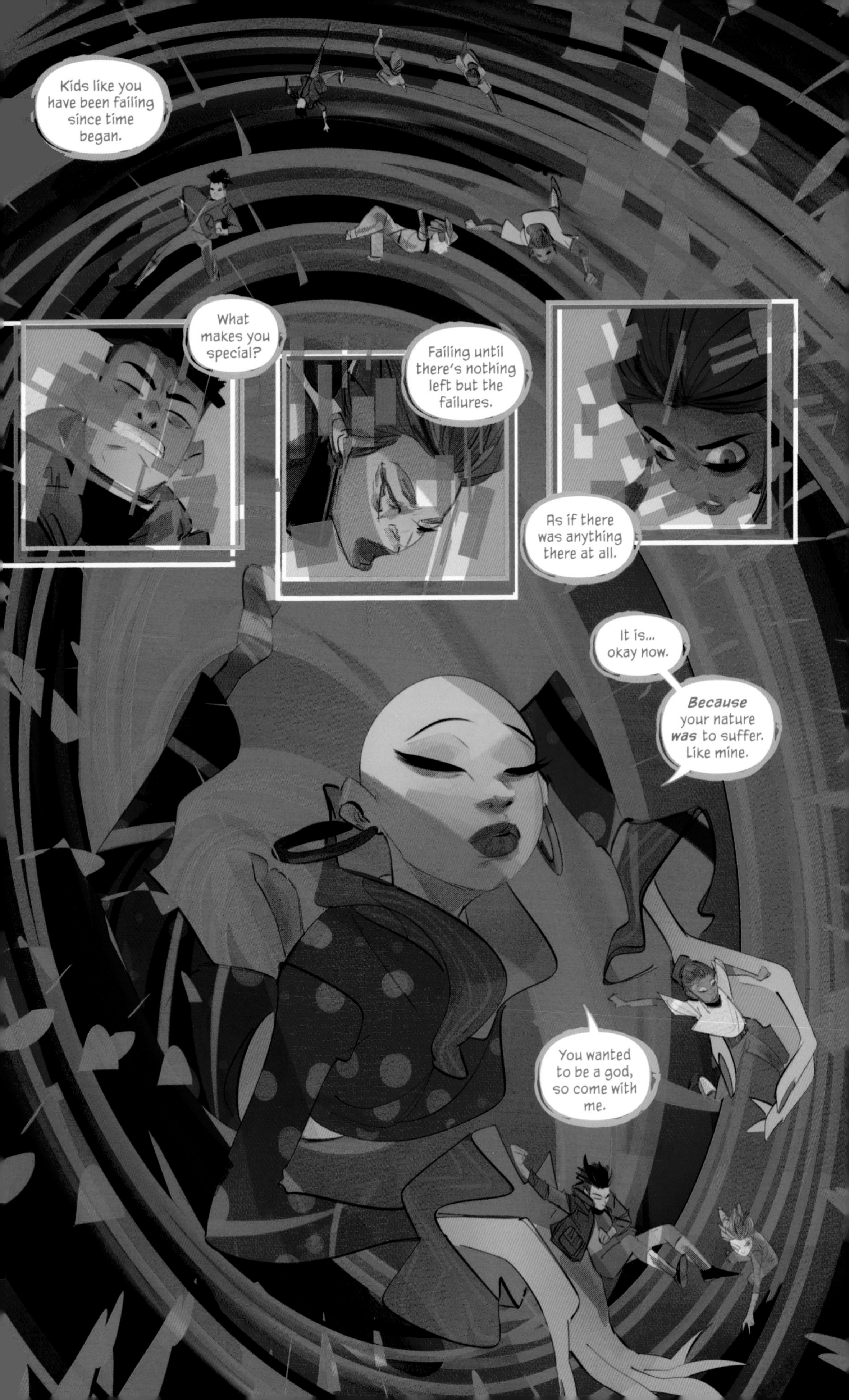
Kids like you have been failing since time began.
What makes you special?
Failing until there's nothing left but the failures.
As if there was anything there at all.
It is... okay now.
Because your nature *was* to suffer. Like mine.
You wanted to be a god, so come with me.

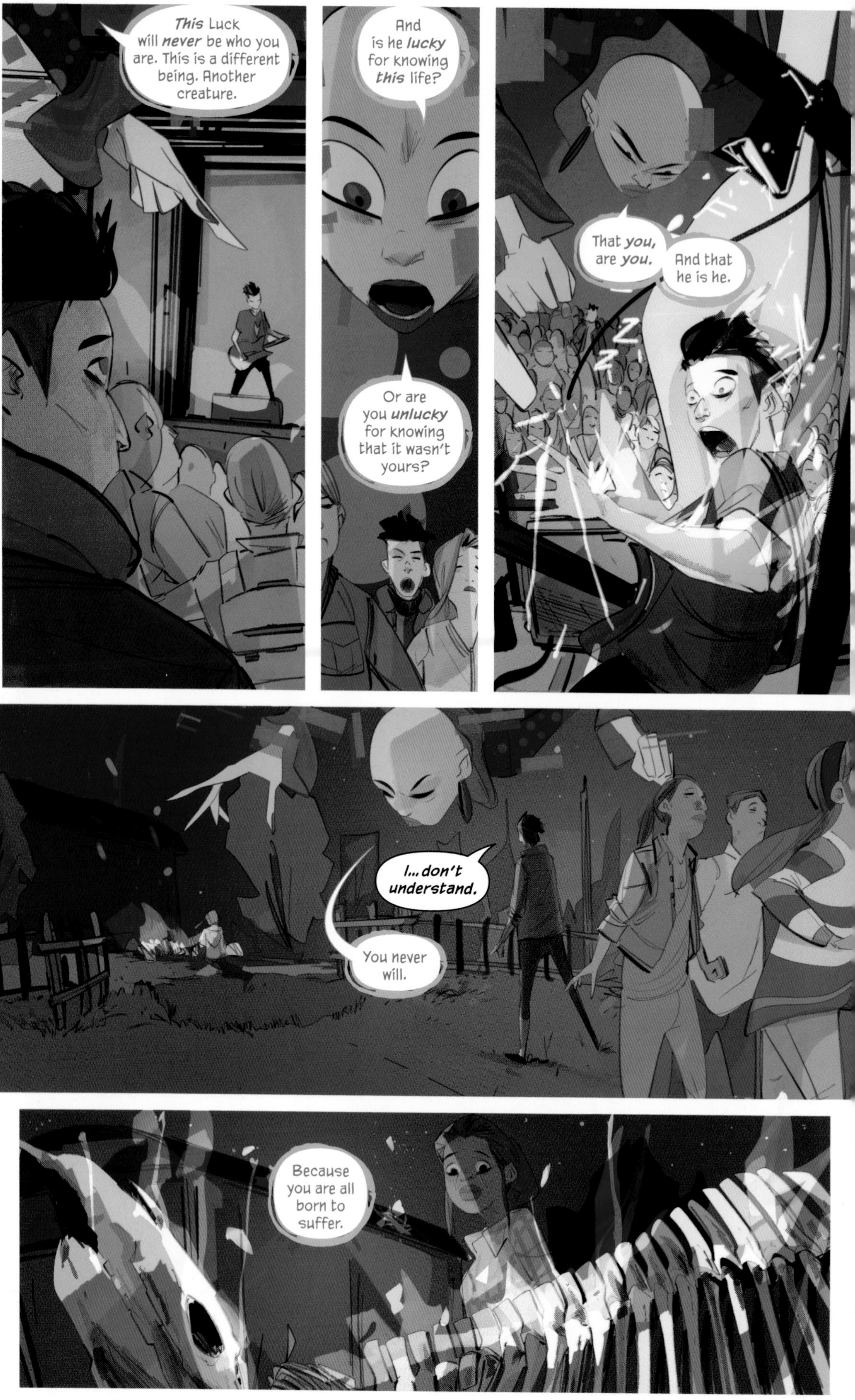
This Luck will never be who you are. This is a different being. Another creature.
And is he lucky for knowing this life?
Or are you unlucky for knowing that it wasn't yours?
That you, are you.
And that he is he.
ZZ
I...don't understand.
You never will.
Because you are all born to suffer.

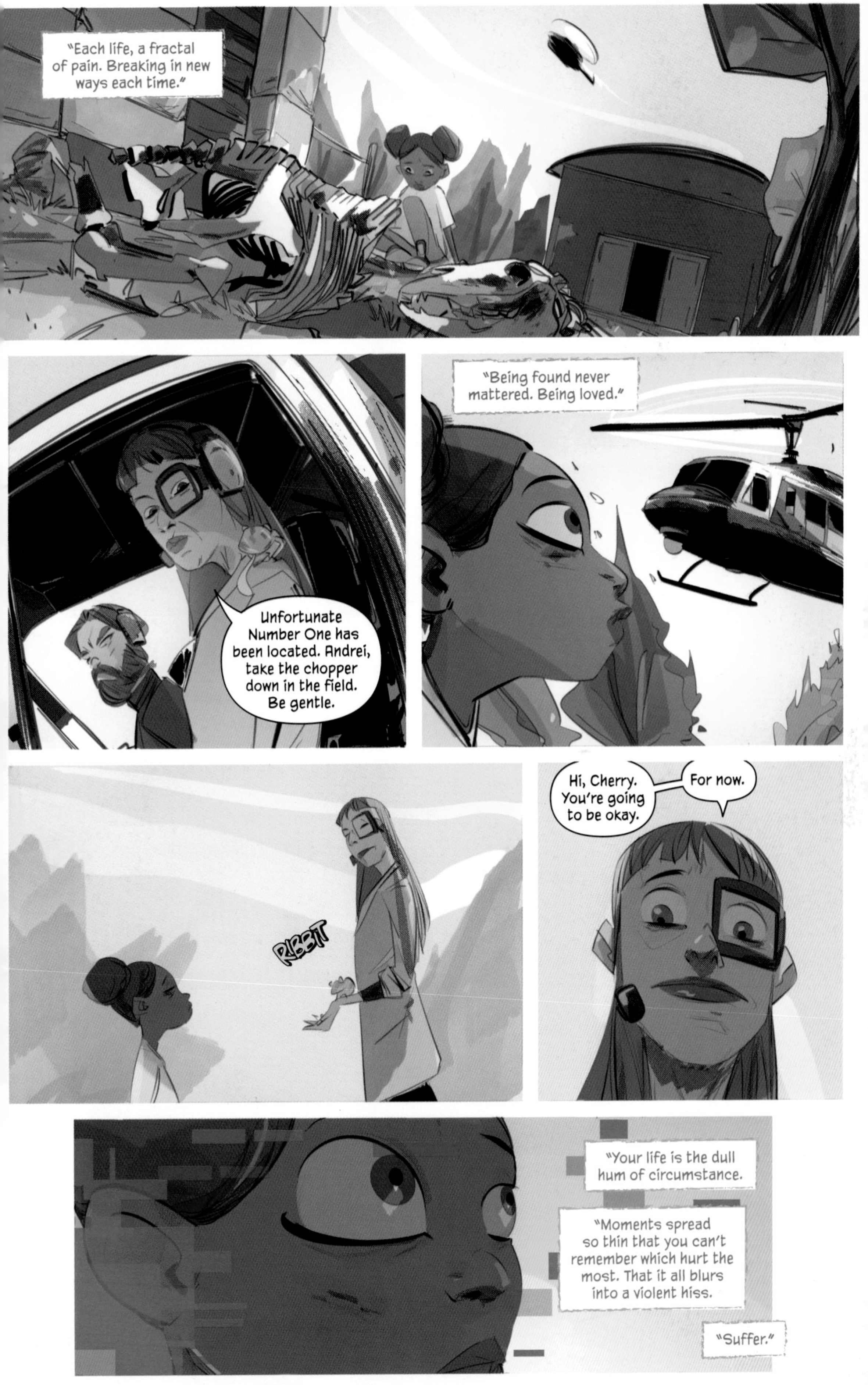
"Each life, a fractal of pain. Breaking in new ways each time."
Unfortunate Number One has been located. Andrei, take the chopper down in the field. Be gentle.
"Being found never mattered. Being loved."
RIBBIT
Hi, Cherry. You're going to be okay.
For now.
"Your life is the dull hum of circumstance.
"Moments spread so thin that you can't remember which hurt the most. That it all blurs into a violent hiss.
"Suffer."

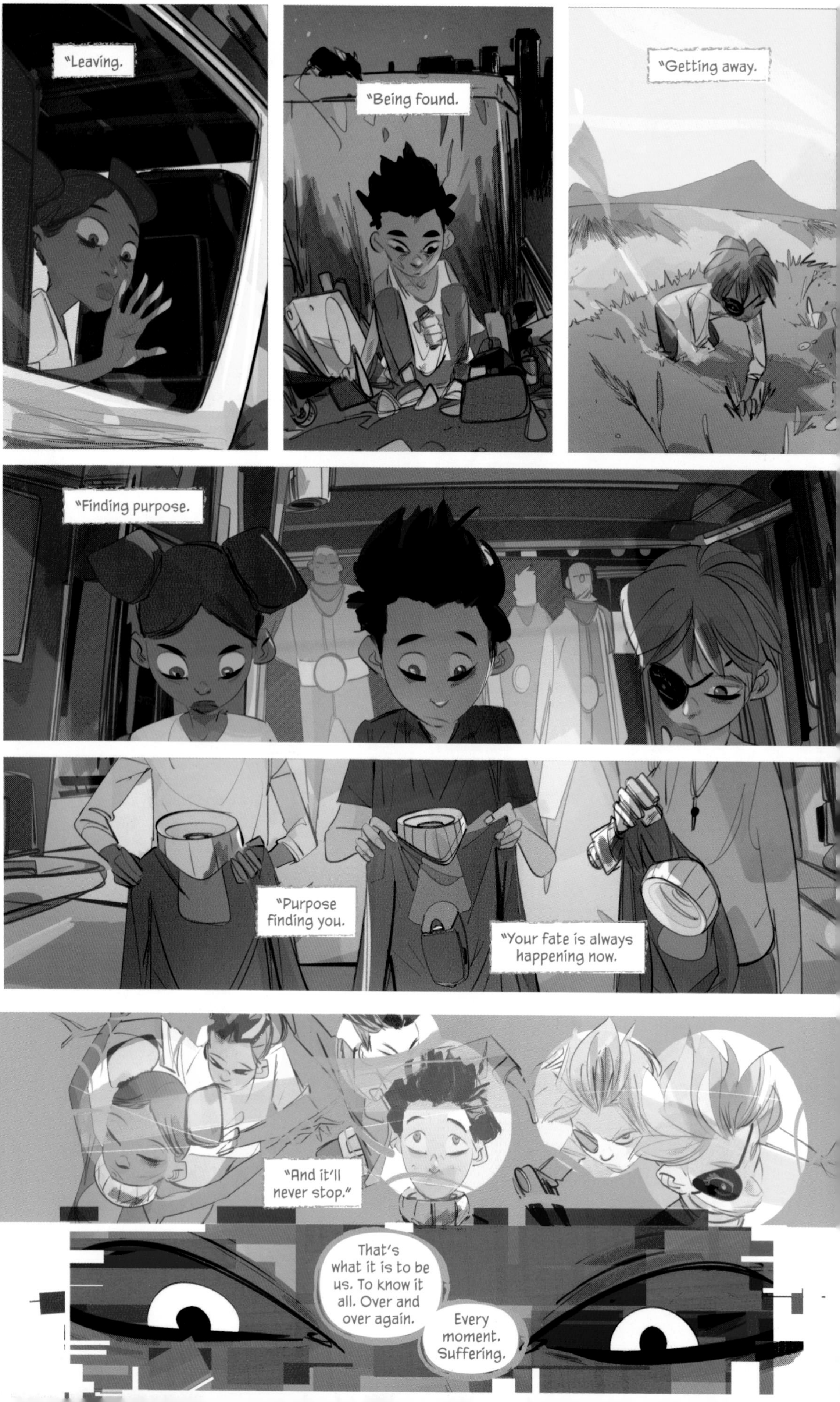
"Leaving.
"Being found.
"Getting away.
"Finding purpose.
"Purpose finding you.
"Your fate is always happening now.
"And it'll never stop."
That's what it is to be us. To know it all. Over and over again.
Every moment. Suffering.

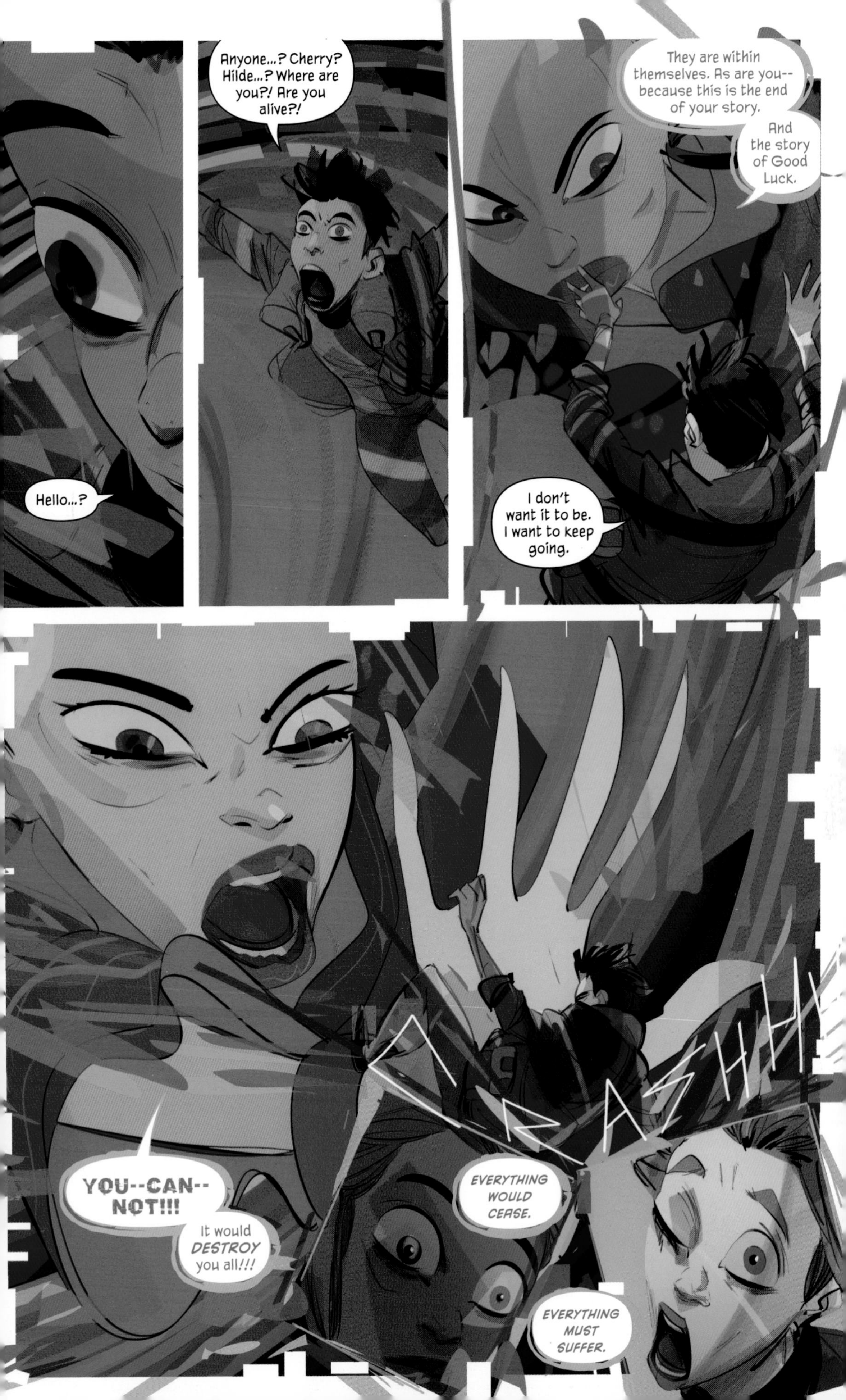
Hello...?
Anyone...? Cherry? Hilde...? Where are you?! Are you alive?!
They are within themselves. As are you-- because this is the end of your story.
And the story of Good Luck.
I don't want it to be. I want to keep going.
YOU--CAN--NOT!!!
It would DESTROY you all!!!
CRASHH
EVERYTHING WOULD CEASE.
EVERYTHING MUST SUFFER.

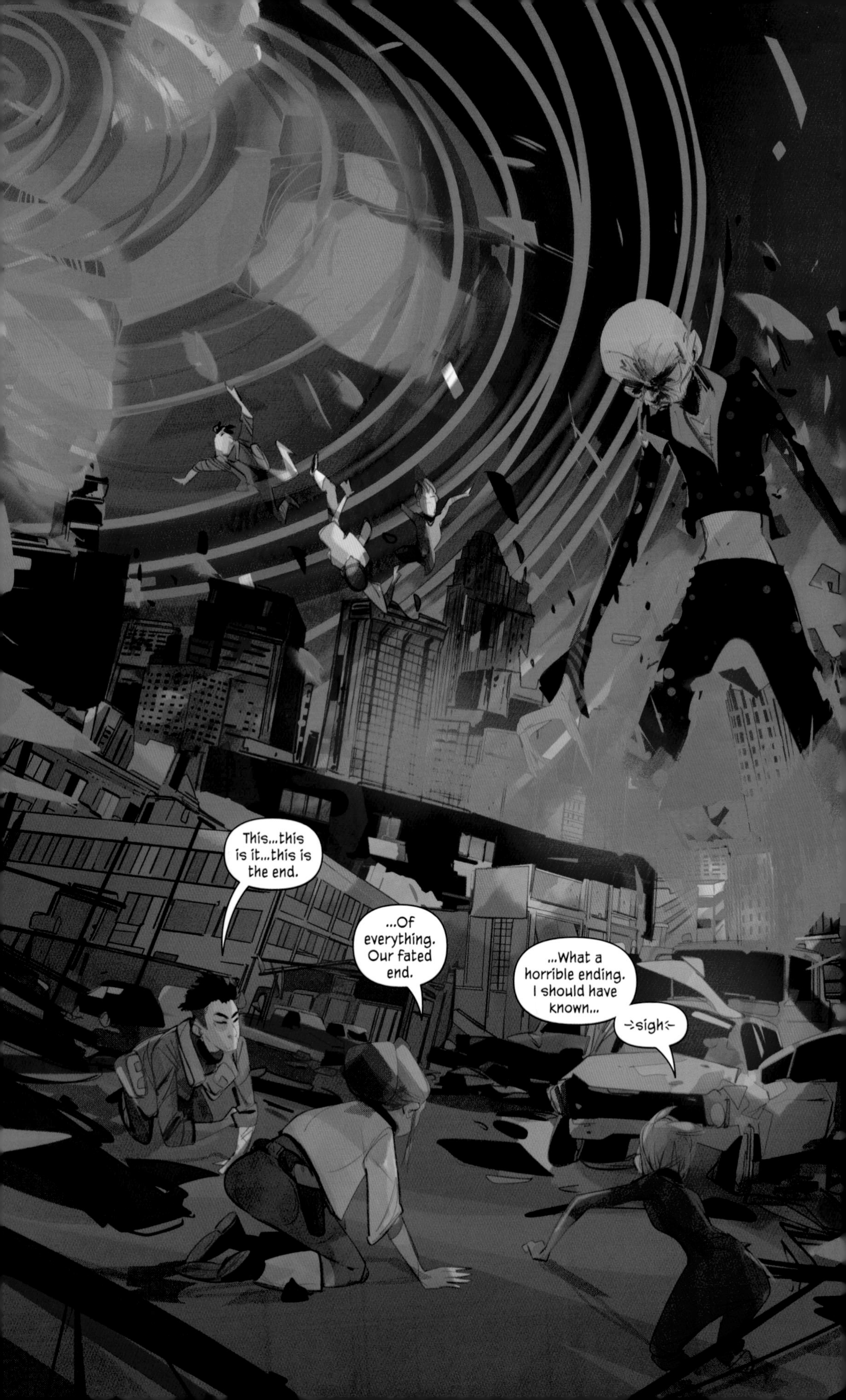
This...this is it...this is the end.
...Of everything. Our fated end.
...What a horrible ending. I should have known...
-sigh-

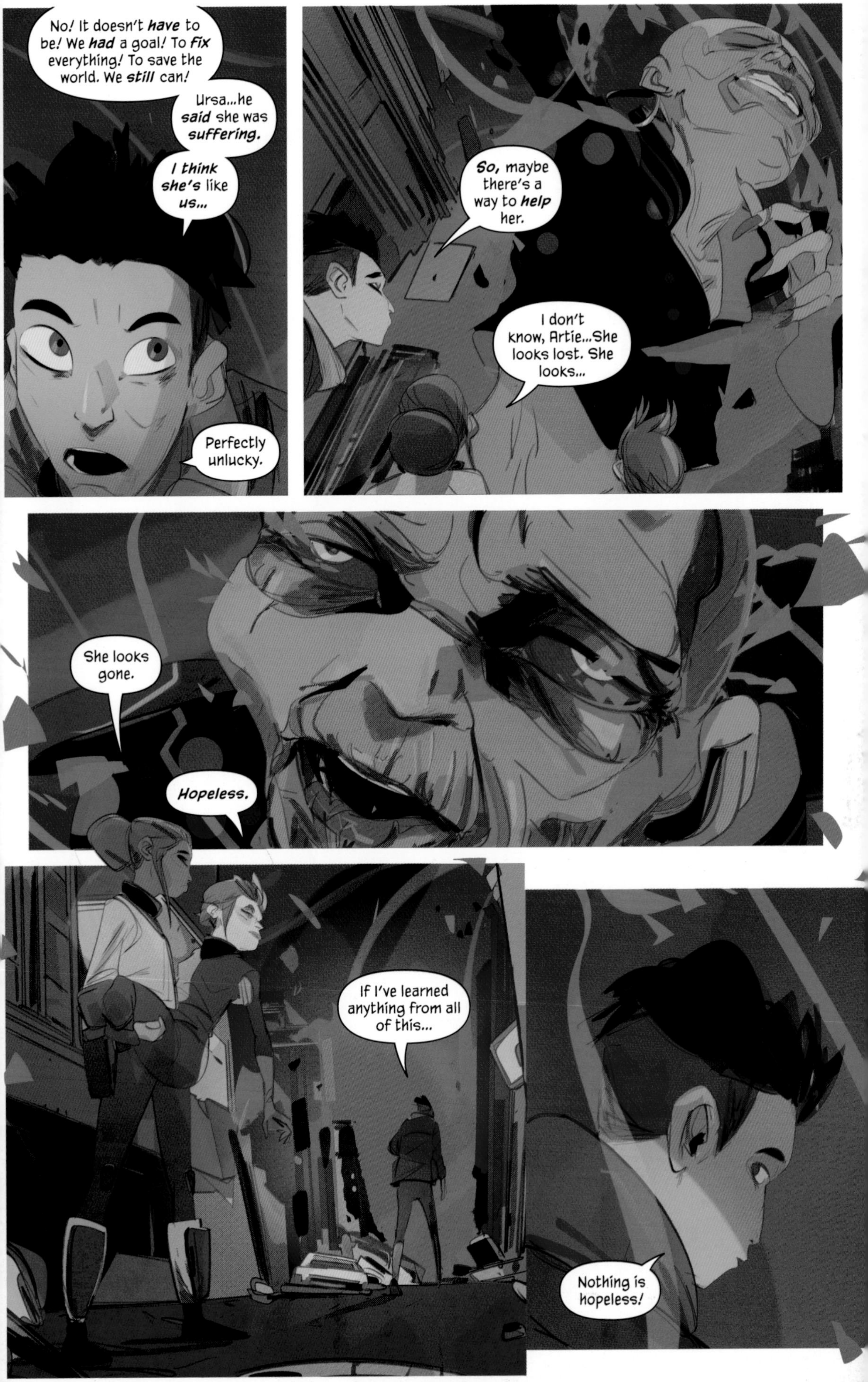
No! It doesn't *have* to be! We *had* a goal! To *fix* everything! To save the world. We *still* can!
Ursa...he *said* she was *suffering.*
I think she's like *us...*
Perfectly unlucky.
So, maybe there's a way to *help* her.
I don't know, Artie...She looks lost. She looks...
She looks gone.
Hopeless.
If I've learned anything from all of this...
Nothing is hopeless!

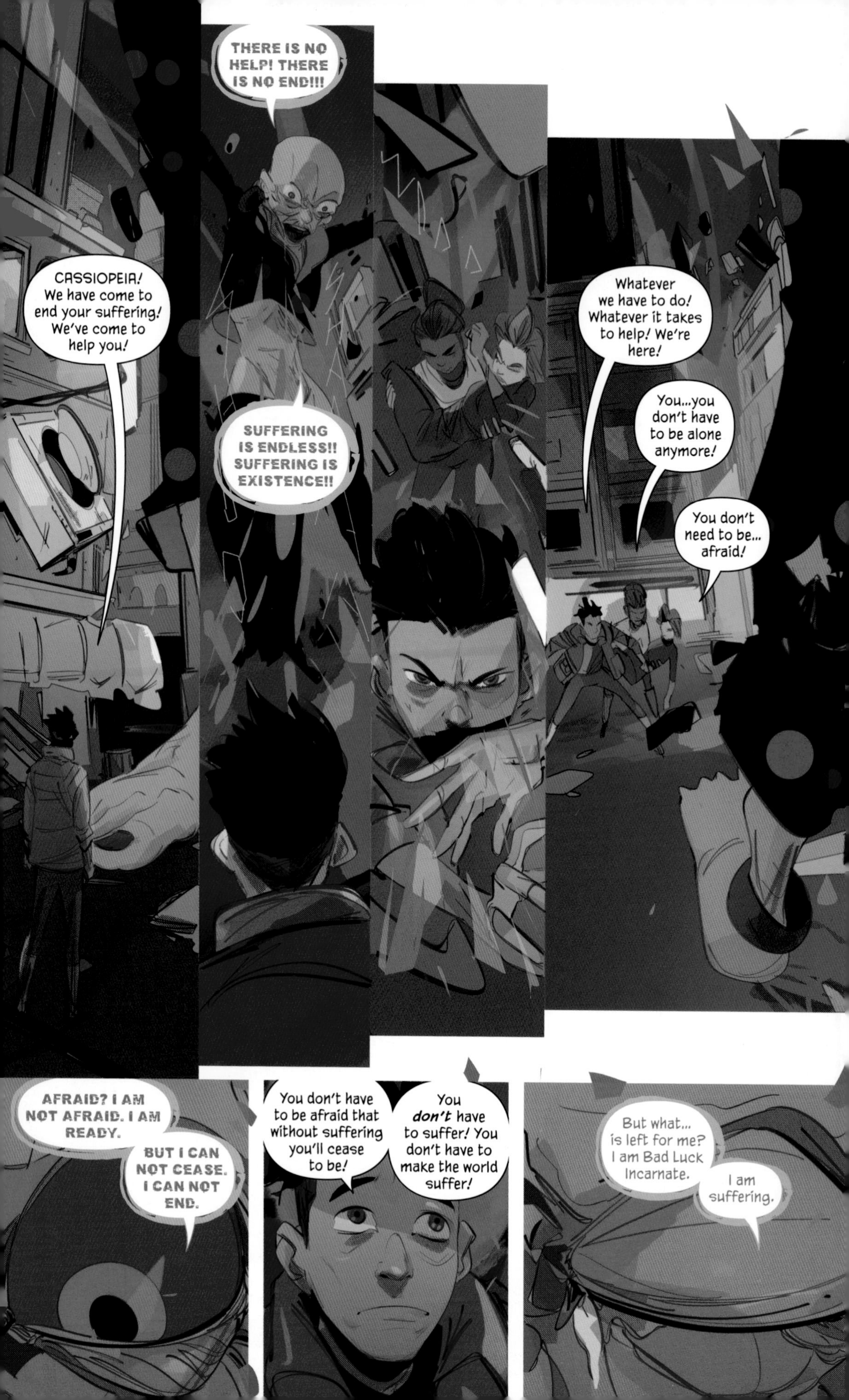
CASSIOPEIA! We have come to end your suffering! We've come to help you!
THERE IS NO HELP! THERE IS NO END!!!
SUFFERING IS ENDLESS!! SUFFERING IS EXISTENCE!!
Whatever we have to do! Whatever it takes to help! We're here!
You...you don't have to be alone anymore!
You don't need to be... afraid!
AFRAID? I AM NOT AFRAID. I AM READY.
BUT I CAN NOT CEASE. I CAN NOT END.
You don't have to be afraid that without suffering you'll cease to be!
You *don't* have to suffer! You don't have to make the world suffer!
But what... is left for me? I am Bad Luck Incarnate.
I am suffering.

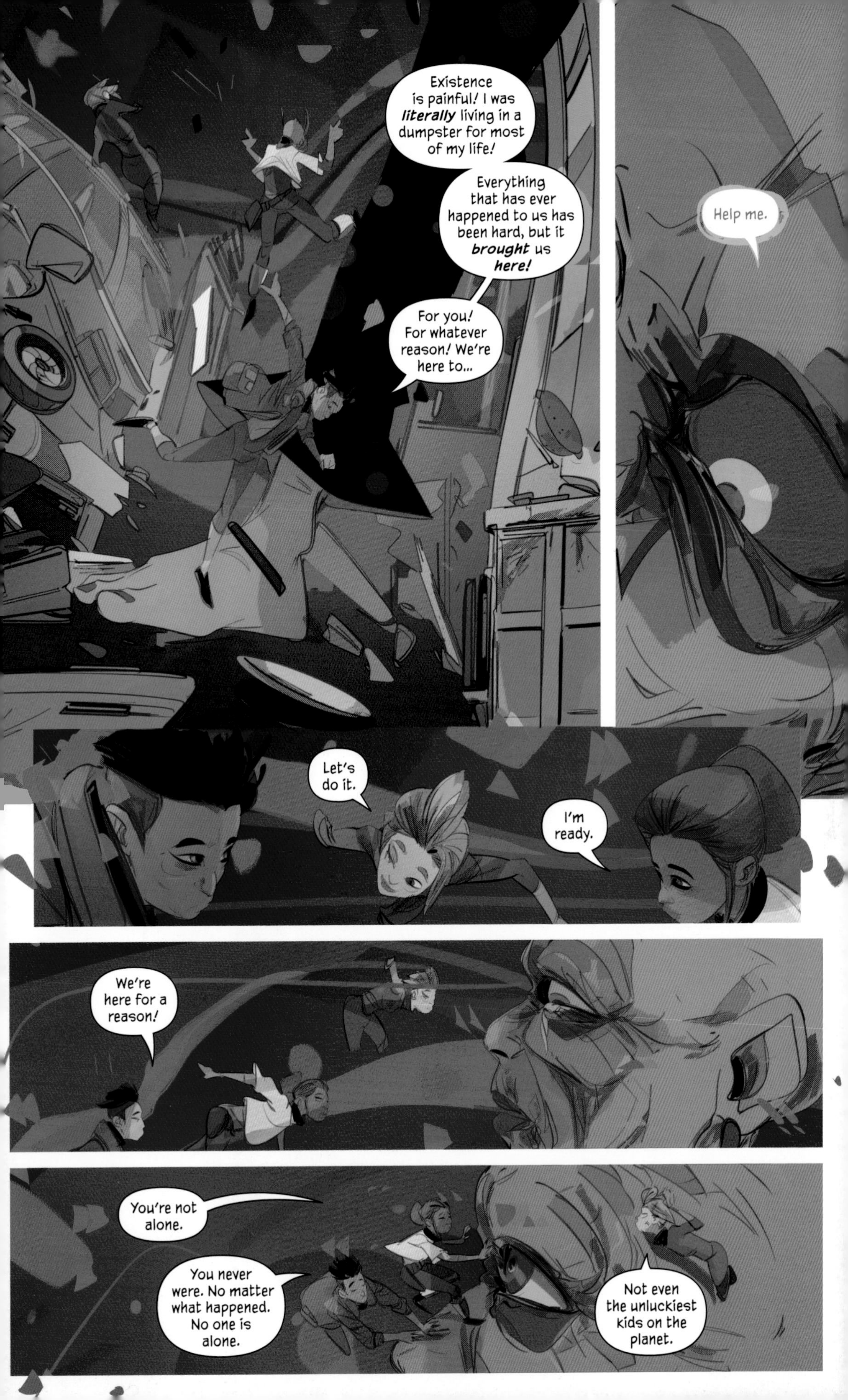

Existence is painful! I was ***literally*** living in a dumpster for most of my life!
Everything that has ever happened to us has been hard, but it ***brought*** us ***here!***
For you! For whatever reason! We're here to...
Help me.
Let's do it.
I'm ready.
We're here for a reason!
You're not alone.
You never were. No matter what happened. No one is alone.
Not even the unluckiest kids on the planet.

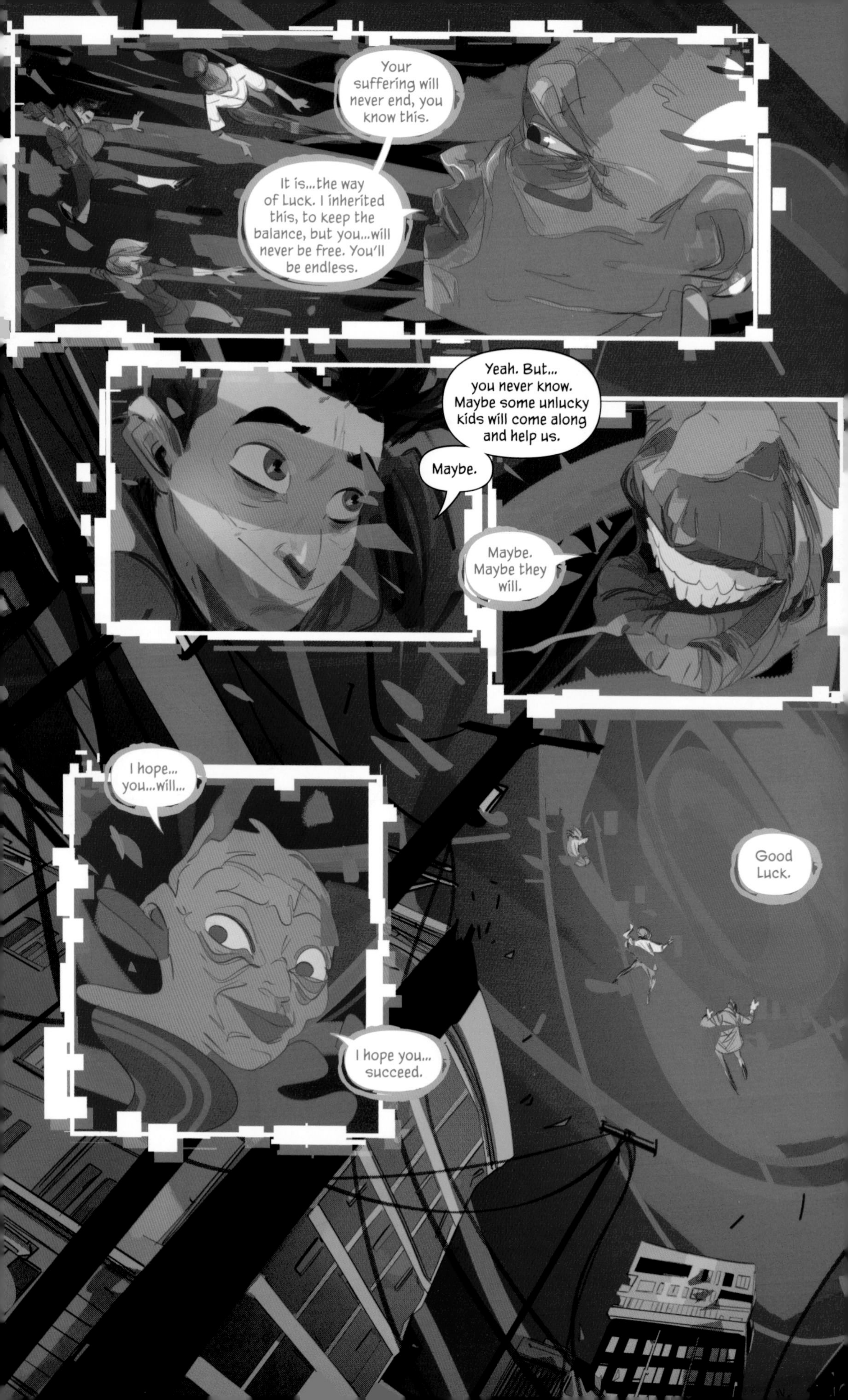
Your suffering will never end, you know this.
It is...the way of Luck. I inherited this, to keep the balance, but you...will never be free. You'll be endless.
Yeah. But... you never know. Maybe some unlucky kids will come along and help us.
Maybe.
Maybe. Maybe they will.
I hope... you...will...
I hope you... succeed.
Good Luck.

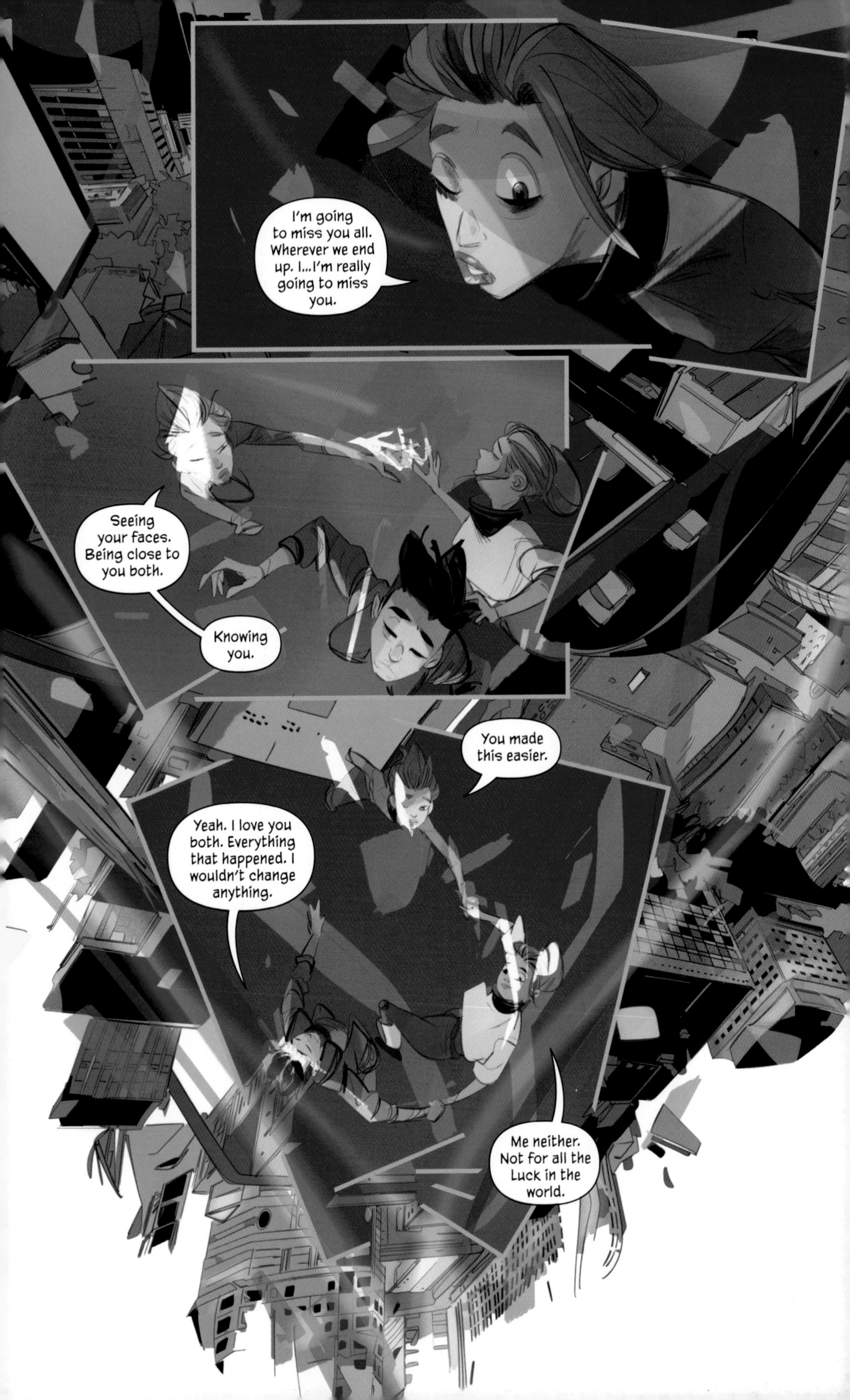
I'm going to miss you all. Wherever we end up. I...I'm really going to miss you.
Seeing your faces. Being close to you both.
Knowing you.
You made this easier.
Yeah. I love you both. Everything that happened. I wouldn't change anything.
Me neither. Not for all the Luck in the world.

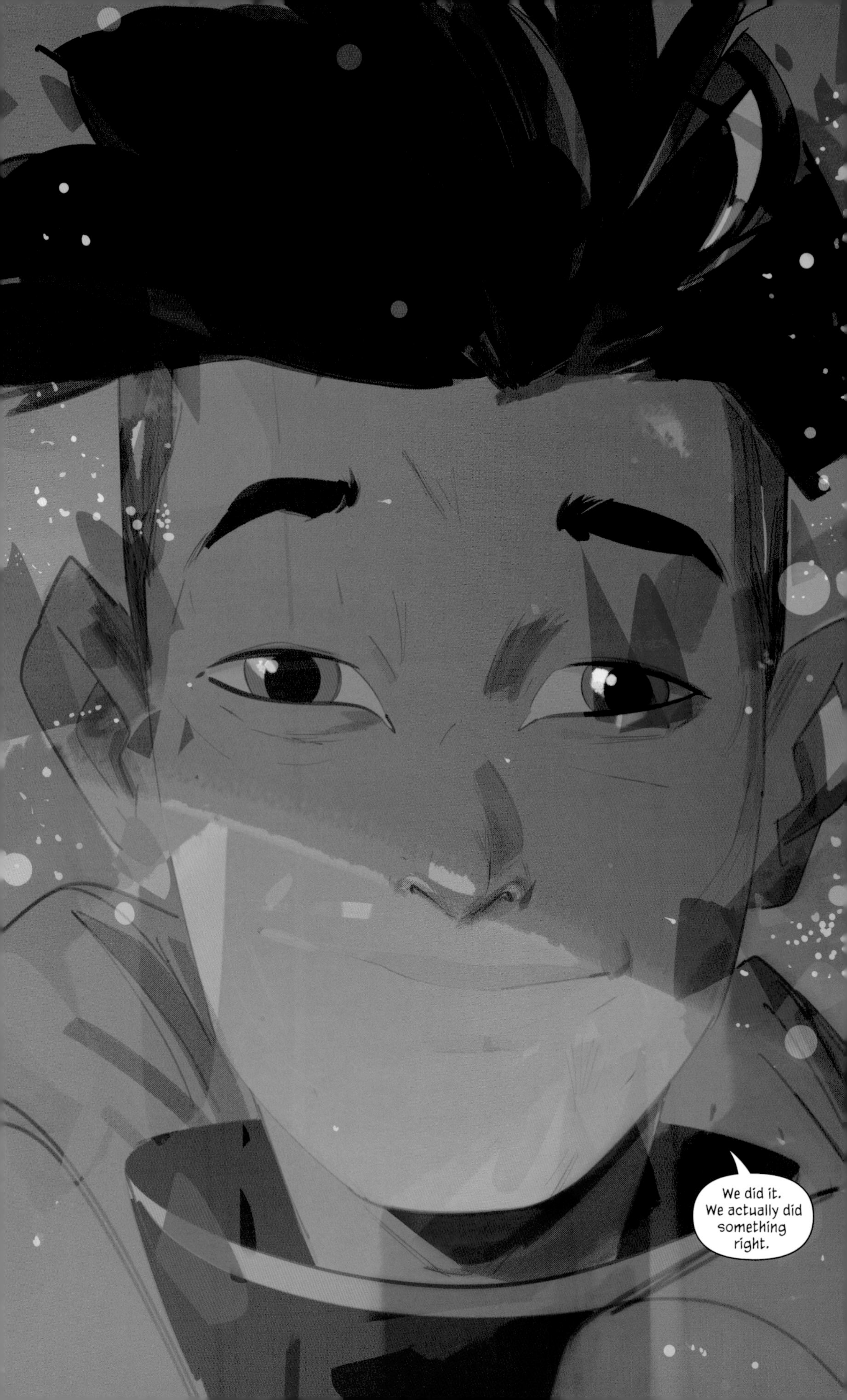
We did it. We actually did something right.

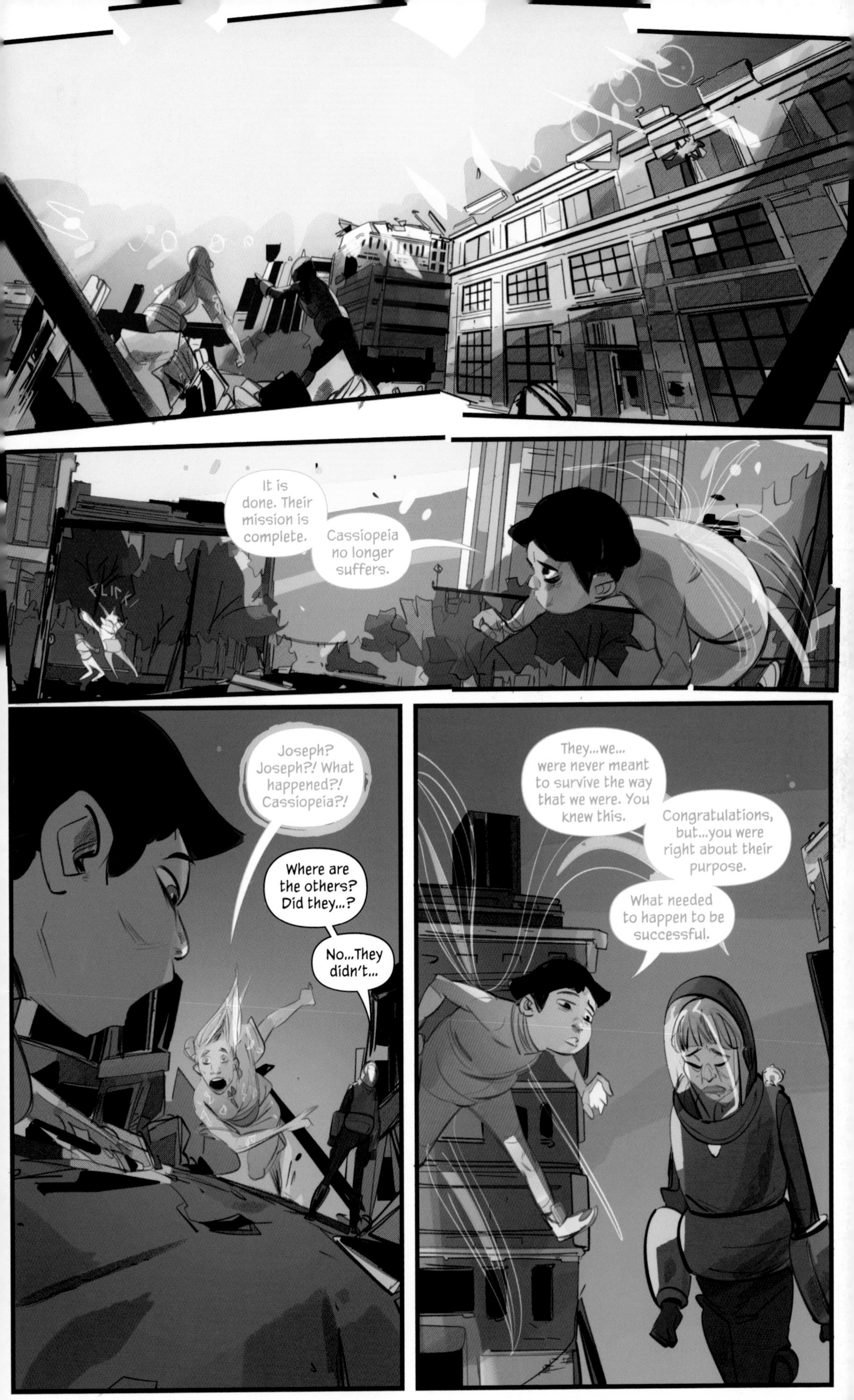
PLICK!
It is done. Their mission is complete.
Cassiopeia no longer suffers.
Joseph? Joseph?! What happened?! Cassiopeia?!
Where are the others? Did they...?
No...They didn't...
They...we... were never meant to survive the way that we were. You knew this.
Congratulations, but...you were right about their purpose.
What needed to happen to be successful.

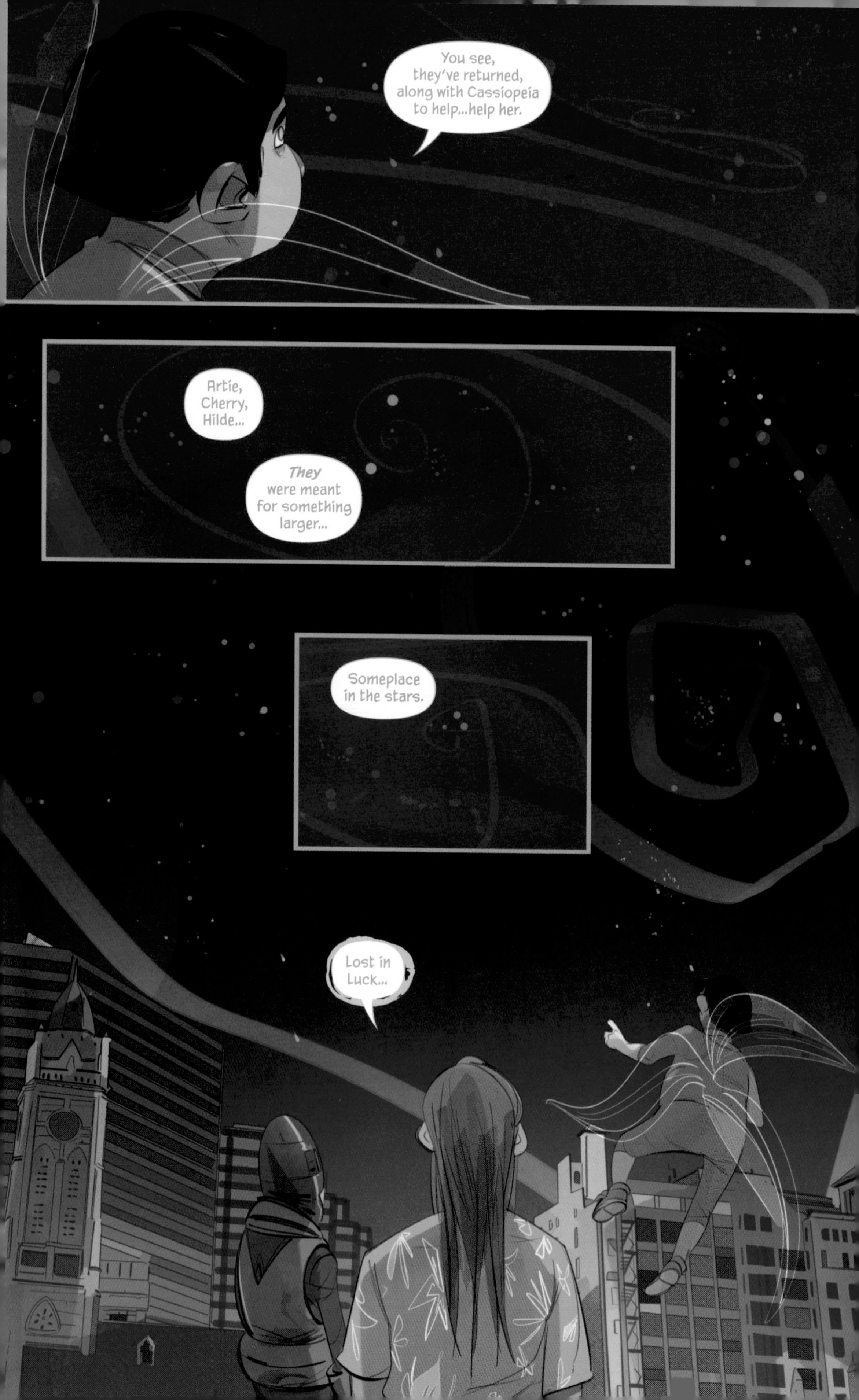
You see, they've returned, along with Cassiopeia to help...help her.
Artie, Cherry, Hilde...
They were meant for something larger...
Someplace in the stars.
Lost in Luck...

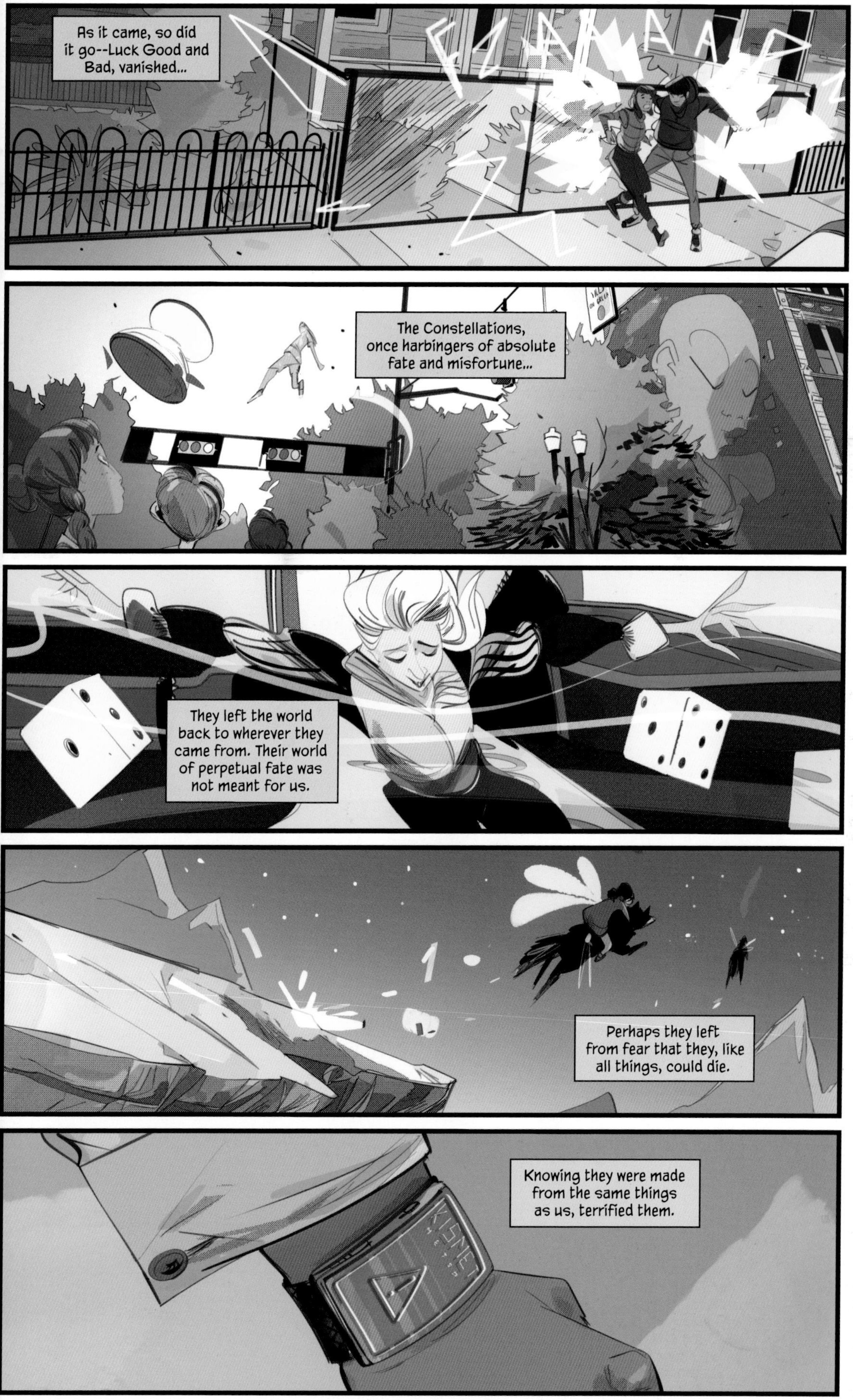
As it came, so did it go--Luck Good and Bad, vanished...
The Constellations, once harbingers of absolute fate and misfortune...
They left the world back to wherever they came from. Their world of perpetual fate was not meant for us.
Perhaps they left from fear that they, like all things, could die.
Knowing they were made from the same things as us, terrified them.

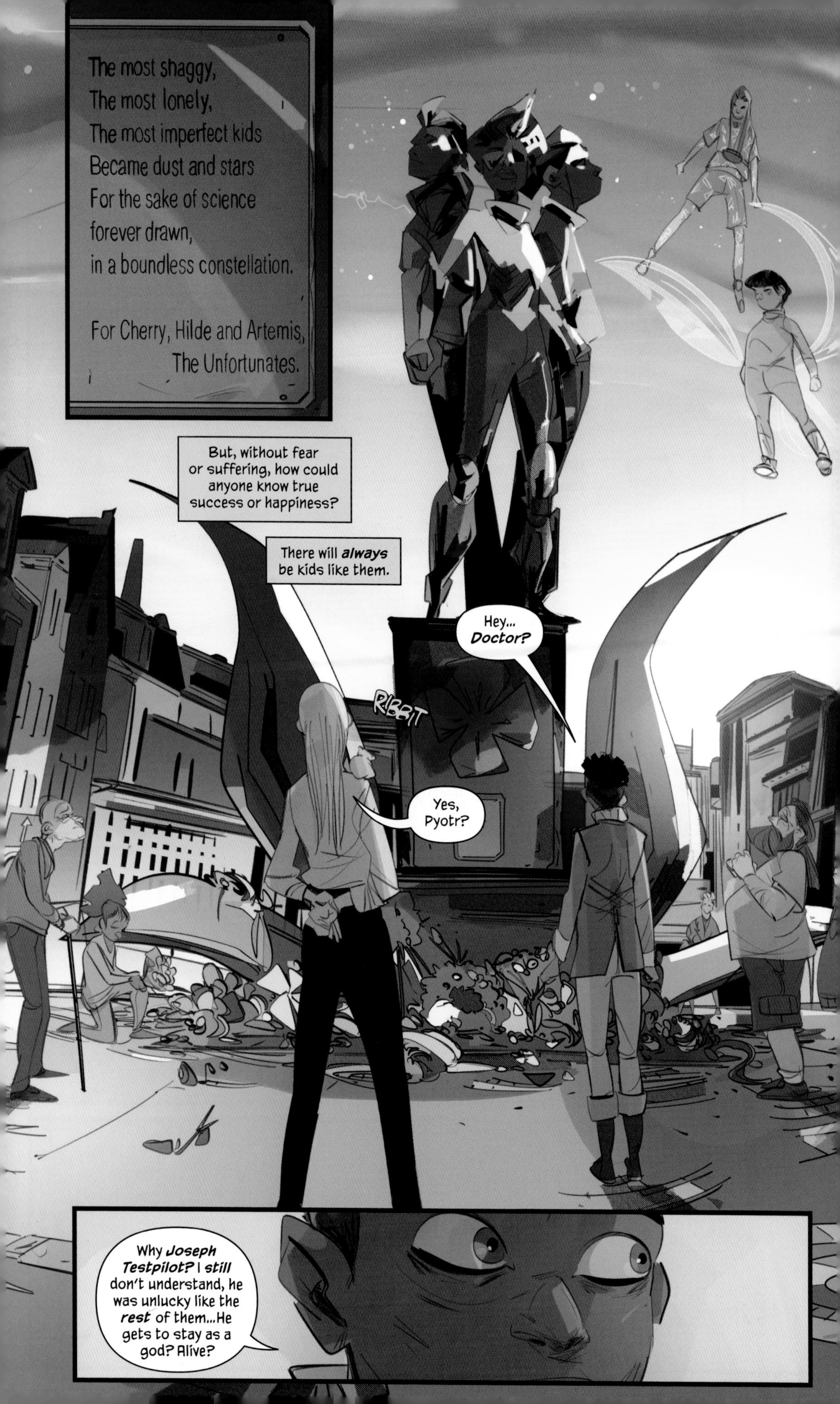
The most shaggy,
The most lonely,
The most imperfect kids
Became dust and stars
For the sake of science
forever drawn,
in a boundless constellation.
For Cherry, Hilde and Artemis,
The Unfortunates.
But, without fear or suffering, how could anyone know true success or happiness?
There will *always* be kids like them.
Hey... *Doctor?*
RIBBIT
Yes, Pyotr?
Why *Joseph Testpilot?* I *still* don't understand, he was unlucky like the *rest* of them...He gets to stay as a god? Alive?

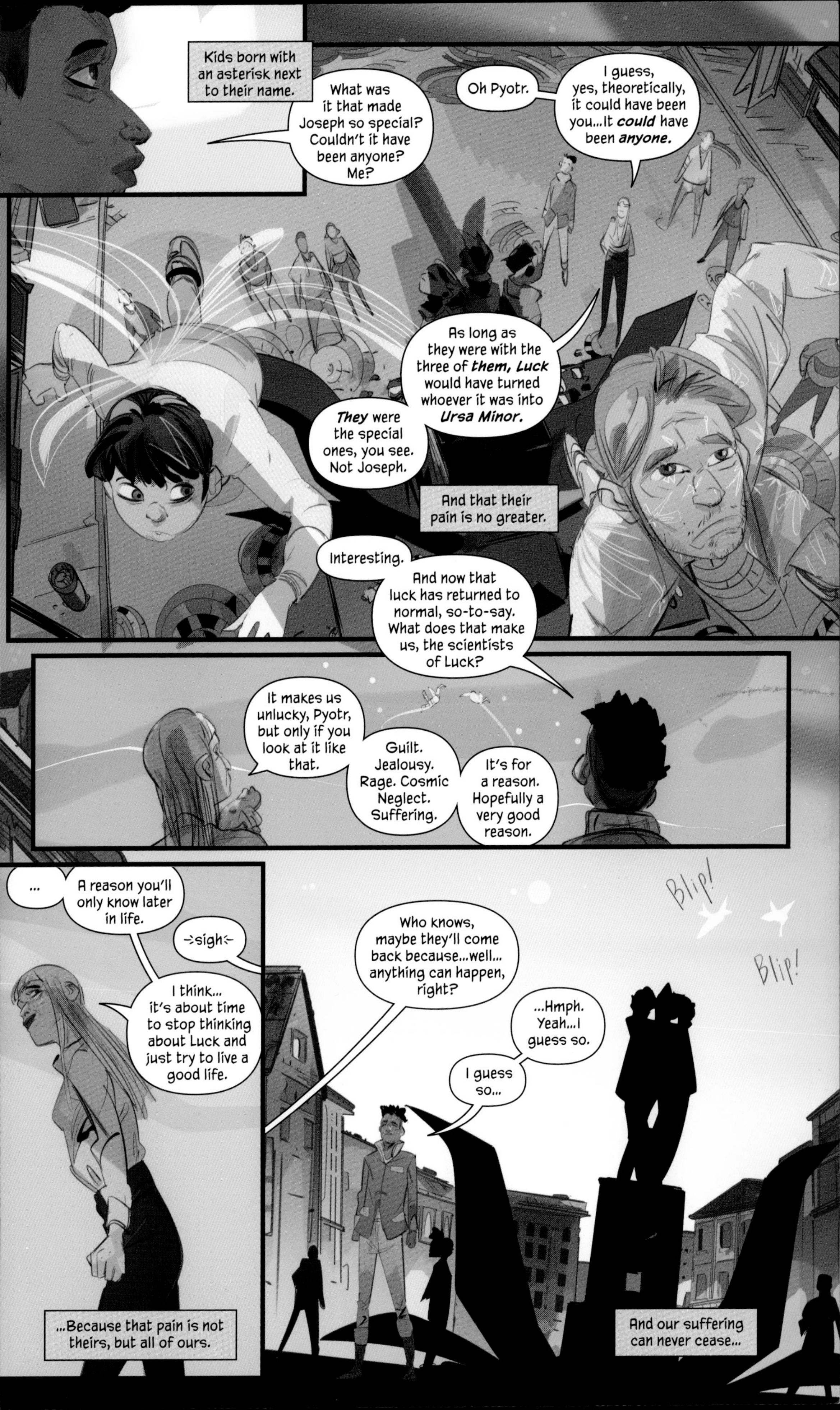
Kids born with an asterisk next to their name.
What was it that made Joseph so special? Couldn't it have been anyone? Me?
Oh Pyotr.
I guess, yes, theoretically, it could have been you...It *could* have been *anyone.*
As long as they were with the three of *them, Luck* would have turned whoever it was into *Ursa Minor.*
They were the special ones, you see. Not Joseph.
And that their pain is no greater.
Interesting.
And now that luck has returned to normal, so-to-say. What does that make us, the scientists of Luck?
It makes us unlucky, Pyotr, but only if you look at it like that.
Guilt. Jealousy. Rage. Cosmic Neglect. Suffering.
It's for a reason. Hopefully a very good reason.
...
A reason you'll only know later in life.
~sigh~
I think... it's about time to stop thinking about Luck and just try to live a good life.
Who knows, maybe they'll come back because...well... anything can happen, right?
Blip!
Blip!
...Hmph. Yeah...I guess so.
I guess so...
...Because that pain is not theirs, but all of ours.
And our suffering can never cease...

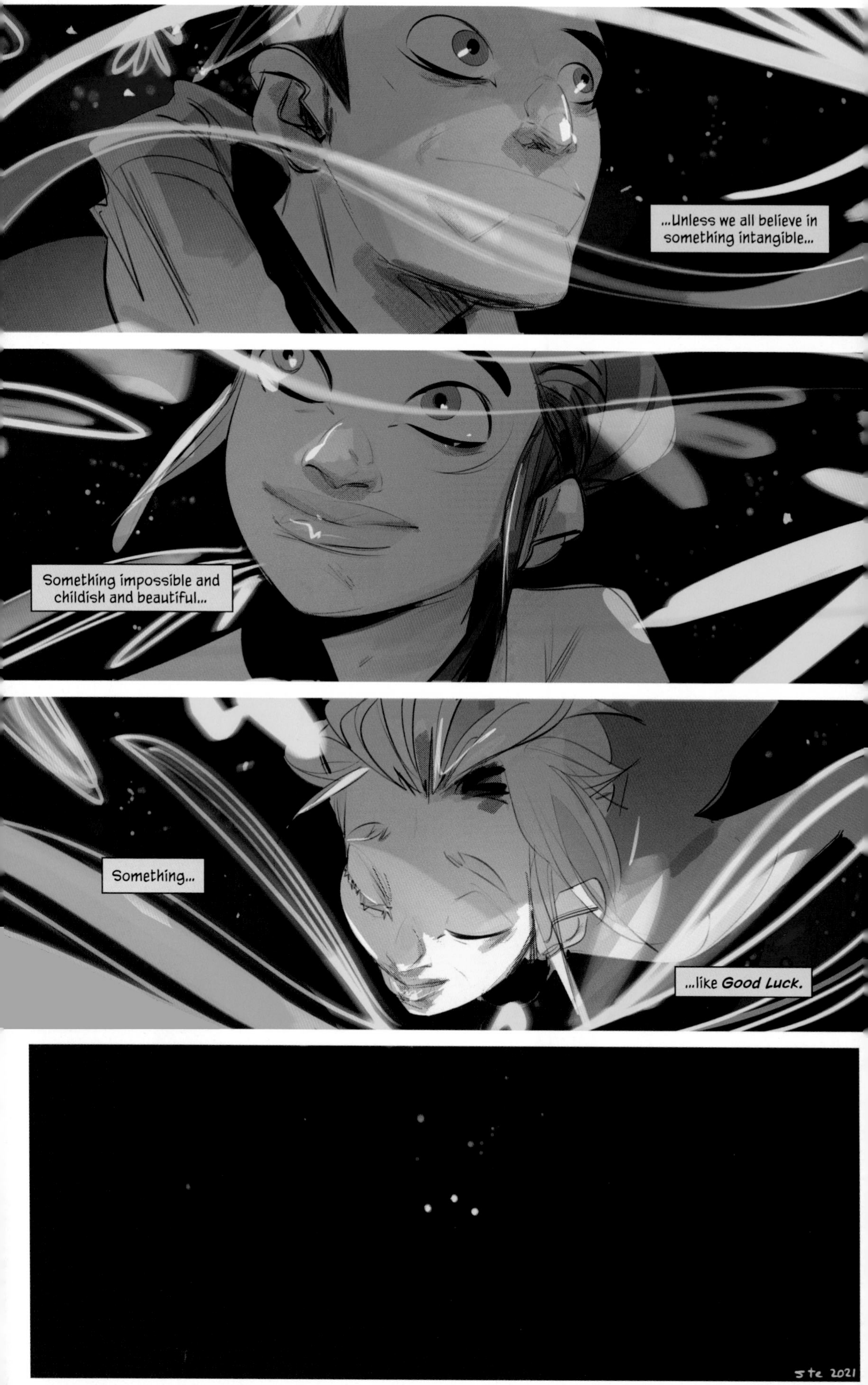
...Unless we all believe in something intangible...
Something impossible and childish and beautiful...
Something...
...like **Good Luck.**
ste 2021

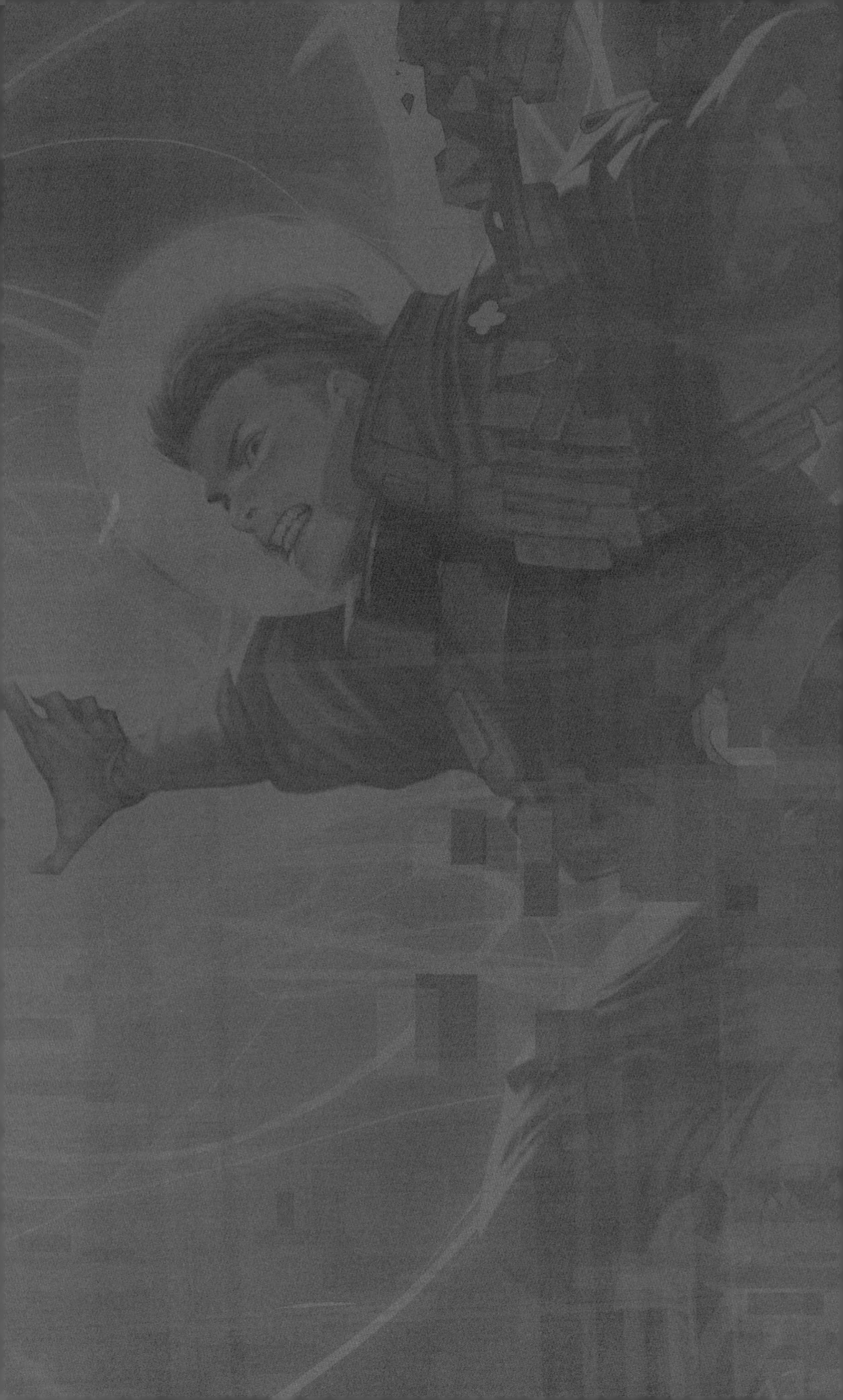

COVER
GALLERY

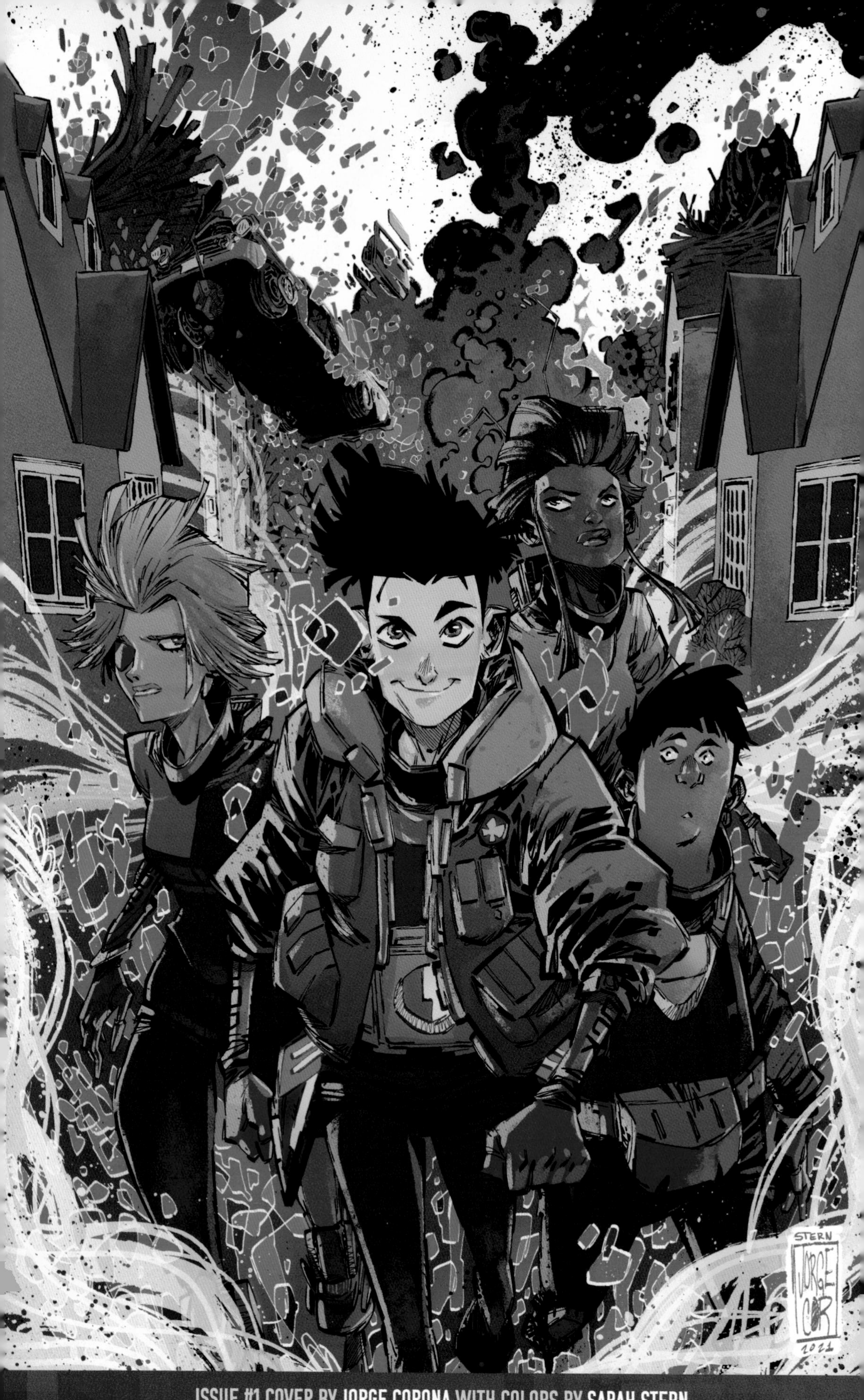

ISSUE #1 COVER BY JORGE CORONA WITH COLORS BY SARAH STERN

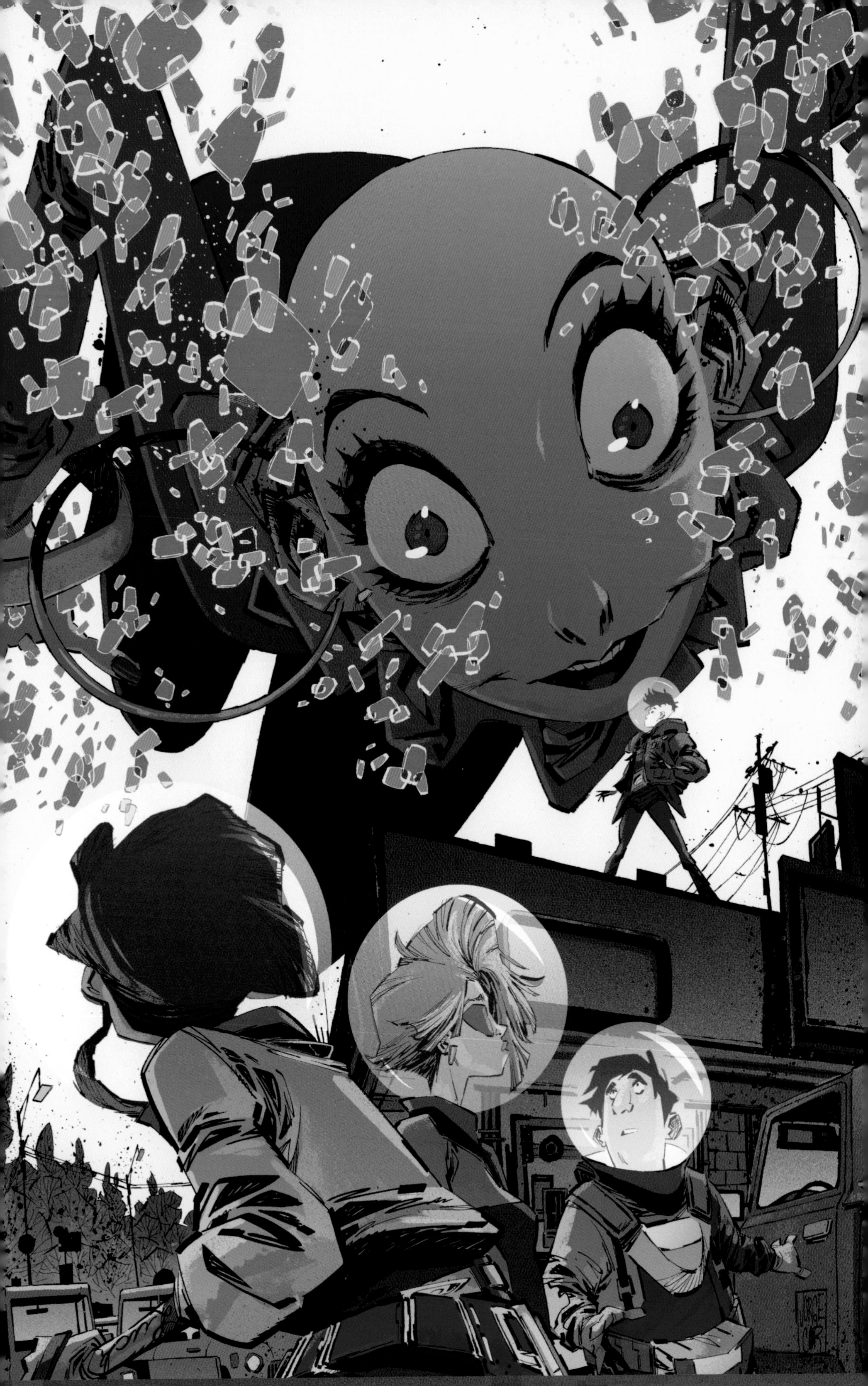

ISSUE #2 COVER BY **JORGE CORONA** WITH COLORS BY **SARAH STERN**

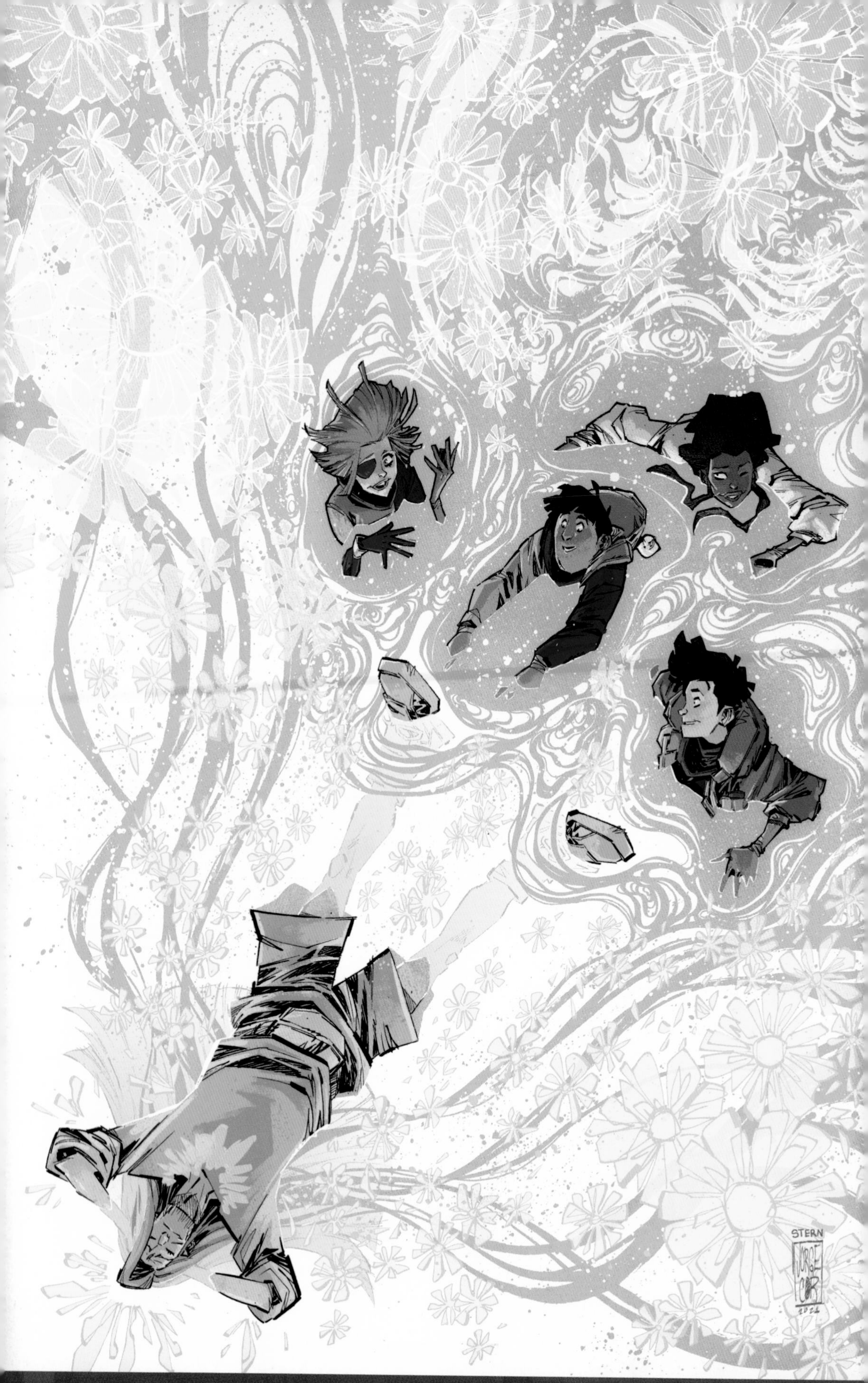
STERN
JORGE COR
2021

ISSUE #3 COVER BY **JORGE CORONA** WITH COLORS BY **SARAH STERN**

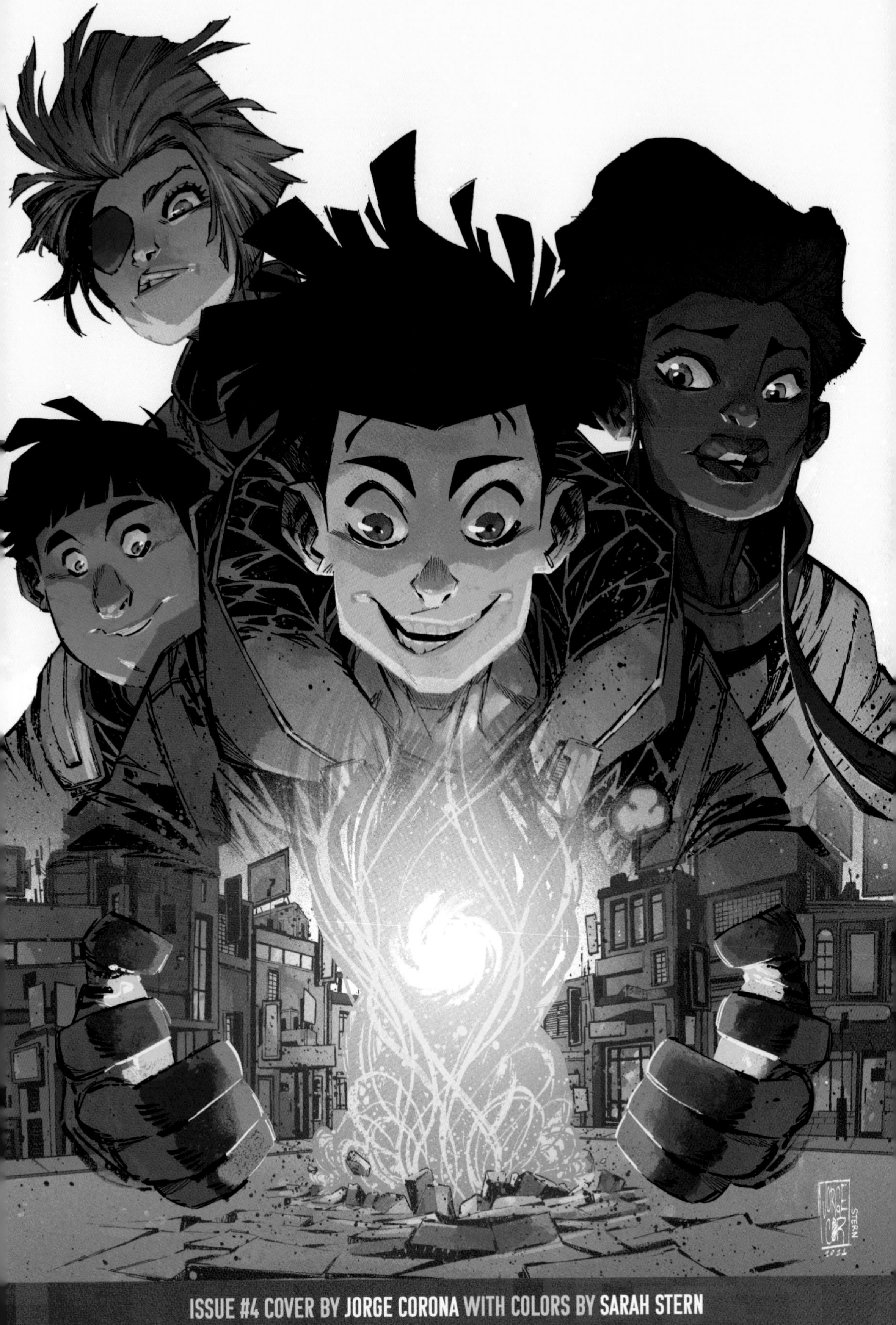

ISSUE #4 COVER BY **JORGE CORONA** WITH COLORS BY **SARAH STERN**

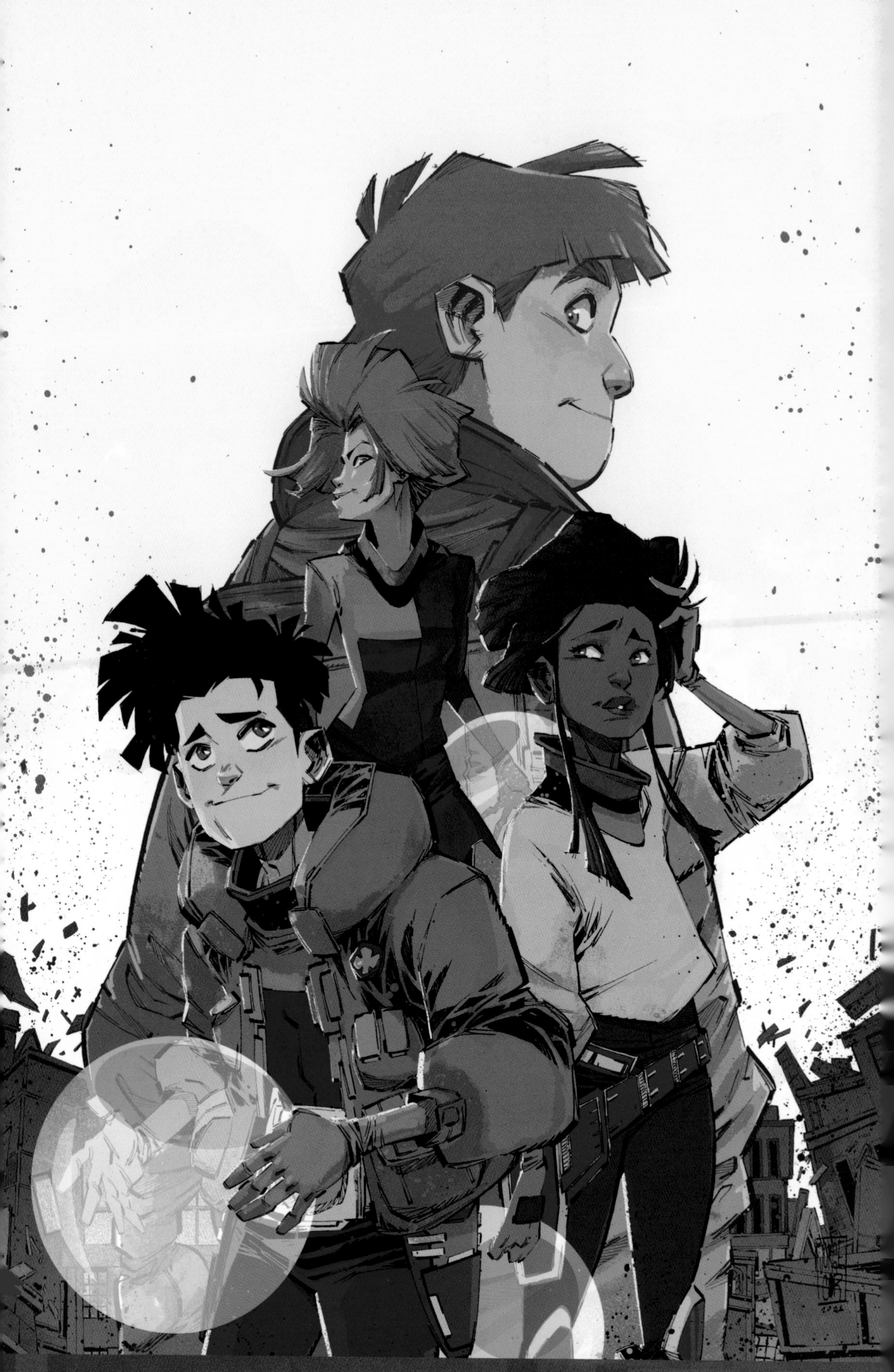

ISSUE #5 COVER BY JORGE CORONA WITH COLORS BY SARAH STERN

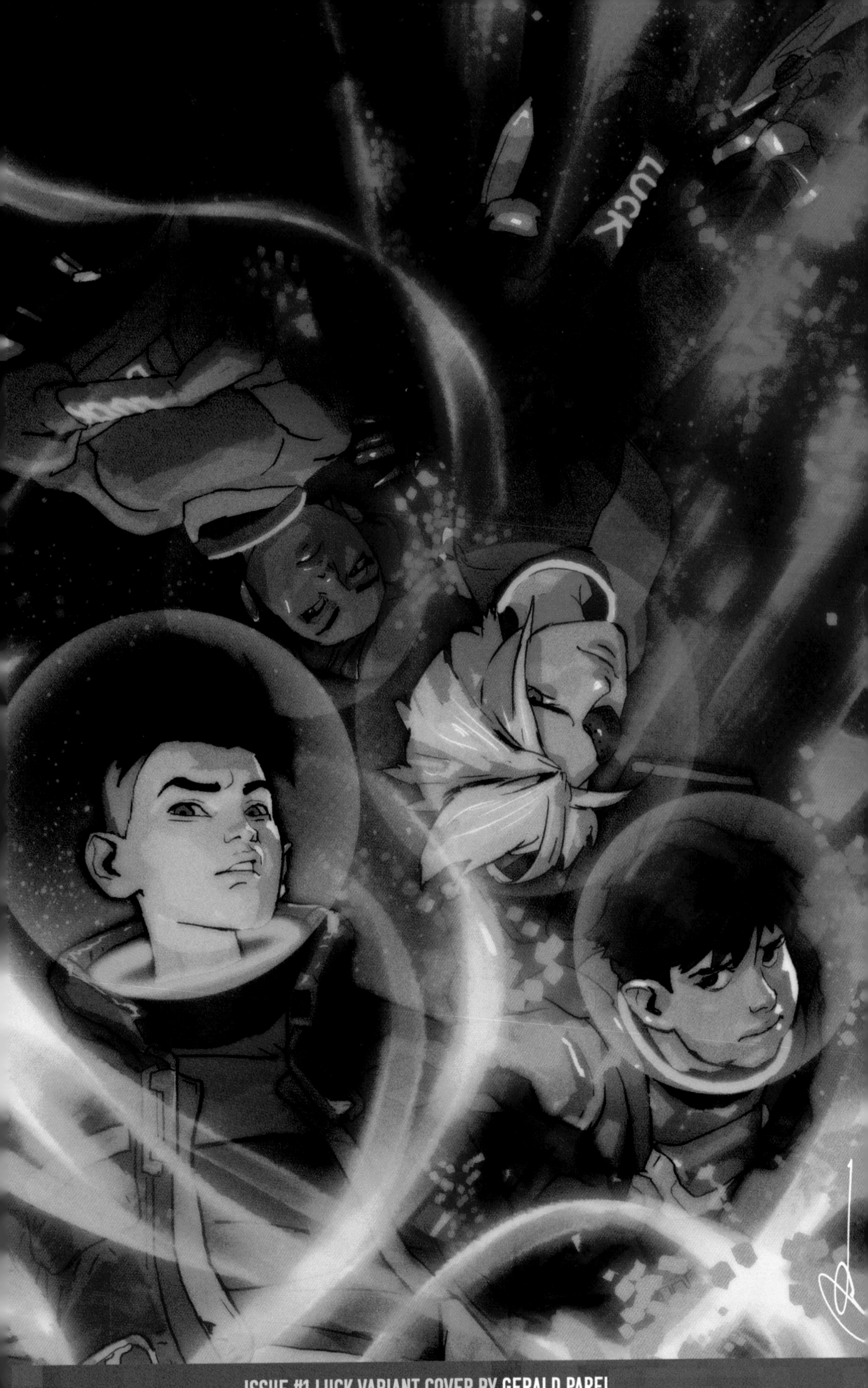
LUCK

ISSUE #1 LUCK VARIANT COVER BY **GERALD PAREL**

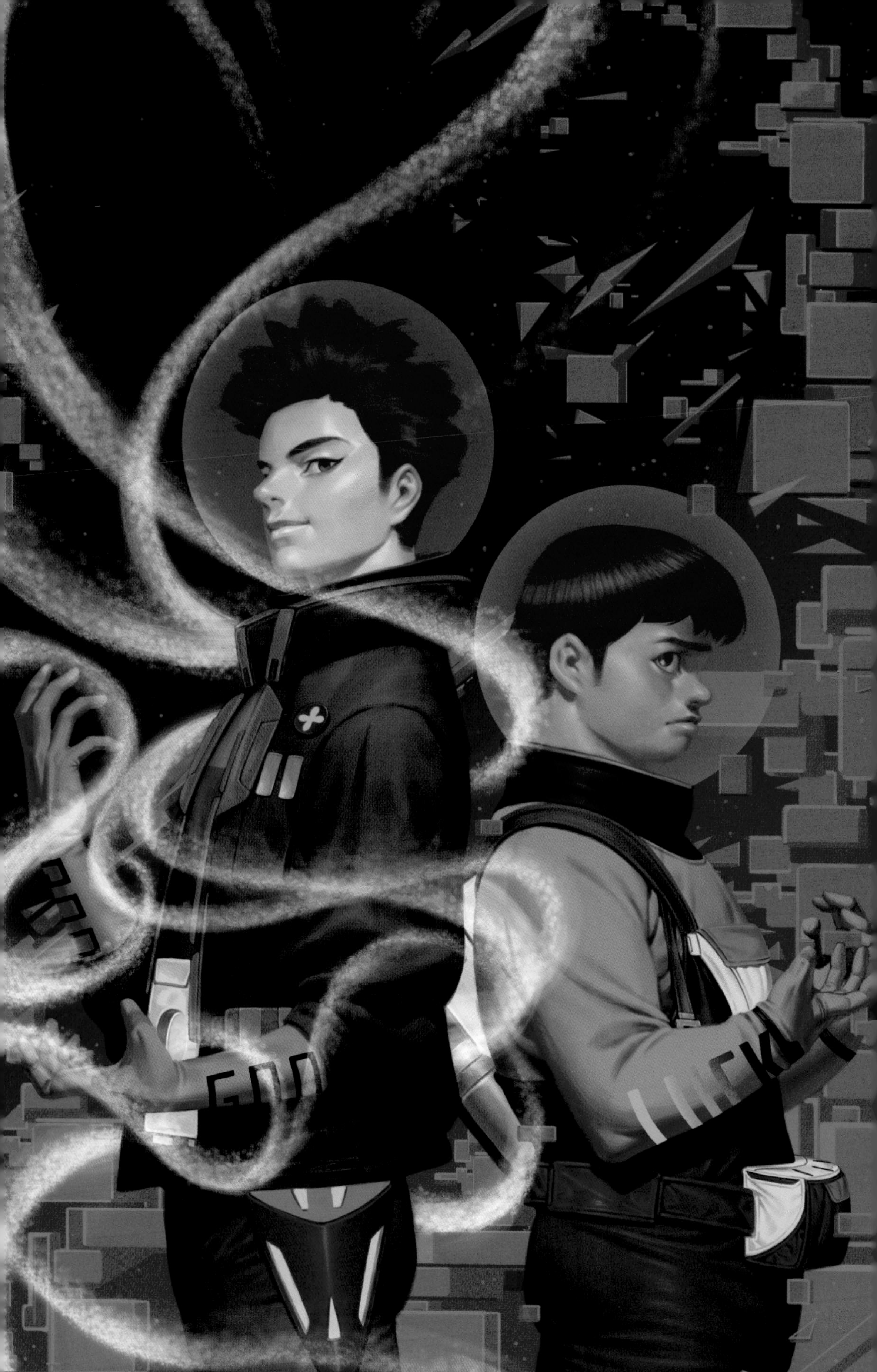

ISSUE #1 VARIANT COVER BY **JUNGGEUN YOON**

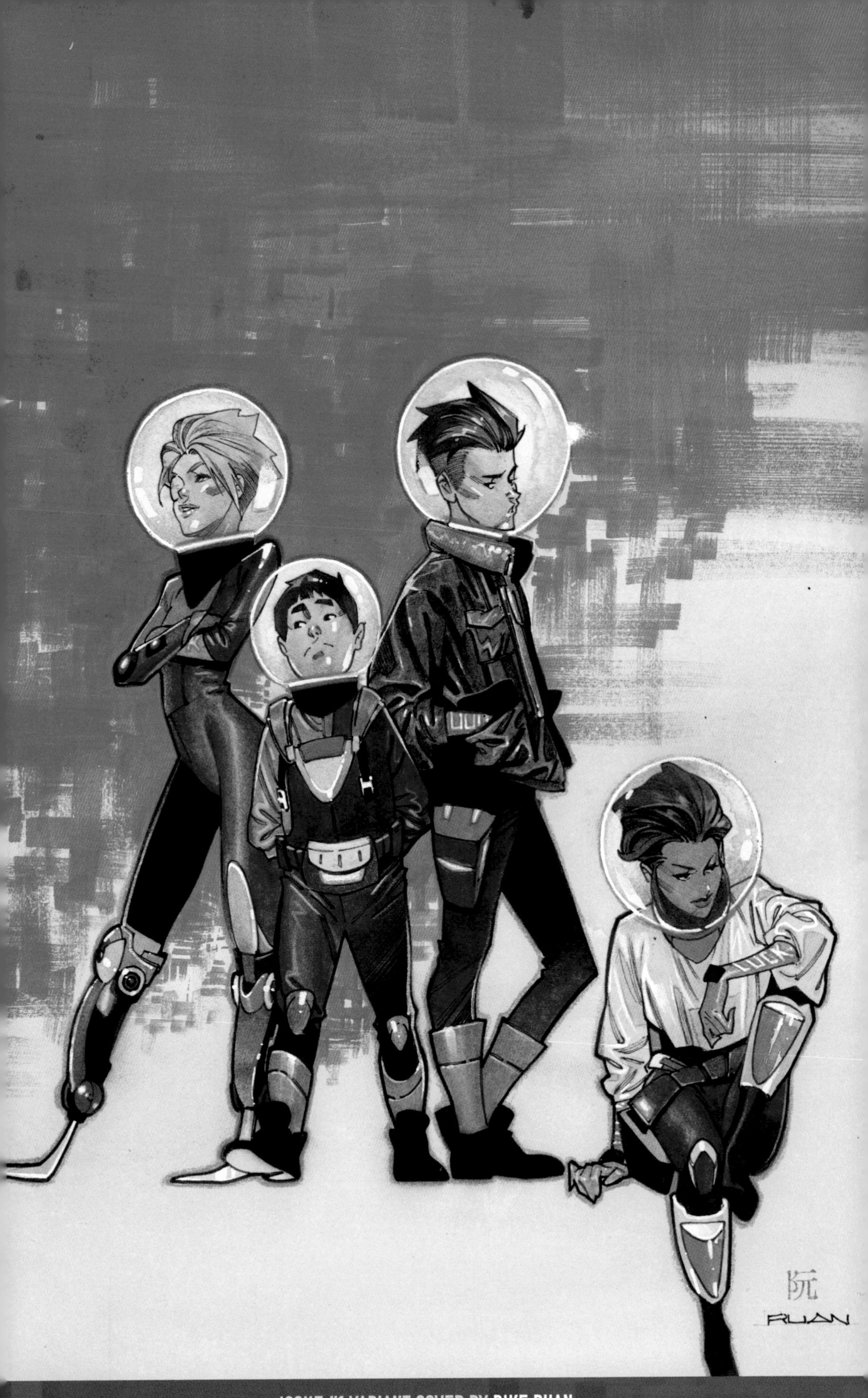
LUCK
阮
RUAN

ISSUE #1 VARIANT COVER BY **DIKE RUAN**

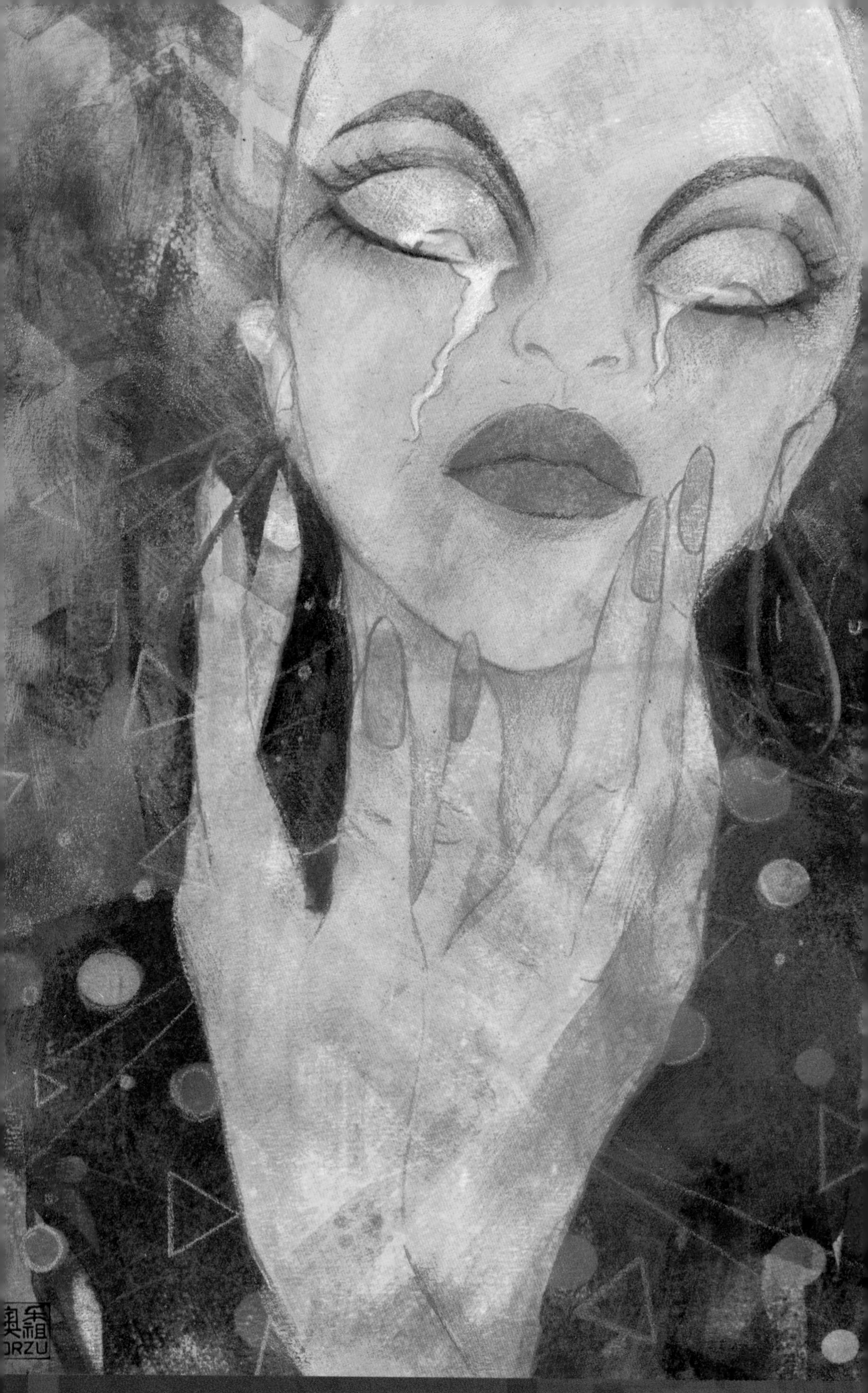

ISSUE #1 VARIANT COVER BY ZU ORZU

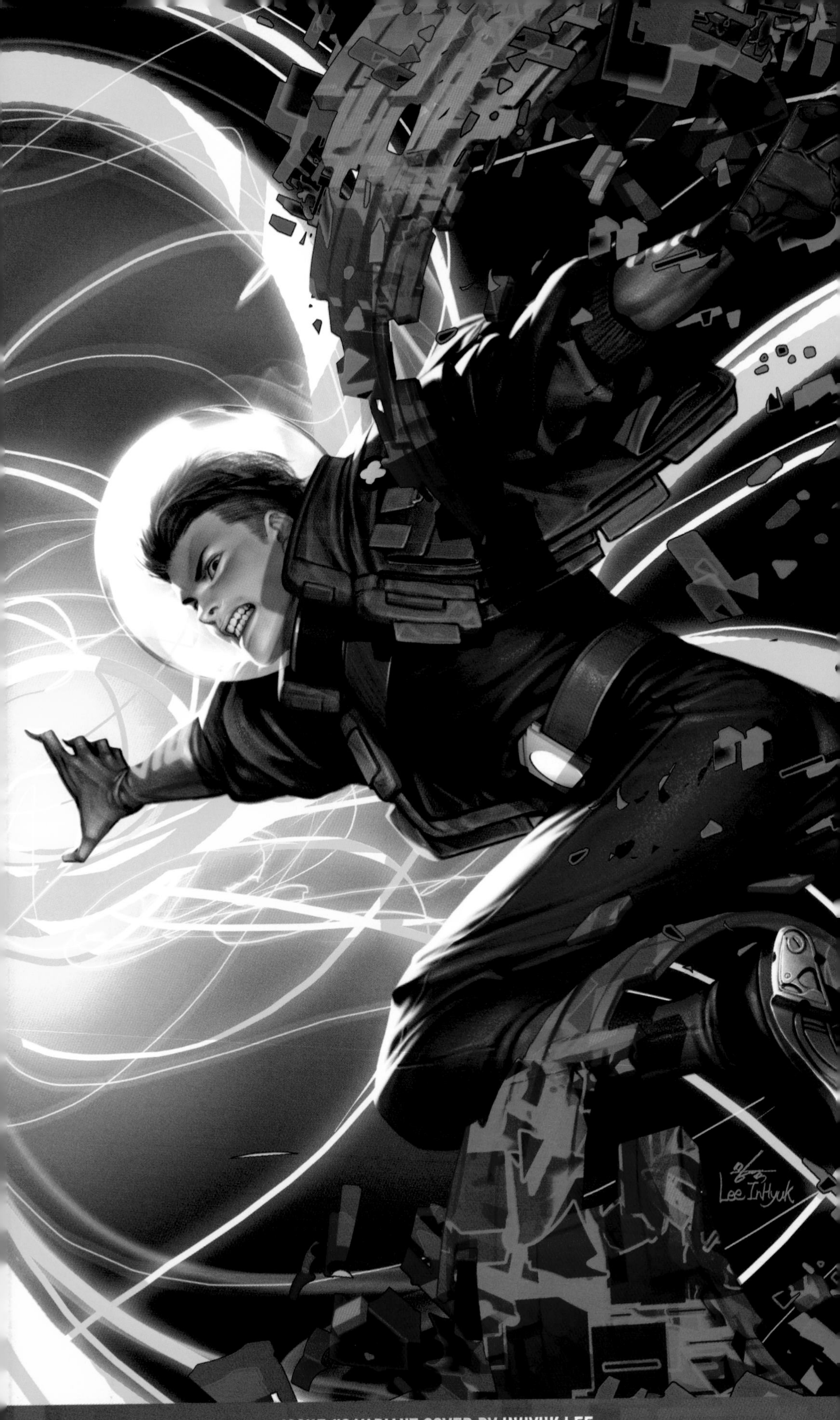
Lee InHyuk

ISSUE #2 VARIANT COVER BY INHYUK LEE

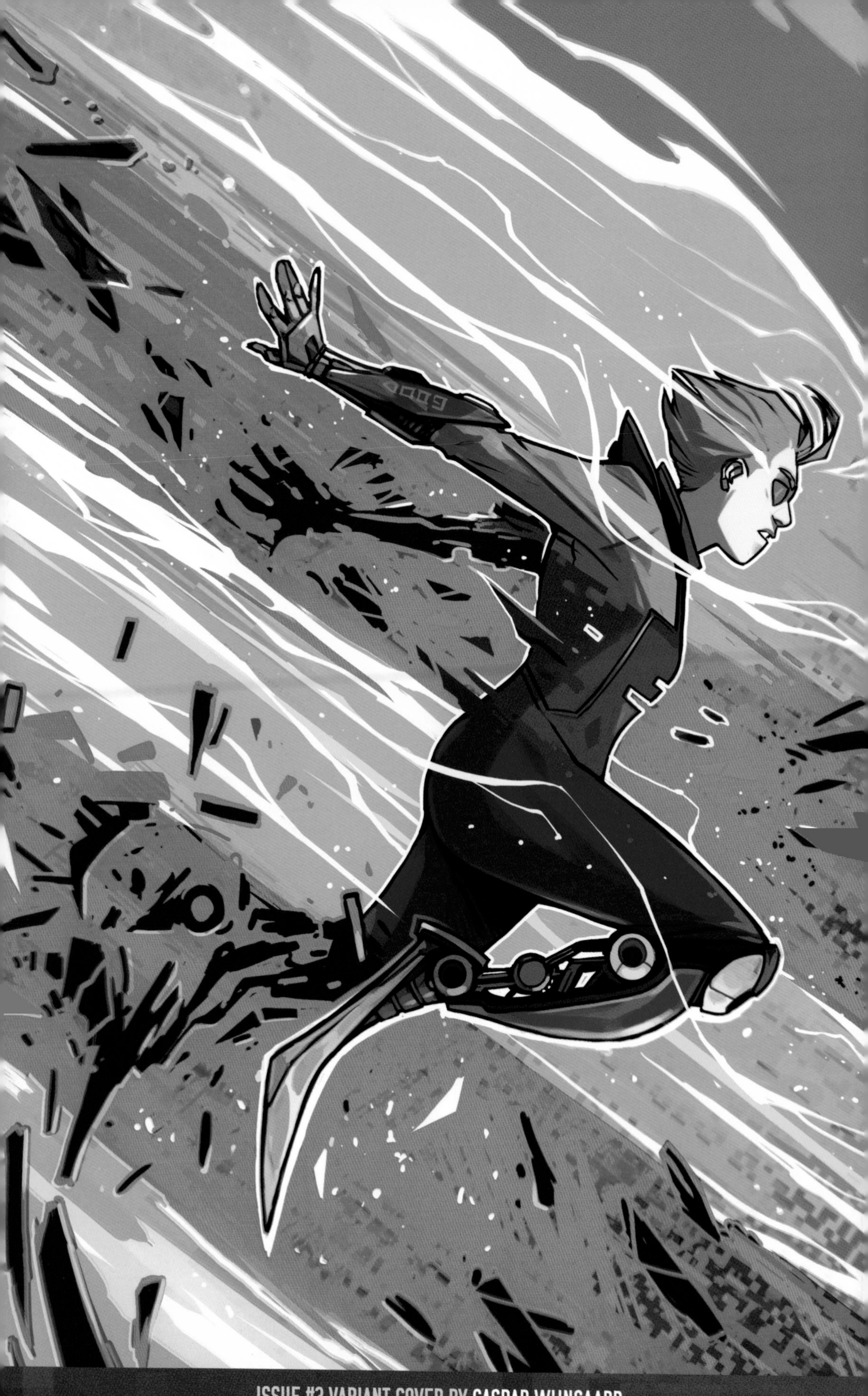

ISSUE #3 VARIANT COVER BY **CASPAR WIJNGAARD**

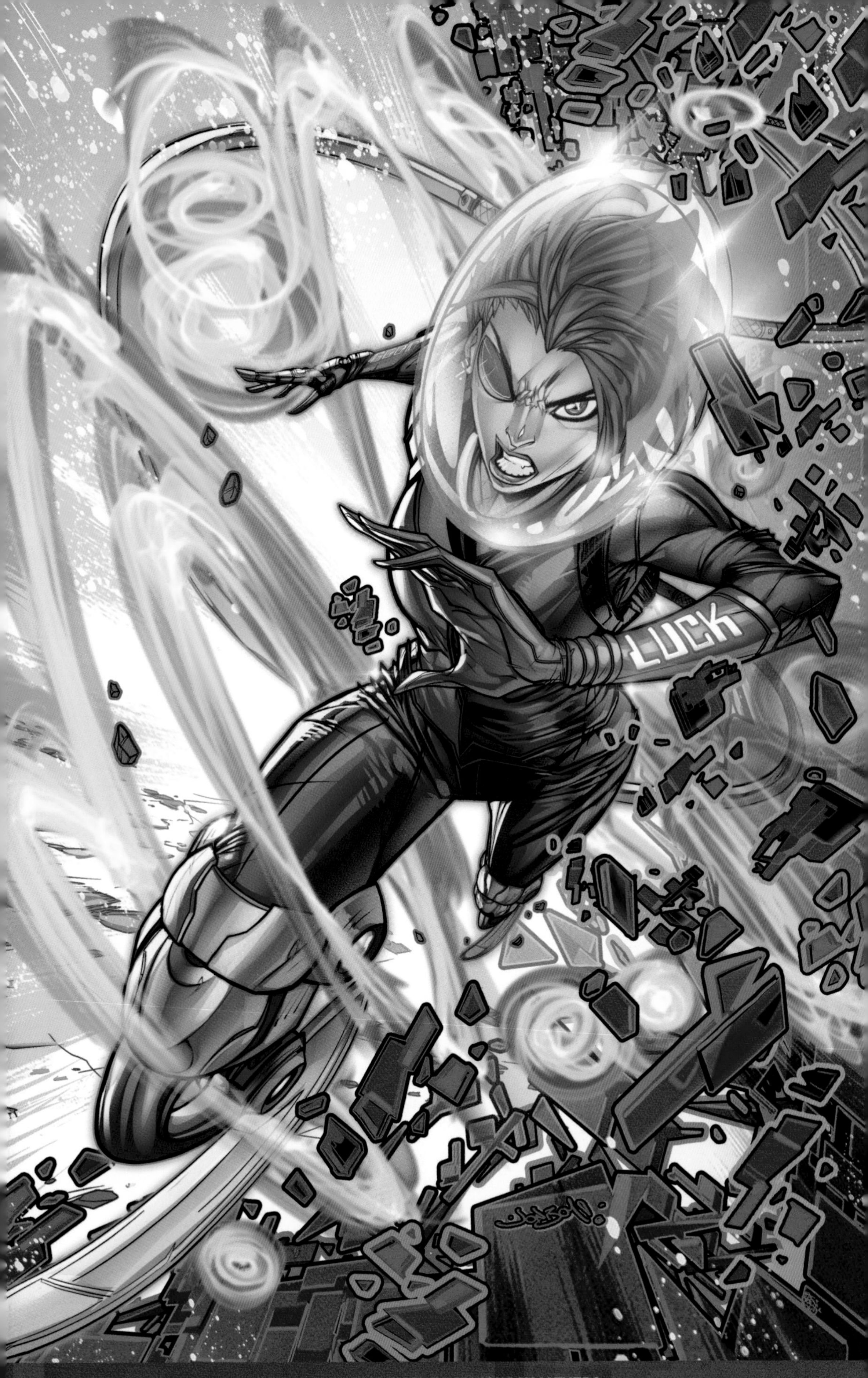
LUCK

ISSUE #4 VARIANT COVER BY JONBOY MEYERS

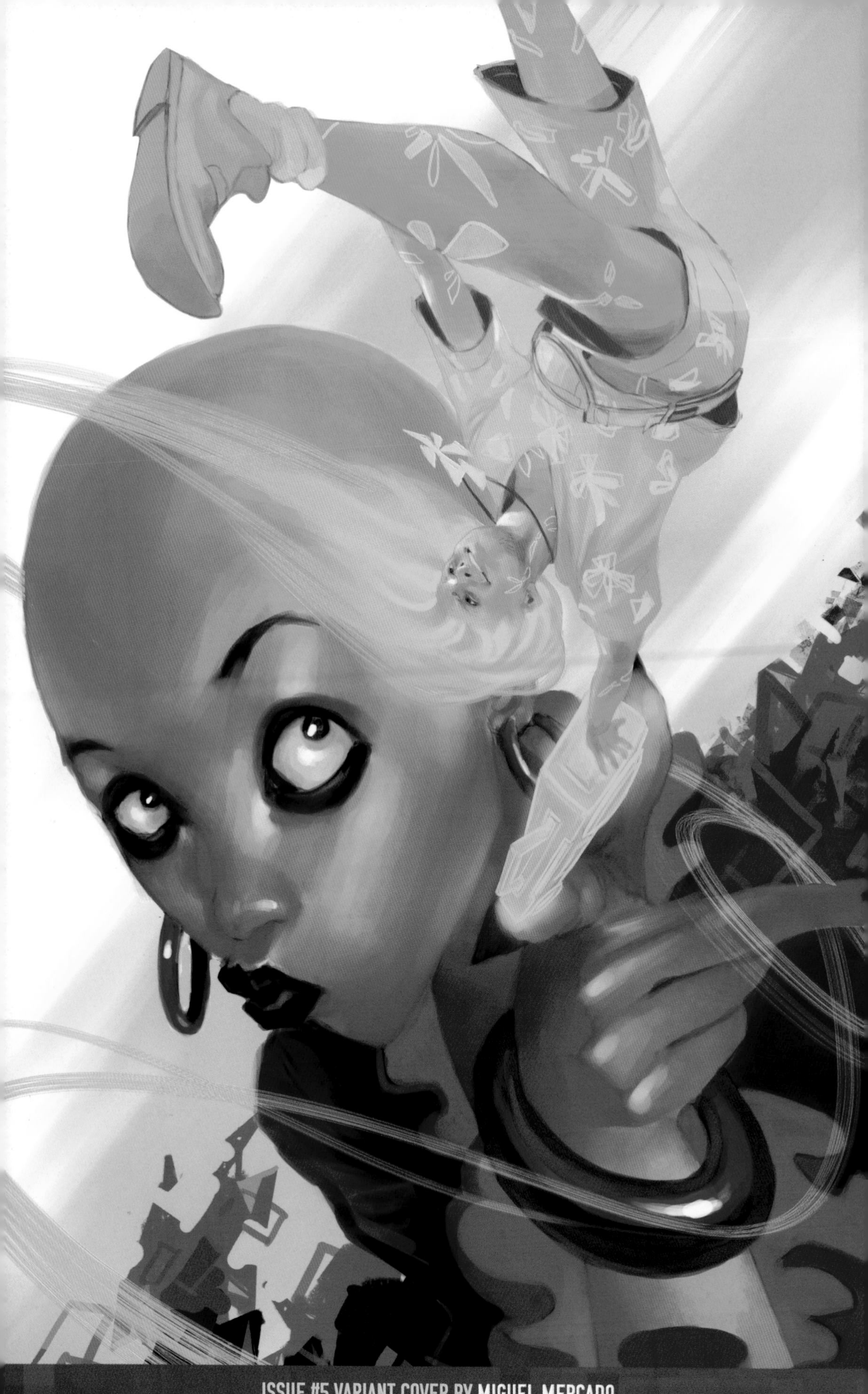

ISSUE #5 VARIANT COVER BY MIGUEL MERCADO

CHARACTER DESIGNS

BY STEFANO SIMEONE

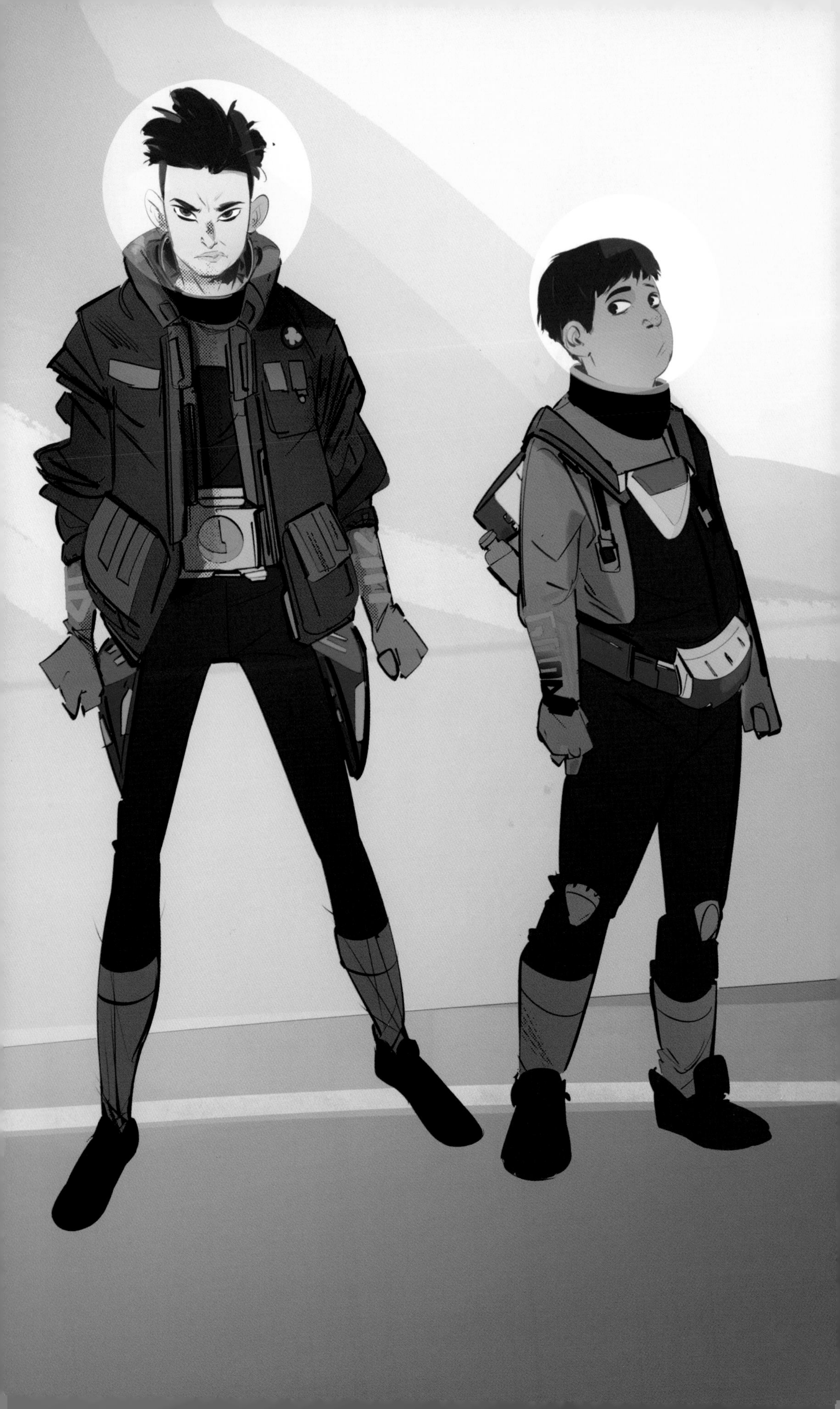

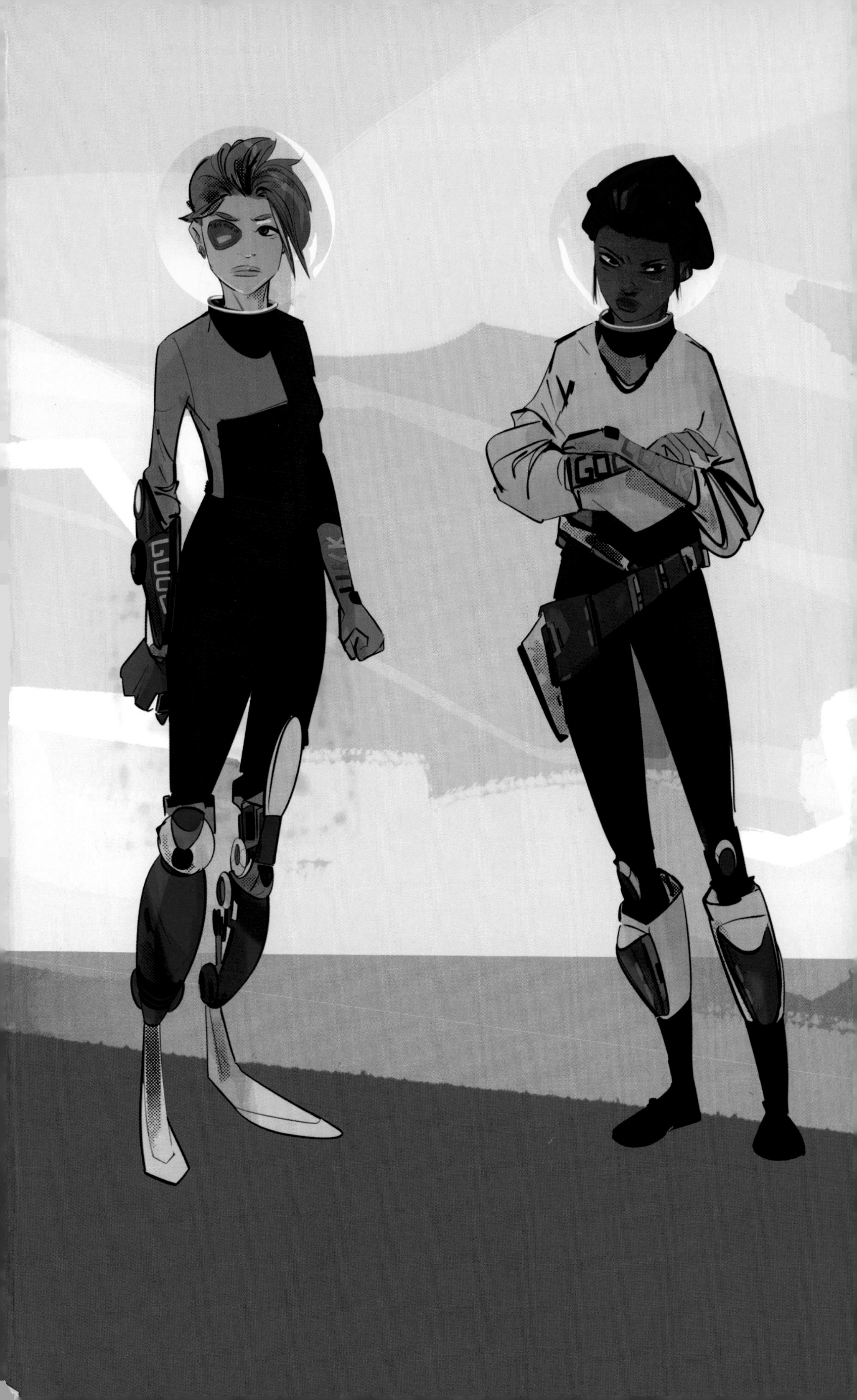